THE FICTION OF FACT-FINDING

THE FICTION
OF
FACT-FINDING

MODI AND GODHRA

Manoj Mitta

HarperCollins *Publishers* India

First published in India in 2014 by
HarperCollins *Publishers* India

Copyright © Manoj Mitta 2014

ISBN: 978-93-5029-187-0

2 4 6 8 10 9 7 5 3 1

Manoj Mitta asserts the moral right to be identified as
the author of this work.

The views and opinions expressed in this book are the author's own
and the facts are as reported by him, and the publishers are
not in any way liable for the same.

HarperCollins *Publishers*
A-53, Sector 57, Noida 201301, India
77-85 Fulham Palace Road, London W6 8JB, United Kingdom
Hazelton Lanes, 55 Avenue Road, Suite 2900, Toronto, Ontario M5R 3L2
and 1995 Markham Road, Scarborough, Ontario M1B 5M8, Canada
25 Ryde Road, Pymble, Sydney, NSW 2073, Australia
31 View Road, Glenfield, Auckland 10, New Zealand
10 East 53rd Street, New York NY 10022, USA

Typeset in 11/15 Aldine401 BT at
SÜRYA

Printed and bound at
Thomson Press (India) Ltd.

For
my mother Indira,
who instilled in me the value of scepticism,
and
in the memory of
journalist Shoebullah Khan,
who paid with his life in 1948,
for advocating the merger of Hyderabad, my native place,
with an India he had trusted would remain pluralist

Contents

Author's Note

The government of Atal Bihari Vajpayee was never able to live down a meek surrender; it handed over three terrorists to the Taliban in Afghanistan in December 1999, in exchange for a hijacked aircraft along with its crew and passengers. What is less remembered, however, is that two years later, it gave in to another extremist ideology, this time to homegrown Hindutva. On 13 March 2002, the Vajpayee government pleaded with the Supreme Court to let the Vishva Hindu Parishad (VHP) perform, two days later, a 'symbolic' ritual near the disputed site in Ayodhya where Lord Ram was believed to have taken birth. The situation was fraught, surreal. Barely a fortnight earlier, fifty-nine Hindus had been killed as bogies of a train were set on fire at Godhra, following a communal clash at the railway station there. The frenzied ranks of the VHP had since been on the rampage in Gujarat, leading to a carnage in which over 1,000 people, mostly Muslims, had been killed.

For all that violence, the VHP leaders were showing no signs of relenting on their Ayodhya campaign, which had sparked the Godhra incident. They prevailed upon the Vajpayee government to acquiesce to their plan of marking 15 March 2002 as the launch date of the much-touted Ram temple construction. And that's why attorney general Soli Sorabjee was before the Supreme Court, batting for the VHP on behalf of the government.

The bench, headed by Chief Justice B.N. Kirpal, was,

however, unwilling to trust the VHP's assurance that they would confine themselves to a symbolic puja. This was not only because the same organization was complicit in the ongoing post-Godhra violence. There was a prior reason too. The last time the court had trusted the VHP's promise to hold a symbolic ritual in Ayodhya, it had led to the demolition of the Babri Masjid, arguably the greatest blow to secularism in India since Partition. 'We don't want a repeat of the December 6, 1992 incident,' the bench observed, seeing through the ploy of the symbolic puja.

Within hours, the VHP chief, Ashok Singhal, proclaimed to the media in Ayodhya that the Supreme Court order had actually gone in the organization's favour. The cause for his jubilation was an error in the 13 March order. Had this error not been corrected in the little time that was left, it could have helped the VHP escalate communal tension across the country.

The error lay in the description of the 67 acres of government-acquired land that was covered by the status quo injunction. Though the acquired land encompassed over 100 revenue plots, the Supreme Court order directing status quo inadvertently referred only to two revenue plots. This gave scope to the VHP to pretend that it could still lawfully perform puja in the government-acquired land surrounding the disputed site. In my report in *The Indian Express* on the Supreme Court proceedings, I pointed out the error and explained how it had crept into the order. Seeing my report on the morning of 14 March, Justice Kirpal corrected the 'ambiguity' by holding an unscheduled hearing before his bench the same day. The prompt corrective put paid to the VHP's chances of pulling off the puja the next day. Contemporaneous accounts of this politico-legal drama referred to the catalytic role played by my report. Take jurist A.G. Noorani's analysis in the *Frontline* magazine of 30 March 2002: 'Thanks entirely to Manoj Mitta's mention of an inadvertent error in the description of the acquired plot, the court clarified on March 14 that the entire acquired land of 67.703 acres was covered.'

The purpose of this recollection is not to blow my own trumpet. Rather, it is to convey that, as a journalist tracking the Indian legal system for almost three decades, I have always sought to expose mistakes, even if these were committed by no less an august body than the Supreme Court. The one on the acquired land in Ayodhya was a rare instance, though, of a mistake being acknowledged, and promptly at that. The exception happened because the mistake in question was, as Noorani pointed out, inadvertent. Where the mistake was deliberate, as would be the case most times, the authority concerned would tend to be in denial.

This book is about mistakes committed in the course of fact-finding on the Gujarat carnage, an offshoot of the Ayodhya dispute. The material on fact-finding was gleaned not just from the reports of committees and commissions set up to probe the carnage, but also the reports of investigating agencies, and even the judgments and orders of courts. Serious as they were, a lot of these mistakes covered up political and administrative complicity in the post-Godhra violence. The distortions in the findings were thanks to the insidious manner in which issues had been framed, facts selected, evidence recorded or inferences drawn.

This is my second book on the vagaries of fact-finding in India, and this is again in relation to a carnage. The first was on the anti-Sikh violence in Delhi in 1984, the very event that is often cited as the benchmark of comparison to the 2002 violence in Gujarat. Common to both books is an unsparing look at the cover-up done under the guise of fact-finding, irrespective of whether its ultimate beneficiary was Rajiv Gandhi or Narendra Modi. Published in 2007, *When a Tree Shook Delhi* questioned the oft-quoted view of academic Ashutosh Varshney that 'the riots in Gujarat were the first full-blooded pogrom in independent India'. Little wonder then that in his memoirs brought out in 2008, BJP leader L.K. Advani referred to my book in a chapter devoted to the Gujarat carnage. The scale of the killings was greater in 1984, the violence more one-sided and the cover-up more intractable. It was all the same an easier book for me because of my co-author, senior advocate H.S. Phoolka, the spearhead of the entire struggle for justice in the anti-Sikh violence. The present work has turned out to be more challenging, partly due to the absence of a Phoolka-like counterpart involved with all the rounds of fact-finding.

To catch the nuances of the cover-up in the Gujarat context, I have had to interact with at least three different sets of lawyers, activists and whistleblowers. Though the narrative in the book is entirely mine, these participants in fact-finding have been immensely helpful to me in deconstructing official documents. About the commission headed by retired Supreme Court judge G.T. Nanavati, my key source of information was advocate Mukul Sinha, who was the main representative of victims before this fact-finding body on the Godhra and post-Godhra violence. As regards the trial in the Godhra train burning case, I received much help from lawyers who appeared in the trial court, particularly A.A. Hasan and A.D. Shah, and those who appeared in related proceedings, such as Colin Gonsalves and Somnath Vatsa. When it came to the probe by the Supreme Court-appointed special investigation team (SIT) into riot victim Zakia Jafri's complaint against the Modi regime, my most valuable sources were activist Teesta Setalvad and whistleblower R.B. Sreekumar. Sadly, however, there was a lack of coordination among all these people fighting for truth or justice, and this added to the complexity of my Gujarat project.

Another reason it has been more challenging to unravel the fact-finding on the 2002 violence is the aura of the Supreme Court's monitoring of the SIT investigations. The monitoring did make a dent in India's record of impunity for perpetrators of communal violence. The most notable example was, of course, the conviction of a minister in the Modi government, Maya Kodnani, for plotting a massacre in which ninety-six people had been killed in Naroda Patiya in Ahmedabad. But how did Modi himself and other influential persons accused by Jafri of the larger conspiracy behind the post-Godhra violence get a 'clean chit' from the SIT, despite the same monitoring by the Supreme Court? Audacious as the question is, this book addresses it for the first time ever, while tracing the trajectory of Jafri's complaint. In the process, the book brings out infirmities in the monitoring, which allowed vital pieces of evidence to fall through the cracks and distortions to go unchallenged. The book dissects, among other things, the 541-page closure report filed by the SIT before an Ahmedabad magistrate in February 2012. The magistrate's order upholding the SIT closure report came in December 2013, just as this book was going to press. Constrained perhaps by the quality of the evidence placed by the SIT, the magistrate rejected Jafri's protest petition against the closure report.

The timing of the book is fortuitous. It has become more relevant than ever before because of Modi's emergence as a prime ministerial candidate in the upcoming election. All the same, I could not have attempted it earlier because much of the official findings have been published only in the last three years—beginning with the trial court verdict in the Godhra case in February 2011 and ending with the magistrate's endorsement of the SIT's clean chit to Modi in December 2013. Such delays are endemic to the deeply flawed legal system in India. It took twenty-three years for Phoolka and me to come out with the book on the 1984 carnage because there was an even greater delay in that case in the release of official fact-finding material.

Though both were exonerated of all culpability for the massacres associated with them, Modi's role was scrutinized more closely than that of Rajiv Gandhi. As it happened, Modi's exoneration gave me a first-hand experience of the SIT's cavalier approach to facts. The closure report made an allegation against me, while assailing the motives of anybody seeking to uncover political complicity in the 2002 violence. On the basis of email hacking, the SIT named me among the people who had 'strategized' with controversial police officer Sanjiv Bhatt before he filed an affidavit against Modi in the Supreme Court in 2011. It claimed that on seeing his draft affidavit, I had advised Bhatt 'to incorporate a few more paragraphs drafted by' me. This was a conscious exaggeration of my role, as evident from the very email annexed by the SIT by way of evidence. The only drafting that the email shows is all of one sentence, in which I suggested to Bhatt that he explain his compulsion for approaching the Supreme Court. From its viewpoint, the SIT could well have criticized me for treating Bhatt as a whistleblower or for not being neutral about Modi's accountability. Instead, by passing off that solitary sentence as 'a few more paragraphs', the SIT gave me a taste of its pliability.

The SIT's attempt to malign me, however trifling in the larger scheme of things, proved to be a blessing in disguise. It drove me to discover another questionable aspect of fact-finding, which had a bearing on the flawed composition of the SIT. This was the appointment of the former CBI director, R.K. Raghavan, to the crucial post of SIT chairman. Raghavan had himself been a subject of inquiry, a decade prior to the Gujarat carnage. It was for the security lapses surrounding the assassination of Rajiv Gandhi. Despite his indictment, Raghavan got away lightly and was rehabilitated by the Vajpayee government. What remained a closely guarded secret was that even his indictment in the first place had been a diluted one: a commission of inquiry headed by Supreme Court judge J.S. Verma had glossed over damaging contents of Raghavan's own affidavit. I owe the chance discovery of the affidavit to K. Ragothaman, who was the CBI's chief investigating officer in the Rajiv Gandhi assassination case. It also helped that, in the course of my journalistic work in 1991-92, I had attended the commission's proceedings and interacted with almost the entire gamut of players involved in that probe, from Verma to Raghavan himself and his lawyers. The evidence of Raghavan's unsuitability to the post and other such revelations in the book put in perspective the kind of fact-finding carried out by the SIT, whether in the Godhra case or on the complaint against Modi.

Hence an oxymoronic title for this work of nonfiction on 'the fiction of fact-finding'. The book is more than just about, as they say, speaking truth to power. Written from a human rights perspective, the book is ultimately a commentary on the people of India. It interrogates their claim to being a liberal democracy, committed to pluralism and the rule of law. In varying ways, Rajiv Gandhi's unparalleled success in the 1984 election and the growth of the Modi phenomenon, whether because of or in spite of the 2002 violence, reflect the social sanction enjoyed by communal politics. The sanction extends to the process of fact-finding, allowing it to be reduced, as in most cases, to an insidious variant of the dictum that history is written by victors. Barring honourable exceptions such as the Jaganmohan Reddy Commission's report on the Gujarat riots of 1969 and the B.N. Srikrishna Commission's report on the Bombay riots of

1992-93, the fact-finding on communal violence in India has largely been fictitious. Wrapped as it is in legal authority, this subversion of fact-finding often drives Indian politics without any of the fiction being exposed for what it is. Though Modi has been catapulted to the national stage only after he had been exonerated by the SIT report, there is little understanding of the great deal of fiction underlying it. Here's an attempt to fill a vital gap in the public discourse.

Besides the contributions already acknowledged on the research front, I must express my gratitude to the friends who enriched the book with their comments on its drafts. The feedback given by senior advocate Anupam Gupta has helped me immensely in making the book sharper and more rigorous. We have long been comrades-in-arms in various battles for secularism. Incidentally, Anupam was instrumental in helping me expose the mistake mentioned at the beginning of this note in the 2002 Supreme Court order on Ayodhya. He was then, in his avatar as counsel for the Justice Liberhan Commission, in the thick of cross examining a range of leaders for the demolition of the Babri Masjid. Anupam has lately been in the news as counsel for Haryana officer Ashok Khemka, who had dared to thwart property deals of Sonia Gandhi's son-in-law Robert Vadra.

I must also record my deep appreciation for the critical inputs I got from independent law researcher Usha Ramanathan, another old friend. Usha went beyond my expectations by sending me an intern, law student Anviti Chaturvedi, who referenced all the documents I had collected during my research. Anviti's meticulous work is partially reflected in the 'Further Reading' section towards the end of the book. The first reader of my raw copy, chapter by chapter, was my childhood friend Himadeep Muppidi, a US-based political scientist, who provided me the confidence to proceed with the project. Another major source of moral support has been Amit Bhattacharya, who is also a colleague in *The Times of India*. His journalistic feedback on the manuscript has been most reassuring. Others who contributed to the book in different ways include Dilip Simeon, Ramachandra Guha, B.G. Verghese, Aakar Patel, Shabnam Hashmi, Waqar Qazi, Ashish Khetan and Aniruddha Bahal. This book would not perhaps have been possible without the patience, trust and acumen displayed by my editor at HarperCollins, Amit Agarwal. While the book has benefited immeasurably due to the help and advice from all these friends, I am solely responsible for its deficiencies, in style or substance.

Though my study is essentially based on official documents, I have also drawn material from media reports and books, most notably my former boss Shekhar Gupta's interviews with two BJP leaders, books by Advani, D.R. Kaarthikeyan and P. Chandra Sekharan, and stories appearing in *The Times of India* and *The Hindu*. I have acknowledged all such sources in my narrative.

1

The Enormity of Godhra

On the fateful morning of 27 February 2002, the Sabarmati Express was overcrowded. Besides its complement of authorized passengers, the train was teeming with kar sevaks. Identifiable by their saffron bandanas, the kar sevaks crammed even reserved coaches. They were returning from the holy town of Ayodhya after participating in an ongoing ritual. Such round trips had been organized across the country by the VHP as a prelude to its grand plan of constructing a temple on the disputed site where Lord Ram was believed to have taken birth.

The train arrived at Godhra, the second halt in Gujarat, at 7.40 am, which was almost five hours behind schedule. When they got down on platform number one for tea and breakfast, kar sevaks started shouting slogans, most commonly 'Jai Shree Ram'. The hawkers on the platform were predominantly Muslims as the station was right next to Signal Faliya, a huge ghetto of the minority community.

What followed was a group clash in the course of which coach S-6 of the train was burnt down, with horrendous consequences. It was an unprecedented mass crime. As many as fifty-eight persons perished on the spot, charred beyond recognition. One of the injured persons died four days later. Of

1

the fifty-nine fatal casualties, fifty-two were Hindus while nine have remained unidentified till date. In any event, a lot of the casualties were kar sevaks, the targeted group. Twenty-nine of the deceased were men, twenty-two women and eight children. Besides, forty-eight persons sustained burn and other injuries.

The arson erupted about a kilometre from the platform, within 15 minutes of the train's arrival at the Godhra railway station. The train had stalled close to a railway watch tower called 'A' cabin. It was the second time that the train had stalled since its 'departure' from the Godhra station. The first time was when a part of the train was still along the platform, near what is called the 'parcel office'.

The exact sequence of events from the arrival of the train at the platform to the arson near 'A' cabin—or how exactly it came to be stalled twice—has remained shrouded in mystery. This is despite a 785-page trial court verdict on the Godhra incident on 22 February 2011. The mystery endures partly because the two persons who were said to have been instrumental in stalling the train were produced by the prosecution as witnesses rather than as accused persons. Muddying the waters, these witnesses, Iliyas Husen Mulla and Anwar A. Kalander, turned 'hostile' in March 2010 as they declared during the trial that their testimonies had been extracted under torture. The trial court still relied on their pre-trial testimonies, thereby salvaging a key portion of the prosecution's account. The judgment is of course subject to the outcome of appeals against it before superior courts. The overarching issue in this very important case was whether the arson was a premeditated crime or the consequence of a spontaneous riot.

The trial court upheld the conspiracy charge even as it confirmed that the arson had been preceded by a group clash triggered by kar sevaks. Conducted in a specially created court premises at the Sabarmati Jail in Ahmedabad, the trial did serve to resolve contested facts such as this group clash. Though the prosecution had sought to play down the provocative behaviour aimed at Muslims on the platform, the defence counsel succeeded in drawing out the truth while cross-examining prosecution witnesses. In the conclusions drawn in his verdict, trial judge P.R. Patel found that 'some quarrel took place on platform between kar sevaks and hawkers in respect of payment of price of tea-breakfast and compelling for speaking of slogan Jai Shree Ram'. Tellingly, the judgment added: 'Not only that, some kar sevaks had also misbehaved with Muslim girls on the platform.'

The pre-arson violence was not confined to the platform. The trial threw up tell-tale details of a quarrel inside the ill-fated coach S-6, shortly after the train's arrival in Godhra. 'In cross examination, it has also been admitted that in coach S-6, when a Muslim hawker having a beard entered for selling tea, some kar sevaks misbehaved with him and prevented him from selling tea, and then, pushed him out of that coach,' the judgment said.

The judicial confirmation of the various forms of misbehaviour by kar sevaks at the Godhra station did not of course detract from the barbarity that followed in the form of the arson. No amount of provocation could have justified the extent of the retaliation and its tragic consequences in Godhra. Apart from it being cruelly disproportionate, there was no scope to verify whether any of the fifty-nine killed in the arson had been personally involved in the skirmishes a few minutes earlier. It would also be inhuman to dismiss the women and children figuring among the casualties in the Godhra arson as collateral damage. Recalling that the town was 'known for its past history of communal riots', the trial court said: 'For Godhra, this is not the first incident of burning alive innocent persons belonging to Hindu community.'

All the same, having acknowledged the provocation offered by kar sevaks for the pre-arson skirmishes, the trial court could have attributed the mass killings entirely to a spontaneous reaction, which in legal parlance would have translated to an 'unlawful assembly' driven by a 'common object'. Had the finding been of unlawful assembly instead of conspiracy, it would have substantially altered the import of the Godhra incident. The rejection of the pre-meditation charge might have reduced the quantum of punishment. More importantly, the judgment might then have undermined the political rhetoric that had been used by the VHP and others to incite or justify post-Godhra killings.

In the event, the trial court's finding was that the arson had resulted from both conspiracy and unlawful assembly. 'Taking advantage of (the) quarrel (which) took place on (the) platform and (the) misbehaviour by kar sevaks with Muslim girls,' two of the conspirators were found to have 'raised shouts, called Muslim people from nearby area of Signal Faliya etc., by misleading (*sic*) that kar sevaks were abducting (a) Muslim girl inside the train and also instructed to stop the train by chain pulling'. Accordingly, one of the conclusions drawn by the trial court was that the 'gathering of the mob was not only spontaneous, but unlawful assembly came to be formed with a view to fulfil the common object by the assailants'. Referring to the totality of the evidence that had emerged during the trial, the judgment also said that 'the alleged incident was not a simple reaction (to) a small quarrel (which) took place on the platform, but it was a pre-planned attack on the kar sevaks, as part of a conspiracy hatched . . . on the previous day'. The mix of the conspiracy and unlawful assembly charges upheld in Godhra is reminiscent of the proceedings in the Ayodhya case. The difference, though, is that for the demolition of Babri Masjid in 1992, kar sevaks have been arraigned for conspiracy while BJP leaders such as L.K. Advani, Murli Manohar Joshi and Uma Bharti are being tried separately for unlawful assembly.

The evidence that convinced the trial judge about the conspiracy charge had a lot to do with the ferocity of the counter attack on the train, during the two times it had stalled after its Godhra halt. When it stalled for the first time, 'stone pelting (was) started by the members of the mob of Muslim community, from behind Parcel Office, i.e., Signal Faliya, and on the other hand, some kar sevaks had also thrown metals towards that mob'. The situation escalated further when the train stalled at a lonely stretch near 'A' cabin. The violence turned one-sided at this point as those inside the train, vulnerable as they were, could do little beyond shutting all doors and windows. 'Immediately, a mob consisting of more than 900 Muslim persons of nearby area, attacked the train with weapons like sticks, iron-pipes, iron-rods, dhariyas, guptis, shouting slogans and also started pelting stones, acid bulbs-bottles, burning rags etc on the train coaches.' Adding to this frightful situation was 'the instigation', as the trial court put it, from somebody shouting on a loud speaker from the nearby Ali Masjid.

Within minutes of the train stalling near 'A' cabin, coach S-6 was engulfed in flames. Attributing the fire to conspiracy, the trial court gave a finding that the conflagration was caused by petrol. Amid the stone-pelting, members of the mob were found to have entered the coach and splashed petrol from 20-litre carboys or jerry cans. It was held that those conspirators had forced their way inside by cutting the canvas vestibule between coaches S-6 and S-7 and breaking open the sliding door to coach S-6. Judge Patel said: 'As the assailants could not succeed in setting on fire the coach by throwing burning rags etc., some assailants found out another way and after cutting canvas vestibule of coach S-7, succeeded in opening eastern side sliding door of coach S-6 forcibly and after entering into the coach, the East-South corner door of coach S-6 came to be opened, from which some others entered with carboys containing petrol and poured petrol sufficient enough in the coach and then by a burning rag, the entire coach S-6 set on fire.'

Despite this categorical finding, the cause of the fire, like the cause of the stalling, remains a mystery. Since a conspiracy is typically hatched in secrecy, it is common for this charge to be upheld purely on the basis of circumstantial evidence. It is, however, debatable whether such latitude in evidence could be extended to the *execution* of the conspiracy. This is especially when the crime admittedly took place, as in Godhra, in the presence of several persons. Besides forensic reports, the trial court accepted the prosecution's narrative of the incineration on the basis of the testimonies of some hawkers as well as the retracted confession of an accused person. But then, none of the authorized passengers and kar sevaks travelling in that coach vouched for the dramatic manner in which the coach was said to have been burnt from inside. There was no corroboration even from the passengers and kar sevaks who happened to be in that very part of the coach where the conspirators had allegedly entered and splashed petrol from 20-litre cans. They testified to have neither seen nor physically felt the petrol in the overcrowded coach. Making light of this infirmity in the prosecution's account, the trial court said: 'Admittedly, at the time of the incident (around 8 am), all the doors and windows of the entire train were closed because of the tense atmosphere and the passengers were not in a position to see or identify the assailants and that too, unknown assailants.' The judgment was walking a fine line as the issue was not so much of identifying the assailants. The real gap, which remained unaddressed, was that nobody inside the coach had seen or felt anybody break open the door and splash petrol.

On balance, the trial court found enough evidence in the Godhra case to convict thirty-one Muslims, on the charges of murder, conspiracy and unlawful assembly. In its 41-page sentencing order on 1 March 2011, the trial court found the role played by eleven of those convicted persons to be serious enough to warrant no less than the death penalty. They included Jabir Binyamin Behra, whose confession was central to the conspiracy charge and was relied upon despite its retraction. Among the factors pointing to his complicity was that Behra had gone underground for almost a year after the Godhra incident. The confession was recorded on 5 February 2003 following his arrest a fortnight earlier. The judgment used Behra's confession to convict twelve co-accused persons, seven of whom were also awarded the death penalty. The trial court laid much store by Behra's testimony for the sheer magnitude of its disclosures and admissions.

The testimony began with the disclosure that, on the eve of the Godhra incident, Behra and other accused persons had bought 140 litres of petrol in seven carboys from the nearby Kalabhai Petrol Pump and stored them in Aman Guest House, across the road from the railway station. And then, after the eruption of the violence in the morning on platform number one, Behra was involved, by his own admission, in rushing those seven carboys of petrol in a three-wheeler from the guest house to the vicinity of 'A' cabin, where the train had stalled. More importantly, he confessed to having been one of the few assailants directly involved in three vital aspects of burning coach S-6: cutting the vestibule, breaking open the sliding door and splashing petrol from carboys. He confessed to having then got down from the coach along with other assailants on the 'off side', where the survivors of the arson had taken refuge. Further, Behra confessed to have attacked a couple of survivors—one was a passenger and the other a kar sevak—as he engaged in looting money and ornaments.

The testimonies of those two survivors and a Muslim witness in relation to the looting served as corroboration of Behra's confession. There was further corroboration in the testimony of a doctor who had treated Behra the same morning for an injury he had sustained during the violence. At the time of his arrest on 22 January 2003, Behra was found to be still bearing the mark of the injury on his forehead. The prosecution even produced a jeweller to whom Behra was found to have sold a ring, which he had looted from one of the arson survivors. Such meticulous corroboration of minute details persuaded the trial court to rely on Behra's confession even after he had retracted it during the trial, and despite the procedural objections that had been raised by the defence counsel. Taken together, the corroborative evidence adduced by the prosecution did establish that Behra was in the mob which had attacked the train and that he had looted some of the survivors. But whether it also proved more crucial issues such as the conspiracy charge and the prosecution's account of the arson was open to question. Insofar as his confession related to how he and his accomplices had entered the congested coach and splashed petrol from carboys, there was not a word of supporting evidence from any of the survivors. Luckily for the prosecution, this serious gap in the corroborative evidence, as mentioned earlier, was overlooked by the trial court.

Another question mark on Behra's confessional statement

was about the advance purchase of the petrol that had apparently been used in the arson. Though the prosecution produced two witnesses to buttress Behra's confession on this vital aspect, their testimonies were marred by U-turns and flimsy explanations. The testimonies were of two employees of the Kalabhai Petrol Pump, from where Behra and his accomplices were found to have bought 140 litres of petrol in seven carboys. Their corroboration was accepted despite the fact that in their initial testimonies, recorded on 10 April 2002, barely a month after the arson, deliveryman Ranjitsinh Patel and cashier Prabhatsinh Patel had given no indication of that suspicious transaction. They vouched for it only after Behra had confessed in February 2003 that petrol had been bought from the Kalabhai Petrol Pump on the eve of the Godhra arson. In their fresh testimonies recorded before a judicial magistrate in March 2003, the two petrol pump employees claimed that they had not admitted it in the first instance because the police had then asked them only about the transactions that had taken place on the morning of the Godhra incident. Four years later, in a sting investigation by *Tehelka* magazine, Ranjitsinh Patel was caught admitting that he had been induced by the police to echo Behra's confession. Ranjitsingh Patel said on camera that he and Prabhatsinh Patel had each been paid Rs 50,000 in 2003 by investigating officer Noel Parmar to depart from their earlier testimonies. When he deposed in the trial court on 4 March 2010, Ranjitsinh Patel gave yet another twist to his shifting claims. Debunking his original April 2002 testimony, he said he had given it under the influence of the petrol pump owner, who was a Muslim. This stretched credulity because, when the state was still reeling from the post-Godhra violence and the petrol pump had long been sealed in connection with the Godhra case, his former employer was unlikely to have had the clout to thwart the same investigation. The trial court, however, found Ranjitsinh's explanation plausible. Its finding simply stated that his April 2002 statement 'came to be recorded at the instance of (the) owner of the petrol pump'. Equally surprising was the trial court's acceptance of Ranjitsinh's disclaimer on his bribery allegation in the *Tehelka* sting against the police officer. In his deposition during the trial, Ranjitsinh claimed that undercover reporter Ashish Khetan, whom he referred to as 'Dilliwala Bhai', had misled him into believing that he was being considered for a 'TV serial'. Claiming that he had been paid Rs 2,000 for an audition, Ranjitsinh said that he had been asked to make the allegation as part of the deal. 'I did take Rs 2,000 from him and, out of greed for more money, I made the statement saying that Noel Parmar had paid me Rs 50,000 in order to identify as accused those whose photos he had shown me,' Ranjitsinh testified. Without referring to his curious tale about the prospect of acting in a TV serial, the trial court went by Ranjitsinh's attempt to play down his bribery allegation. The judgment said that the 'story of payment of Rs 50,000 to each of (these witnesses) and that too by an investigating officer is highly improbable'. It added: 'No prudent man would dare to take such a risk of giving false evidence, against huge number of accused belong(ing) to Muslim community without thinking about his entire future life.'

Such is the tenuous foundation of the prosecution's whole story about petrol having been bought the previous night as part of the conspiracy behind the arson. Though it got away with this infirmity, the prosecution was not so lucky with other gaps and flaws in its evidence. The very judgment that convicted thirty-one accused persons went on to exonerate as many as sixty-three. In other words, two-thirds of the ninety-four persons who had been tried in the Godhra case were acquitted. Unlike their Hindu counterparts in the post-Godhra massacre cases, who had generally been granted bail sooner than later, most of those found innocent in the Godhra case had languished behind bars for periods ranging up to nine years. One such example was none other than the president of the Godhra municipality, Mohammad Hussain Kalota, who had spent nine years in incarceration before he was acquitted by the trial court. The discriminatory treatment on the bail front ensued partly from the application of the draconian Prevention of Terrorism Act (POTA) to the Godhra case. By the time the trial began in June 2009, POTA charges had, however, been withdrawn, on the basis of a statutory committee's recommendation and the Gujarat high court's endorsement of it.

Of the sixty-three acquittals in the Godhra case, the most telling by far was that of the alleged mastermind, a cleric and timber merchant called Maulvi Hussain Ibrahim Umarji. He was not accused of being present at the scene of the crime nor even at the two meetings allegedly held the night before the Godhra incident, in Aman Guest House. Umarji was still implicated in the conspiracy because the crime had allegedly been committed at his instance. According to the prosecution, one of the conspirators present at the meetings, municipal councillor Bilal Haji, conveyed a message from Umarji 'ordering' them to burn Coach S-6 of the Sabarmati Express returning from Ayodhya in a few hours. This alleged message apparently came to light through the confession of Behra, who was among the conspirators present at the second meeting. Umarji was arrested immediately after Behra's confession had been recorded before a magistrate on 5 Feburary 2003. Early the next morning, in fact, even before sunrise, the police arrested Umarji from his home in a high-security operation. The police took elaborate precautions for his arrest because he had been the most widely quoted spokesperson for his community, the Ghanchi Muslims, who had been accused of complicity in the Godhra crime. A 2002 book, *Gujarat: The Making of a Tragedy* edited by Siddharth Varadarajan, referred to a statement issued by Umarji and other prominent Ghanchi Muslims condemning the Godhra incident. The statement, though in Gujarati, was apparently glossed over by the local media. The book also said that Umarji had participated in peace meetings called by district collector Jayanti Ravi and had 'apologized on behalf of his community'. He did have a credible standing with the district administration: in the wake of the 2002 riots, Umarji was the only one to have been authorized by it to run a relief camp in Godhra. In his bail application before the Supreme Court in 2003, Umarji alleged that he had been framed for embarrassing Chief Minister Narendra Modi during Prime Minister Atal Bihari Vajpayee's visit to Godhra in April 2002. Umarji had given a representation to Vajpayee on the alleged persecution of Muslims in Godhra. When Vajpayee had asked him to elaborate, Umarji pointed to Modi and said sarcastically that he would 'know better'. However, having failed to obtain bail from any of the courts, Umarji secured freedom only on his acquittal, after he had suffered eight years of incarceration.

His acquittal in 2011 was a letdown for the Modi regime. For it had leveraged his arrest to bring back terror charges into the Godhra case. The terror charges had been restored on 19 February 2003, barely a fortnight after Umarji's arrest. When the terror law had been first invoked in 2002, it was within three days of the train burning. The terror law at the time was an ordinance promulgated in the wake of 9/11. The only arrests made by then were of the twenty-eight picked up on the first two days (without any justification, as we shall see). But then, within three weeks of applying them, the Modi regime suffered the mortification of 'suspending' the terror charges. This was even after the number of arrested persons had increased by then to fifty. The turnaround was due to the exigency faced by the Central government of replacing the terror ordinance with a long-term law. Having failed to push the necessary terror bill through the Rajya Sabha, the Vajpayee government convened a joint sitting of the two Houses of Parliament as a last resort. The Modi regime withdrew the terror charges on 25 March, right on the eve of that joint sitting. This was to allay the concerns of some of the political parties, which were sceptical about the terror twist given to the Godhra case. After all, lawmakers had first-hand experience of an actual terror attack, a couple of months before Godhra. It was a shootout inside the Parliament complex as five gunmen had sneaked in, in a car laden with the powerful RDX. The Modi regime's climbdown served the intended purpose of helping the Vajpayee government mobilize enough support within Parliament for the enactment of POTA. The irony deepened a year later when Umarji's arrest heralded the return of terror charges in 2003. The terror charges this time were under POTA, the law that could be passed the previous year only after the Modi regime had dissociated terror from this very case.

So what was so compelling about the evidence against Umarji that the Modi regime was emboldened to reintroduce the terror law in the Godhra case? None of the evidence that had been marshalled against him stood the test of judicial scrutiny. Even before the Godhra trial began in June 2009, the terror charges had once again been withdrawn. This was on the recommendation of a statutory review committee set up by the Manmohan Singh government after repealing POTA. The recommendation was upheld by the Gujarat high court in February 2009. All the accused persons, including Umarji, were still tried for conspiracy—but only under the general criminal law. The trial court went on to uphold the conspiracy charge even as it let off the alleged chief conspirator.

The judgment laid bare the tenuous case that had been made out against Umarji. Besides Behra's confession, all that the prosecution produced against Umarji was the testimony of hawker Sikandar Shaikh, who had seen him for the first time only after the Godhra incident. Between them, the testimonies made two broad allegations. The first, common to both, was that, besides running a relief camp for victims, Umarji gave financial aid to those involved in the arson. The trial court held that the allegation pertained to 'subsequent help' and that it was 'to some extent hearsay'. The second allegation made by Behra alone was about Umarji's name figuring in the conspiracy meeting. The trial court said: 'Except the bare words alleged to have been told by co-accused Bilal Haji, (there was) no other supporting evidence against this accused.' From all this discussion, it concluded: 'Under the circumstances, in (the) absence of sufficient evidence on record, it would not be safe to hold the accused guilty in such (a) serious crime. This accused is, therefore, entitled to get (the) benefit of (the) doubt.' True, he only got the benefit of the doubt; Umarji was among the seven accused persons whose acquittal was not unqualified. But that he was let off at all was remarkable, given the odds that had been stacked against Umarji and how much was riding on his alleged guilt. Umarji's eight-year stint in jail reportedly took a toll on his health. He passed away at the age of sixty-five in January 2013, less than two years after he had been released.

Because of the exoneration of the alleged mastermind, the trial court was silent in its conclusions on how exactly the conspirators had come to meet at the guest house. It just said: 'Conspiracy came to be hatched on the previous day i.e. 26-2-

2002 during the meeting held in Aman Guest House between the conspirators . . .' One of the conspirators found to have been involved in the meeting was Bilal Haji, who had been accused of contributing to the plot by conveying Umarji's message to others in the guest house. This councilor was also found to have been present at the time of the arson and, with the help of his men, blocked the fire tender before it could reach coach S-6. Bilal Haji was among the twelve persons who had been convicted on the basis of, among other things, Behra's confessional statement. Though it awarded the death sentence to Bilal Haji, the conclusions drawn in the judgment steered clear of the prosecution's allegation that it was he who had passed on Umarji's message to other conspirators urging them to target coach S-6. Had it not glossed over this vital aspect in its conclusions, the trial court would have been hard-pressed to explain why the targeting of coach S-6, despite Umarji's acquittal, was specifically a part of the conspiracy.

The judgment was more forthcoming on other egregious flaws in the prosecution's narrative. Take its rejection of the entire lot of evidence given by the nine VHP members who had been presented as independent witnesses. Their testimonies unravelled during their cross examination, partly because of the implausibility of some of their claims and partly because they were clueless about some of the things that had actually happened. One of the issues that damaged the credibility of the VHP witnesses in the eyes of the trial court was their 'ignorance' of the clash between kar sevaks and Muslim hawkers on the platform. Their claim to have been present at the railway station was doubted as, unlike other prosecution witnesses, these local VHP members did not make any admission of the quarrel even during their cross examination.

Having found the testimonies of every one of those nine

'VHP workers' to be 'unreliable', the trial court acquitted as many as thirty-one Muslims who had been named by them as members of the mob that had attacked the train. The thirty-one *acquitted* due to the unreliability of the VHP members should not, however, be confused with the thirty-one *convicted* on the testimonies of other witnesses. The trial court could not help acquitting those thirty-one Muslims, named by one or the other of the nine VHP witnesses, because of an array of contradictions that had emerged during their cross examination. The contradictions prompted the trial court to hold that the VHP members 'cannot be termed as witnesses of truth' and that their testimonies 'can never be accepted as gospel truth'. As a corollary, it awarded convictions only where none of the nine VHP members was cited as a witness or if there was corroboration from other witnesses who were taken to be independent. Out of the thirty-one convicted in the Godhra case, three did happen to be named by one or the other of the nine VHP workers. The trial court made it clear that the convictions of those three Muslims had nothing to do with the discredited testimonies of any of the nine VHP witnesses.

During their examination by the prosecutor, the VHP members parroted the police line claiming that they had all gone to the Godhra railway station as early as 6 am, armed with garlands and food packets, to greet the kar sevaks returning from Ayodhya. But when it came to their cross examination by the defence counsel, the VHP witnesses had no answer as to how they could possibly have planned such a reception given that the Sabarmati Express was originally due to arrive much earlier, at 2.55 am. Such an unearthly hour could only have been, as the trial court observed, 'for peaceful sleeping journey, and can never be accepted as a proper time for welcoming or offering tea-snacks to kar sevaks and thereby to create disturbance to kar sevaks themselves, as also to other passengers'. Even otherwise, the VHP witnesses had no explanation for the timing of their visit to the station despite being unaware of the almost five-hour delay in the running of the train. Nor was there any corroborative evidence of their visit. Though they claimed to have garlanded the kar sevaks and handed over the food packets, none of the kar sevaks testified to have received any such treatment at the station. Neither kar sevaks nor other witnesses, including officials on duty, testified to have even noticed the presence of any of those VHP members. Conversely, VHP witnesses could not explain why they had, even after the train burning, made no effort to approach district police chief Raju Bhargava and collector Jayanti Ravi, who had reached the spot in quick succession. At the end of it all, the trial court was left with no option 'except to discard their evidence in totality with regard to their presence at the time of the incident, at or near the place of occurrence and about witnessing of the incident as narrated by them'.

It was on the testimony of one of the discredited VHP witnesses that the Gujarat police had implicated even Mohammad Hussain Kalota, the Godhra civic chief. Affiliated as he was to the Congress party, Kalota's arrest a fortnight after the incident was touted as the biggest breakthrough in the early phase of the Godhra investigation. His implication in the case was then milked by the BJP to put the Congress on the defensive, in the run-up to the 2002 Gujarat assembly election. After spending nine years as an undertrial prisoner, Kalota, like Umarji, received the benefit of the doubt in 2011.

Despite his prominence in Godhra, the investigators could not get any 'independent' witness from outside the tainted lot of the VHP members. So, while discussing the evidence adduced against Kalota, the trial court pointed out that VHP member

Murlidhar Mulchandani could not be accepted as an independent witness because of the 'political rivalry' between the two. Although the court dismissed Mulchandani's testimony, there was never any doubt about Kalota's presence on the spot. In fact, Kalota himself admitted his presence as he claimed to have, as president of the Godhra municipality, rushed to the spot on hearing about the incident. This was borne out by his mobile phone call records. The prosecution too accepted that he had arrived at the spot only after the outbreak of the violence. Its charge against Kalota was that after his arrival 'he was instigating the members of the mob'. But, 'looking to the conduct of the accused', the court said, 'it is difficult to accept the allegation that he was instigating the crowd'. This was because Kalota, as expected from somebody holding his office, was found to have participated in the rescue operation in various ways: coordinating with police chief Bhargava, helping the fire brigade to access water from a nearby tube well and calling the electricity department to ensure that the water pump worked uninterrupted. The court therefore concluded that Kalota's presence at the place of the incident 'was but natural' and that 'in the absence of any cogent evidence, he cannot be held guilty of any of the charges'.

Next to the discovery of the trumped-up evidence of the VHP members, the biggest setback suffered by the prosecution in the trial court was the exoneration of all the twenty-eight Muslims who had been arrested in Godhra before the eruption of the massacres targeting Muslims. While the unravelling of the mischief related to the VHP witnesses led to thirty-one acquittals, the exposure of the false arrests made in Godhra on 27 and 28 February 2002 led to twenty-five acquittals. Three other persons, who had been arrested along with these twenty-five acquitted persons, died before the commencement of the trial in June 2009. To the Gujarat police, the acquittal in effect of all the twenty-eight persons arrested at the outset in the Godhra case was more damaging than the rejection of the VHP testimonies. For the charges against these twenty-eight accused persons had been based mainly on the testimonies given by policemen themselves.

These twenty-eight persons accused of committing the 'original sin' of the 2002 mass killings happened to be arrested in two batches. In the first batch, fifteen of them were picked up on the day of the crime, allegedly right on the spot. And of these fifteen, one died in custody as an undertrial prisoner. Of the thirteen arrested the morning after the Godhra incident, one died in custody and another when he was out on bail. All the twenty-five that survived the trial in that group of twenty-eight were acquitted as the police witnesses were found to have falsified the circumstances in which they had been arrested. The anticlimax in 2011 came as a vindication of the defence's counter-allegation that all the twenty-eight Muslims had been randomly picked up in the build-up to the post-Godhra massacres.

In the trial court's assessment, what gave away the game was a general claim made by the prosecution about the fifteen arrested on the first day. Besides accusing them of participating in the mob attack on the train, the prosecution claimed that they had all been apprehended 'from the spot', at 9.15 am. The implication of this claim was that even an hour after coach S-6 had caught fire, the Muslim mob, or at least a section of it, was still on the spot and that those fifteen had been caught 'red-handed', as the prosecution was quoted as saying in the judgment. Out of the ninety-four tried in the Godhra case, the charges against fourteen of the fifteen arrested on the first day (one having died before the trial) should, therefore, have been the strongest. Those caught red-handed or nabbed on the spot normally stood the least chance of getting away with the crime. Yet, in the Godhra case, how did these very persons get acquitted—and that too, all of them, without exception?

This paradox betrayed the extent to which facts had been manufactured in the Godhra case, despite the gravity of the mass crime. The rejection of the police testimonies, incidentally, was not because of the absence of corroboration from any independent witness. Citing precedents, the trial court took pains to clarify that it was prepared to go by just the police testimonies, provided they were otherwise found to be reliable. It added, for good measure, that there was 'no principle of law that without corroboration by independent witnesses, their testimony cannot be relied upon'. The court was still forced to reject their testimonies altogether, for a variety of reasons. Not the least was the contradictions in the police's records on the timing and location of the arrests on the first day.

Though the FIR registered at 9.35 am said that 'the mob ran away after (the) assault', the arrests of those fifteen persons were subsequently claimed to have been made on the spot at 9.15 am. Moreover, the police's 'production report' of each of them showed that the arrests had actually taken place a whole 12 hours later, at 9.30 pm. In a bid to reconcile the discrepancy, the police came up with an implausible story. After their arrest at 9.15 am, the fifteen Muslims were, according to the police, 'kept under watch near A cabin up to 12.30 noon (*sic*) and then in the Railway Police Station up to 21.30 hours', till the necessary paperwork was at last carried out. This meant that after they had been nabbed on the spot, the alleged members of the mob were taken away, neither to a police station nor to a magistrate's court. Instead, they were claimed to have been detained for as long as three hours in that 'very tense' atmosphere, at the very place where the rescue operations were going on. None of the eyewitnesses, including officials, corroborated this unlikely police claim. On a 'careful reading' of all the evidence adduced before him, trial judge Patel concluded that 'the story of apprehending of these fifteen accused persons from the spot i.e. near "A" cabin is not believable'. Rather, they were more likely to have been picked up from their homes, as the court said, in the course of a 'combing operation' mounted by the police after 4.30 pm.

Having dismissed the story about the arrests of the first day, the trial court did the same with its sequel too. It rejected the testimonies of the same police witnesses claiming that thirteen more arrests were made the next morning, at 9.30 am. While the police witnesses claimed that those thirteen persons had been 'noticed' by them in the mob that had attacked the train, the defence alleged that they had all been rounded up during the same combing operation in which the previous lot of fifteen accused persons had been picked up. 'Under the circumstances, it would not be safe to rely upon the evidence of said police officials, that they had seen the present accused person in the mob,' the trial court said, adding that there was anyway 'no material on record' against those thirteen Muslims before their arrests.

The sinister pattern of arrests in the immediate aftermath of the Godhra incident is being brought to light for the first time through this book. These false arrests were a measure of the prejudice likely to have been caused to the investigation by Modi's hasty declaration on the first day that the Godhra incident was a terror attack. The police appeared to have come under pressure to make frenetic arrests of Muslims, in a bid to lend credence to Modi's rhetoric. And then, following the eruption of mob attacks on the minority community, there was a prolonged lull in the Godhra case on the arrests front. The next arrest, or rather the next set of arrests, in the Godhra case took place a whole fortnight later, on 14 March 2002, by when hundreds of innocent people had perished across Gujarat.

Around the time of the twenty-eight false arrests at the beginning of the Godhra investigation, the police displayed an equally cavalier attitude to forensic evidence. The trial court was, however, nowhere as exacting in its appraisal of procedural deviations on the forensic front. The police, for instance, showed little concern to preserve the scene of the crime until the arrival of forensic experts. Instead, right from the first day, they never stopped the public from entering the coach and exploring the devastation. Worse, the police took over 30 hours to pick up burnt remnants from the coach as forensic samples for detecting traces of petrol. The saving grace was that for the 'place of occurrence'—the area near 'A' cabin—the police recorded a panchnama (duly documented survey) on the same day. But the panchnama for the coach—the place where the dead bodies had been found—was recorded only the next day, on the evening of 28 February 2002 from 5.45 pm to 7.35 pm. This was when the police got down to preparing a seizure memo of the pieces of evidence collected from the burnt coach, after numerous people had already walked through it. In an even more bizarre delay, it was only on 28 April 2002 that the police requested the Ahmedabad-based Forensic Science Laboratory (FSL) to make a physical inspection of the coach. Consequently, forensic experts visited the scene of the crime for the first time ever on 1 May 2002, which was more than two months since the occurrence of the crime.

Adding a touch of tragi-comedy, the first team of forensic experts got to see the scene of the crime about a month after a team of eminent journalists had visited coach S-6 on 3 April

2002. In their contemporaneous report on behalf of the Editors Guild of India, B.G. Verghese, Dileep Padgaonkar and Aakar Patel said that they were 'surprised to see this prime exhibit standing in the yard unguarded and stray people entering it at will. Anyone could remove or plant anything in the carriage, tampering with whatever evidence it has to offer with none being any the wiser'. This is completely at odds with the official line accepted by the trial court that coach S-6 had been 'kept under the watch of police guard till (the) visit of FSL officials'. In fact, the trial court was dismissive about the concerns over the delay in calling FSL officials or seizing samples from the coach. 'No doubt it is true that help of FSL officers was not taken immediately, but in my view, it makes no difference, because in all 34 muddamal (case property) articles seized from the place of occurrence and the Coach S-6 were sent immediately to the FSL by special messenger.'

The outcome of the FSL's belated inspection was a simulation experiment in May suggesting that the petrol had been thrown from inside the coach. This paved the way for the breakthrough claimed by the police after another two months, on the mystery of how the miscreants had entered the coach. The breakthrough was the testimony given by hawker Ajay Kanubhai Bariya in July 2002. It was on the basis of Bariya's testimony that the police came up with the version spelt out in their second charge-sheet stating that the miscreants had broken into the coach through the sliding door. As a corollary, the sliding door had then been examined by FSL to confirm that it had served as the entry point for miscreants.

The implications of these disclosures contained in the trial court judgment on the quality and integrity of the investigation should be of concern to more than just human rights defenders. The shoddy investigation in the Godhra case—on the forensic front or as evident from the grounds for acquittal—suggests that the police were more into playing politics than finding facts. Without detracting from any of the thirty-one convictions awarded in the case, the judgment can be read as an exposé on the fact-finding done by the Gujarat police and then by the Supreme Court-appointed Special Investigation Team (SIT). Among the nine Gujarat carnage cases entrusted to it in 2008, the SIT deviated the least in the Godhra case from the original police investigation. The only substantive change it made was to arraign one more person and, as it happened, Ibrahim Dhantiya turned out to be among the sixty-three acquitted persons. If Godhra was the result of a conspiracy, as held by the trial court, it was all the more a reason why the investigation should have been of unimpeachable quality. The dirty tricks uncovered by the judgment, wittingly or otherwise, hardly inspire the confidence that real culprits have been brought to justice. The casualties in the Godhra arson deserved better fact-finding, especially under a government that derived so much political mileage from their tragedy.

2

The Dithering Over 'Rajdharma'

It did not happen out of the blue. Just a day before fifty-eight people were killed in the Godhra train burning, members from Opposition parties had repeatedly disrupted Parliament on the Ayodhya issue. The cause for those protests on 26 February 2002 was the initiation, a couple of days earlier, of a mahayagna or a grand ritual in Ayodhya. The mahayagna had been organized by the VHP as a prelude to its programme of starting the construction of the Ram janmabhoomi temple on 15 March 2002. The proposed 'Ram Mandir Nirman' was in defiance of the Supreme Court's status quo injunction, which had been issued in the wake of the demolition of the Babri Masjid in 1992. The MPs demanded that kar sevaks gathering at Ayodhya be arrested and the construction material collected there be seized.

While the Rajya Sabha was adjourned thrice on the issue on 26 February 2002, the Lok Sabha had to forego the question hour in the morning as Opposition MPs protested the government's reluctance to spell out any measures to combat the VHP's plans. Since the government was due to transact

urgent business in the Lok Sabha, Prime Minister Atal Bihari
Vajpayee sought to pacify Opposition MPs in that House by
making a statement. But Vajpayee ended up annoying them
further as he maintained that the mahayagna could not be
stopped unless it created 'a law and order problem'. When the
Lok Sabha reconvened at noon, the government was allowed to
present the economic survey and railway budget. This was
mainly because of Vajpayee's assurance that he would hold an
all-party meeting the same evening.

The all-party meeting, however, failed to yield any consensus
as the BJP-led government held on to its unstated policy of
running with the hare and hunting with the hounds. As *The
Hindu* reported, 'The Government today assured an all-party
meeting that it would maintain status quo in Ayodhya and take
appropriate steps to prevent recurrence of 1992-like situation,
even as the Opposition and some allies of the ruling National
Democratic Alliance expressed dissatisfaction that measures had
not been not initiated or outlined to prevent the build-up of kar
sevaks.' The main Opposition party was evidently so dissatisfied
with the all-party meeting that its president Sonia Gandhi
convened an emergency meeting at that hour of its highest
body, the Congress Working Committee (CWC). The urgency
was increased by the fact that Vajpayee was due to leave the next
evening for Australia. Senior Congress leader Arjun Singh briefed
the CWC about the government's refusal to commit itself to a
plan of action. A prescient line in another report of *The Hindu*
said: 'Mr. Singh told the CWC that the situation was heading
for a catastrophe and the Government was unwilling to commit
itself on how it proposed to prevent the situation from taking a
turn for the worse.'

The worst of the apprehensions expressed at the all-party
and CWC meetings were confirmed the very next morning,

when a train bringing back the first batch of kar sevaks from
Ayodhya to Gujarat was attacked in Godhra. It vindicated the
Opposition charge that the government had been negligent.
Unsurprisingly, Godhra put Vajpayee and his number two,
home minister L.K. Advani, on the defensive. So much so that,
on 27 February 2002, these two avowed votaries of Hindutva
did not utter a word against the Muslim mob alleged to have
caused the death of fifty-eight Hindus. In their statements on
the day of the Godhra incident, Vajpayee and Advani showed
more concern about the VHP's contribution to the crisis. Take
the manner in which their uncharacteristic reticence on the
Muslim role was captured by *The Times of India*, in a report
appearing on the front page on 28 February 2002 headlined
'Govt cajoles and warns VHP'.

> As the death of 55 [*sic*] rail passengers in Godhra brought
> home the incendiary implications of the VHP's Ayodhya
> campaign, Prime Minister Atal Bihari Vajpayee on Wednesday
> asked it to suspend its agitation and said the government
> would maintain law and order at all costs.
>
> Vajpayee clearly linked the incident to the ongoing
> movement for a Ram temple at Ayodhya. 'I appeal to the
> VHP to suspend its movement,' he said, adding that 'the
> Ayodhya problem cannot be solved through a movement or
> violence. There are only two ways, finding a solution through
> negotiations or leaving it to [the] courts.' Asked if the incident
> was linked to the Ayodhya issue, he said, 'An inquiry is being
> held . . . reports indicate the train was stopped because slogans
> were being raised.'
>
> Home Minister L.K. Advani's message to the VHP was
> much more direct. While strongly condemning the incident,
> he warned that the VHP has 'embarked on a course of action
> in Ayodhya which is fraught with dangerous consequences.
>
> 'Thousands are sought to be assembled in Ayodhya to

take part in a mass exercise which can only lead to flagrant
defiance of court orders.' Advising the VHP to show restraint,
Advani said, 'if, however, they persist with the agitation, we
will not hesitate to take action against those who defy court
orders or create problems for law and order.'

While Vajpayee's reaction came out through a brief verbal
interaction with reporters, Advani issued a written statement in
which he called upon VHP leaders to 'abandon their present
course of action'. This press release was his only statement of
the day and, as such, it was widely quoted in the media. The
TOI report was inaccurate, though, in suggesting that Advani
had condemned the Godhra incident on the first day. For the
press release issued hours after the train burning made no
reference to it all, at least not explicitly. As for Muslims, Advani
did refer to them but that was only while he was exhorting
religious leaders of both communities 'to initiate a dialogue' on
the temple dispute. Curiously, Advani's press release of
27 February 2002 was more on Ayodhya than Godhra.

Their initial reactions to Godhra on a day they were
preoccupied in Parliament with the presentation of the General
Budget proved to be a feeble attempt to uphold the rule of law.
No member of the VHP has ever been held to account, legally
or otherwise, for precipitating the Godhra crisis or for the clash
between kar sevaks and Muslim vendors leading to the burning
of the train. Instead, mobs led by VHP cadres and other Hindu
extremists carried out retaliatory violence in Gujarat leading to
a prolonged carnage in which over 1,000 people, mostly Muslims,
were killed.

This was the first communal conflagration after Hindutva
forces had captured power at the Centre in 1998. Just how far
Vajpayee and Advani moved away from the secular concerns
they had expressed on 27 February was evident from their

conduct over the next few days. They were the foremost leaders of the party that was in power at the Centre as well as in Gujarat. Yet, after their initial remarks against the VHP on the day of the Godhra incident, Vajpayee and Advani turned resolutely passive, at a time when their intervention could have reduced, if not averted, the violence against Muslims.

Though Parliament was in session, neither of the leaders made any statement there on the Godhra or post-Godhra violence for the first few days, when the killings were at their peak. This was even after Advani had, in response to Opposition demands, promised the Lok Sabha on 28 February that he would make a statement the following day. The first time he spoke at length in Parliament on the Gujarat riots was on 11 March, replying to a 'short duration discussion' in the Rajya Sabha and a 'discussion under rule 193' (that is, without a vote) in the Lok Sabha. Advani admitted then that he could not keep his promise that he would make a statement on 1 March, but did not advance any reason for that failure. 'In fact, I have with me the statement that I had prepared immediately after the happening and I was to make it in the House, but somehow, I could not make it in this House,' Advani said on 11 March in the Lok Sabha.

Vajpayee made his first appeal to the nation over television on the evening of 2 March, by which time the worst of the massacres had already occurred. And though Advani was the minister in charge of internal security, and an MP from one of the affected areas, he found time to visit Gujarat only on 3 March. The prime minister took another whole month to visit the state, although it continued to be in the grip of communal violence, however sporadic. Neither Vajpayee nor Advani ever again spoke against the VHP, whether in the context of the Godhra or post-Godhra violence. Even when he did break his

'Delphic silence' (as *The Times of India* put it) on 2 March, Vajpayee confined himself to asking the citizens of Gujarat to maintain harmony. 'He did not warn those organizations and individuals which were indulging in a killing spree that they would be dealt with firmly,' *The Times of India* pointed out at the time.

What explains this drastic change in attitude, or the sudden pusillanimity, towards the VHP on the part of Vajpayee and Advani at a critical juncture in India's history? It seems to have been precipitated by a meeting they had with a VHP delegation on the very day on which they had issued their stern statements against it. The two leaders appear to have crumbled under ideological pressure exerted not just by the VHP but also by the Rashtriya Swayamsevak Sangh (RSS), the umbrella organization of both the VHP and the BJP. In that unscheduled meeting on the evening of 27 February, the VHP chief, Ashok Singhal, was accompanied by RSS leaders Madan Das Devi and Rama Jois. Those who participated in it from the government's side included Advani, Law Minister Arun Jaitley, and Defence Minister George Fernandes (who was the only one in that encounter from outside the Sangh Parivar).

Singhal forced the government functionaries at the highest level to take time off to meet him, even after he and other VHP leaders had rubbished Vajpayee's appeal and Advani's warning to the Ayodhya agitators. The VHP's vice president, Giriraj Kishore, for instance, had raised questions insinuating that the government was being partial to Muslims: 'Why is the appeal to maintain peace being made to us? Why is it not being made to those who are creating disaffection? Why is nothing being said (to those) who attacked the train with swords and torches?'

The media widely reported that Singhal had given an earful to Vajpayee and his ministers, and left the meeting in a huff. As

Devi was a senior functionary of the RSS (he was its joint general secretary), his decision to accompany Singhal was taken as a sign that the RSS was on the VHP's side on the Godhra issue. Even the BJP president, Jana Krishnamurthy, was found to be echoing the VHP's thoughts. He declared that the Godhra killings had been perpetrated by those who were 'out to destabilize the country'. The subversives, in Krishnamurthy's mind, could only have been Muslims, as the VHP, however militant and lawless in its activities, is apt to be perceived by other constituents of the Sangh Parivar as being nationalistic. In a report headlined 'VHP rejects PM's appeal', *The Times of India* noted the dissonance on the fateful day between the government and the ruling party:

> If the government appeared to be distancing itself from the VHP, the BJP leadership clearly was not. For while the BJP leaders condemned the incident and pointed fingers at the ISI/terrorist outfits, they said nothing about the provocative slogans raised by the kar sevaks, nor the fact that the VHP buildup in Ayodhya was inciting passions.

Pressure was mounting on Vajpayee and Advani to view Godhra through the lens of ideology rather than governance; to place political interest over national interest. Their initial attempts to rein in the VHP drew sharp reactions from not just the VHP but also the RSS, and hardliners within the BJP. The tipping point was the reaction from Narendra Modi, chief minister of Gujarat.

After going to Godhra the same evening (27 February), Modi declared just the opposite of what Vajpayee and Advani had said earlier in the day in New Delhi. For someone who had been in office for less than five months and who had contested and won an election for the first time in his life just three days earlier, Modi displayed remarkable insouciance. He had no qualms in brushing aside the concerns expressed by the two 'tallest' leaders of his party, whether about the Ayodhya campaign or the provocative behaviour of the kar sevaks. Instead, leveraging his office, Modi lent credence to the counter-allegations made by VHP leaders putting the blame for Godhra squarely on Muslims. In fact, citing no evidence, he made far-reaching assertions. He told the media that the train-burning was a 'pre-planned' crime involving 'terrorists'. As the number of casualties was high and those who died in Godhra were all apparently Hindus, there were ready takers for Modi's version. While making such utterances on Godhra at a sensitive moment, Modi could not have been oblivious to their potential to inflame anti-Muslim sentiment, or add fuel to the fire in a state notoriously prone to communal violence.

What followed the next day (28 February) broadly conformed to the pattern of communal violence in India. Large-scale reprisals erupted, in the course of a statewide bandh called by the VHP and openly supported by the BJP. The ruling party's participation in the bandh, needless to add, had a paralysing effect on the police. It led to lawless situations as in Gulberg Society, a Muslim pocket in a predominantly Hindu neighbourhood of Ahmedabad. This is where former Congress MP Ehsan Jafri was killed along with sixty-eight others, despite the presence of the police and despite repeated phone calls by him to state authorities and political leaders.

A crucial reason for such rampant lawlessness was the reluctance of political leaders, especially from the ruling dispensation, to visit disturbed areas in real time. One honourable exception was George Fernandes, who arrived in Ahmedabad late in the evening on 28 February and visited some localities the next day. It was no coincidence that during the first three days of the post-Godhra riots, when the violence against Muslims was at its height, the only minister who could be spared for this purpose by the BJP-led coalition government was from neither the Sangh Parivar nor Gujarat. The decision to send Fernandes, a veteran socialist, smacked of tokenism. The reason cited for dispatching the defence minister was that Modi had asked for the army's help in controlling the riots. It's another matter though that when the army is sent 'in aid of civil power', the defence minister has little role in its deployment.

As an outsider in more senses than one, his visit to some of the affected areas on 1 March seemed to have had little effect on the rioters or the police. If anything, his motorcade itself came under attack as he attempted to plough a lone furrow. Two days later, in a first-person account carried in *The Times of India* of his peace initiative, Fernandes made no secret of his disappointment that neither Modi nor any of his ministers had accompanied him on his visit. He recalled a visit he had made as an Opposition leader to Ahmedabad in 1969 in the midst of similar riots. Then too, in a bid to restore peace, Fernandes had participated in a walk through the affected areas. The difference, according to him, was that the then chief minister, Hitendra Desai, and his cabinet colleagues had also participated in the walk. 'This time as I went around (my motorcade was also stoned), I realized that our political parties do nothing beyond struggling for power,' Fernandes said, adding, 'There is no civic leadership. There are no tall men around.'

The hint was unmistakable. Fernandes, who was the convener of the ruling NDA coalition, was anguished that Modi did not prove to be tall enough to reach out to the riot-affected people in their hour of need. Fernandes could of course have said the same about Vajpayee and Advani. For all that they did in New Delhi was to issue a joint appeal for peace along with leaders of various other political parties.

Though he had been repeatedly taunted in Parliament for it, Advani never gave any reasons for keeping away from Gujarat during all that violence, till 3 March. The delay was glaring as the subject of communal violence fell under the jurisdiction of his ministry, in the quasi federal arrangement in India. His silence only reinforced allegations of 'state-sponsored riots' or the larger plan to let Hindus give vent to their anger for three days.

Curiously, even his memoirs published six years later shed no light on this vital question of delay, although it devoted a whole chapter to the communal violence in Gujarat. Refuting the charge that 'the Centre turned a blind eye while violence was raging in Gujarat', *My Country My Life* made light of the fact that his visit came after the worst of the massacres—in Gulberg Society, Naroda Patiya, Sardarpura, Best Bakery, etc.—had already played out. 'Within three days of the violence erupting outside Godhra, I visited the state . . .' Advani wrote, somewhat matter-of-factly. While quoting a news report related to his Gujarat visit, Advani steered clear of those that questioned the delay. Take the manner in which *The Telegraph* began its curtain-raiser to his visit: 'L.K. Advani has finally decided to go to Gujarat tomorrow. But, perhaps, he is nearly 100 hours too late. The home minister will be in Ahmedabad when the bloodletting is gradually subsiding.'

Another inconvenient detail evaded by Advani's narrative is the media statements made by him and Vajpayee on the day of the Godhra incident blaming the VHP for the crisis. No question, therefore, of any explanation for their sudden U-turn on the VHP's culpability. In other words, Advani's book does not come clean on why he and Vajpayee, abandoning their misgivings about the VHP, acquiesced to Modi's approach of portraying the kar sevaks as innocent victims in the Godhra incident. Such vital omissions are despite Advani's repeated lament, in his 2008 book and otherwise, that the killings in Gujarat had 'blemished the Vajpayee government's widely appreciated record, until then, of having drastically brought down the number of incidents of communal violence in the country'.

The saving grace, however, is that Advani acknowledged in his memoirs that he and Vajpayee, for all their comradeship over the decades, had not seen eye to eye on Modi's culpability. In fact, he claimed credit for helping Modi remain in office in the face of Vajpayee's reservations. Having left the Muslims of Gujarat entirely at Modi's mercy during the most destructive phase of the post-Godhra violence stretching over three days, Advani remained steadfast in backing Modi in 2002 while Vajpayee, reputedly the more liberal leader, kept vacillating on Modi's culpability.

This pattern began with the contrasting ways in which the two spoke during their respective visits to Gujarat. When he went there on 3 March, Advani seemed to have little in common with the Union home minister who had just four days earlier issued a stern warning to the VHP from New Delhi. Advani's statements from Gujarat confirmed that he had since internalized Modi's line on the Godhra arson: that it was premeditated act of terrorism. Advani demonstrated a similar convergence with Modi on the post-Godhra riots too, as he denied that the Gujarat police were 'inactive' during the attacks on Muslims. All in all, at the end of Advani's visit, Modi could not have asked for a more resounding endorsement from the Centre for his handling of the violence.

Vajpayee's visit a month later, however, threw a spanner in the works. He did not stop with a word of compassion for those who had been targeted by mobs to avenge Godhra. In a tacit indictment of Modi, Vajpayee invoked the traditional Indian benchmark of 'rajdharma', which enjoined upon the ruler to act impartially. It was a throwback to a sermon in the Mahabharata delivered by Bhishma, from his deathbed of arrows, to Yudhishtir on his duty to perform 'rajdharma'. This loaded term cropped up in a press conference at the end of his visit to Gujarat on 4 April 2002. Since he had a bone to pick with officials, Vajpayee was asked if he had a message for the chief minister, too. 'I have just one message for the chief minister: he should adhere to "rajdharma". This word is deeply meaningful. I too follow it. At least, I try to do so. For the king or the ruler cannot discriminate between people, whether on the basis of birth, caste or religion.' Worried over the implication of Vajpayee's reply, Modi, who was sitting next to him, butted in to say, 'Hum bhi wahi kar rahein hain, Saheb' (Even I am doing so, Sir). Vajpayee left him with a face-saver, saying he trusted Modi's claim. Much as the chief minister clutched at that straw, the very invocation of 'rajdharma' came across as an admission from the prime minister that the Modi regime was perceived to be discriminating against Muslims.

One aspect of discrimination that did get highlighted, as an unintended consequence of Vajpayee's visit, was Modi's indifference to the Muslims who had been displaced. Vajpayee, besides going to Godhra, had called on the victims sheltered in Ahmedabad's Shah Alam relief camp, where many of those who had been displaced from Naroda Patiya, the worst hit locality in the carnage, were sheltered. Though it was five weeks after the Godhra incident, it was Modi's first visit to what was the largest relief camp, and even that was thanks to the protocol that required him to accompany the prime minister. Vajpayee's visit also came at a time when Modi was attempting to shut down the camps, which had all been set up by Muslim organizations and which were serving as reminders of his monumental failure as an administrator. Some of the inmates of the Shah Alam camp heckled Modi even as Vajpayee expressed remorse, saying it was 'heart-wrenching that people should become refugees in their own country'. It was not, however, just the refugees' plight that caused him so much pain. Vajpayee admitted that he had his own reasons too. He was due to leave shortly for a visit abroad. Vajpayee said publicly: 'With what face, I do not know, I will go abroad after all that has happened here. *Yeh pagalpan band hona chahiye*' (this madness must end).

When he took off on his visit to Singapore and Cambodia, the fear of losing face on account of the Gujarat riots continued to haunt Vajpayee. This was disclosed in August 2009 by Arun Shourie, the minister who accompanied Vajpayee on that visit. In an interview to *The Indian Express* editor-in-chief Shekhar Gupta on NDTV's 'Walk the Talk', Shourie said that he had asked Vajpayee during the flight why he was looking so sad. Vajpayee's reply: *'Mujhe kyun yahan bheja ja raha hai? Main kis muh se utroonga? Is kalank ko mere munh par laga diya.'* (Why am I being sent here? With what face will I land? They put this taint on my face.) In a bid to relieve Vajpayee of his distress, Shourie suggested to the prime minister that he call up Advani at the earliest and ask him to obtain Modi's resignation. For all his anguish, Vajpayee never rang up Advani because, according to Shourie, 'it is not Atalji's nature to press beyond a point.'

Vajpayee did get to talk with Advani, shortly after his return from that foreign visit. It happened when Shourie again accompanied Vajpayee on a flight, this time to Goa to attend the BJP's national executive meeting from 12-14 April 2002. This was an opportunity for Vajpayee to resolve his Modi dilemma as Advani too was present in the aircraft along with another senior minister, Jaswant Singh. When Vajpayee finally conveyed his unhappiness over Modi's continuance, Advani had little option but to promise that he would take up the matter in Goa with the Gujarat chief minister. It led to a great deal of drama in the party conclave. Modi, however, proved to have greater support than Vajpayee, and survived as hardliners prevailed.

There are three inside accounts of how exactly an agreement on Modi's removal thrashed out by Vajpayee and Advani on the flight to Goa came to be overruled in the party meeting. One is Advani's own, extracted from his 2008 memoirs, while the other two accounts are those of Jaswant Singh and Arun Shourie, from their 'Walk the Talk' interviews, given in quick succession in August 2009.

As Advani recounts in his book, the move to sack Modi in 2002 was one of the two instances when Vajpayee and he had 'significant differences', the other one being the issue of associating the BJP directly with the Ayodhya movement. While Opposition parties as well as some people within the BJP and the NDA demanded Modi's ouster, Advani was convinced that Modi had been 'unfairly targeted' and that he had been 'more sinned against than sinning'. Vajpayee, however, came under pressure because of 'the vitriolic propaganda by our ideological adversaries', damaging the image of BJP and the government. 'Although Atalji had not expressed his view explicitly on this matter, I knew that he favoured Modi's resignation. And he knew that I disfavoured it.'

As Advani describes it, during the two-hour journey to Goa, Vajpayee fell into a 'contemplative mood' in the course of a discussion on Gujarat. Jaswant Singh broke a long spell of silence by asking Vajpayee what he thought about Modi. Vajpayee replied: *'Kam se kam isteefa ka offer to karte.'* (He should have at least offered to resign.) Advani then said, 'If Narendra's quitting is going to improve the situation in Gujarat, I am willing to tell him to offer his resignation. But I do not think that it would help. Also, I am not sure whether the party's National Council or Executive would accept the offer.'

Advani goes on to say that as soon as they arrived in Goa, he called up Modi and told him that he should offer to resign. Modi readily agreed. In the party meeting, Modi put the Godhra and post-Godhra violence in the perspective of Gujarat's long history of communal tension. He ended his speech saying, 'Nevertheless, as head of the government, I take responsibility for what has happened in my state. I am ready to tender my resignation.'

However, the hundred-odd members of the party's top decision-making body and special invitees gave a thunderous response: '*Isteefa mat do, isteefa mat do*' (Don't resign, don't resign.) Advani adds that he then consulted senior leaders present there. Each one of them, 'without exception', said that he must not resign. 'Thus ended the debate inside the party on an issue that had generated deeply divided opinions in Indian society and polity.'

About a year after the publication of Advani's memoirs, Jaswant Singh came up with a substantially different account of the drama within the BJP. This came at a time when Jaswant Singh was temporarily out of the party because of a sympathetic book he had written on Pakistan's founder, M.A. Jinnah, one that had been banned by the Gujarat government.

In his 'Walk the Talk' interview with Shekhar Gupta, Jaswant Singh recounted that on the fateful flight to Goa, Vajpayee asked his three co-passengers, '*Gujarat ka kya karna hai?*' (What should be done with Gujarat?) After a spell of silence, Vajpayee persisted, '*Gujarat ke bare mein sochna hai.*' (We have to think about Gujarat). Then Advani went towards the toilet. Pointing to Advani, Vajpayee asked Singh: '*Poochhiye fir kya karna hai.*'

(Ask him then what should be done). When Singh conveyed Vajpayee's message to him, Advani just uttered one phrase: *'Bawal khada ho jayega party mein.'* (There will be a commotion in the party). Asked by Shekhar Gupta whether this meant that Advani had come to Modi's rescue while Vajpayee had called for action, Singh said: 'I think that is correct.'

Shourie's own account in 'Walk the Talk' of what transpired at the time was even more interesting. Having seen Vajpayee's distress over Modi's continuance during the foreign tour in April 2002, Shourie said he returned with a resolve that the matter should be thrashed out one way or the other. He made a remarkable confession: 'I was more affected by Atalji's pain than by what had happened in Gujarat. Maybe this is my inhumanity or something. I can't claim that I was that great liberal.'

At the end of the conversation between Vajpayee and Advani on the flight to Goa, 'it was definitely decided that when we get down, Advaniji will ring up Modi and say that in the meeting in the evening, offer to resign'. In the event, when Modi offered to resign, he told the gathering, *'Main nahin chahta ki* party should have any difficulties because of me.' (I don't wish that the party should . . .)

'And as if on cue, people from different parts of the hall started saying, "absolutely no . . . *koi galti nahin hai* . . . "' (You have committed no mistake). Sitting at the back, Shourie saw Vajpayee's 'bewilderment because he thought this was a done deal. This was like an orchestrated coup against him.'

Shourie intervened in the meeting, saying, 'Narendra Modi *ne abhi jo yeh kaha hai,* it's in pursuance of the decision which these senior leaders have taken in the flight . . . I was present.' (What Narendra Modi said just now, it's in pursuance . . .) There was consternation, but immediately again 'the chorus started' and eventually Vajpayee or the party president announced that as it was time for the scheduled public meeting, the Modi issue could be decided the next day. This was again greeted with protests. 'So there is absolutely no doubt,' according to Shourie, 'that Atalji was completely thwarted.'

Whether Vajpayee was 'completely thwarted' on 12 April 2002, and indeed whether there was any high principle involved in his objection to Modi, is open to question. That very evening at the public meeting in Goa, Vajpayee delivered a speech echoing Modi's claims on the Godhra and post-Godhra violence. This changed the complexion of the Modi debate within the BJP. Once he too agreed that Muslims alone were accountable for Godhra and that the retaliatory violence was spontaneous and unavoidable, there was little reason left for Vajpayee to seek Modi's ejection. Therefore, notwithstanding the announcement that had been made at the end of the first day's session of the national executive (as claimed by Shourie), no one bothered the next day to resume the discussion on Vajpayee's proposal of penalizing Modi for his handling of the violence.

Given the dramatic change in his stand in the course of a single evening, it would seem that Vajpayee had been swayed by hardliners after hearing their protests at the national executive meeting. Whatever the reason for the shift, Vajpayee's speech at the public meeting in Goa on the evening of 12 April had much to cheer the BJP leaders who had outmanoeuvered him earlier in the day. What stood out was his sudden insensitivity to the feelings of Muslims, and that at a time when they had just been subjected to a series of massacres in Gujarat. He said:

> Wherever Muslims live, they don't like to live in co-existence with others, they don't like to mingle with others; and instead of propagating their ideas in a peaceful manner, they want to

spread their faith by resorting to terror and threats. The world has become alert to this danger . . .

What happened in Gujarat? If a conspiracy had not been hatched to burn alive the innocent passengers of the Sabarmati Express, then the subsequent tragedy in Gujarat could have been averted. But this did not happen. People were torched alive. Who were those culprits? The government is investigating this. Intelligence agencies are collecting all the information. We should not forget how the tragedy of Gujarat started. The subsequent developments were no doubt condemnable, but who lit the fire? How did the fire spread?

This was a far cry from Vajpayee's earlier perspective. Once he reframed the lighting of the fire in Godhra as the starting point, it suggested that Vajpayee was no longer concerned about the provocation that had been offered by kar sevaks. The Goa speech of 12 April was also a complete disconnect from the one he had delivered just eight days earlier at the Shah Alam camp in Ahmedabad invoking 'rajdharma'. In a sixteen-hour discussion that took place in the Lok Sabha on Gujarat on 30 April, several Opposition MPs made an issue of the divergence between his 4 April and 12 April speeches. Responding to the discussion under rule 184 (which allows voting), Vajpayee denied that he had been changing his statements. 'What I said in Gujarat is not different from what I said in Goa,' he insisted, adding, 'It seems that a speech in one day has finished me. The allegation has become a never-ending source of agony for me.' He took pains to clarify that his Goa speech was not an attack on all Muslims but on the form of Islam that 'is now being used in militancy, which has no place for tolerance. It runs on the slogan of jehad and dreams of bringing the entire world under its aegis.'

Considering the context in which he was referring to jehad, Vajpayee's conversion to the Modi line on Godhra appeared to be complete by the time he spoke in the Lok Sabha on 30 April. This was reinforced by a disclosure he made during a similar discussion in the Rajya Sabha, which concluded its session on 6 May. He said that he had decided to remove Modi the previous month but then had thought the better of it. 'I had gone to Goa making up my mind on changing the ruler in Gujarat but according to my own assessment, I felt that the change in leadership would only worsen the situation.' This was the closest Vajpayee came to admitting in the immediate aftermath of the Gujarat carnage that he, the liberal face of the BJP, had surrendered to the hardliners in the larger Sangh Parivar. For all his protestations that he had never discriminated against anyone on the basis of religion, Vajpayee's speeches in Goa and Parliament presaged a further erosion of secularism in India.

This is because it emboldened Modi to derive political mileage from the carnage. Having sold his narrative of a Muslim terror conspiracy and spontaneous Hindu backlash, Modi sought to cash in on it when feelings were still running high. Although elections were due only the following year, he dissolved the assembly prematurely on 19 July 2002. His stated reason though for seeking early elections was 'to challenge the forces maligning Gujarat's image and get people's verdict'. However, the Election Commission, after surveying the situation on the ground, said that it would not be able to hold free and fair elections earlier than November or December that year. Rather than deferring to the opinion of the institution tasked to maintain the integrity of elections, the Vajpayee government went out of its way to challenge the commission. It resorted to the extraordinary device of making a presidential reference to the Supreme Court.

Then, when Modi pulled off a thumping victory in December 2002, winning 127 out of 182 seats, Vajpayee was swept by the euphoria that had engulfed the Sangh Parivar. It prompted him to make another extraordinary gesture, this time of attending Modi's swearing-in function in Ahmedabad's Sardar Stadium on 22 December. Modi proclaimed on his website: 'First incidence in the country where the prime minister attended the oath-taking ceremony of a chief minister.' It appeared that by the end of what was a traumatic year for the country, the Sangh Parivar, recovering from Vajpayee's pangs of conscience, was back to being one large happy family.

In a curious twist of history, Vajpayee returned to playing the spoiler. The liberal in him resurfaced, or his conscience pricked him once more in June 2004, shortly after he had found himself out of office. Brooding over his party's unexpected defeat in the Lok Sabha elections, Vajpayee felt that the failure to sack Modi for the Gujarat violence was one of the principal underlying reasons. 'The impact of the Gujarat riots was felt nationwide. This was unexpected and hurt us badly; Modi should have been removed after the incident,' Vajpayee said in an interview to Zee TV on 13 June 2004. Much in the spirit of his 'rajdharma' exhortation at the Shah Alam camp two years earlier, Vajpayee revived the proposal to remove Modi for his handling of the riots. The only difference this time was that Vajpayee mustered the courage to say openly what he had swallowed at the party meeting in Goa in April 2002. Also, notwithstanding the fiasco in Goa, he made bold to announce through the interview that the issue of leadership change in Gujarat would figure in the upcoming meeting of the BJP national executive in Mumbai from 22-24 June 2004. However, having caved in to the hardliners in Goa while he was prime minister, Vajpayee had little chance of standing up to them in Mumbai, without the clout and prestige of that high office. Equally critical in saving Modi from Vajpayee's renewed attack was this intervening circumstance: the Gujarat police's sensational encounter with a nineteen-year-old student from Greater Mumbai, Ishrat Jahan, and three others, who were all allegedly on a mission to kill Modi. It was brilliantly timed for Modi as his 'would-be assassins' were killed near Gandhinagar on 15 June, just two days after Vajpayee's scathing observations on him. Much as it helped Modi consolidate his position in 2004, the Ishrat Jahan encounter has since been registered by the CBI as a 'fake encounter' case on the orders of the Gujarat high court, and several senior police officers have been jailed for their alleged involvement in the conspiracy.

Despite the mileage derived by Modi from the Ishrat Jahan encounter, Vajpayee's interview created a stir, especially as it revived the memory of his abortive bid to remove Modi in the immediate aftermath of the riots. The accounts given by Advani, Jaswant Singh, and Shourie came much later. While those three leaders in different ways said that he had been overruled by others in the party, Vajpayee in the Zee interview stuck to the claim he had first made in the Rajya Sabha in May 2002: that the decision to let Modi remain in office had in the end been his. The interview quoted Vajpayee as saying: 'There were two opinions on the question of [the] removal of Modi after the riots. Some people wanted his removal. I was of the same opinion. But the entire responsibility was put on me and I had to take a decision keeping in mind all shades of opinion.'

Vajpayee's claim that the 'entire responsibility' of deciding Modi's fate had been devolved to him by members of his party suggested that he was the leader in command in 2002. This proved to be at odds, for instance, with Shourie's version in 2009 that at the BJP conclave in Goa, Vajpayee had found himself 'completely thwarted' on the issue of Modi's resignation.

Regardless of who took the call in Modi's favour in April

2002, none of the four leaders who came out in the open about the abortive attempt to get rid of him pretended to be overly concerned about his widely perceived complicity in the post-Godhra massacres. Steeped as they were in the Hindutva ideology, they made no bones about conflating democracy with majoritarianism. Whatever the majority wanted was acceptable to them, even if it compromised constitutional values such as secularism and the rule of law. That is why Vajpayee was unembarrassed to admit in 2004 that although he had favoured Modi's removal in 2002, he had felt that holding elections in Gujarat 'would be more beneficial'. If he was again seeking Modi's removal after he had himself been ejected from office, it was more for strategic than moral reasons. 'Whatever damage could have happened has happened,' he said, adding, 'But we did not realize that this strategy would be exploited so much outside Gujarat.' He was indirectly admitting that he might have been better off had he not bowed to the majority opinion in his party in 2002.

Having backed off in 2002 from a conflict with hardliners in the Sangh Parivar, Vajpayee could as well have admitted in 2004 that he had underestimated the hold that Modi had, for better or for worse, come to acquire over such elements. To them, it was unthinkable that any action could be contemplated against Modi, and that too, on the issue of the riots. Sure enough, the BJP president, Venkaiah Naidu, with the backing of stalwarts such as Advani, Jaitley, and RSS chief K.S. Sudarshan, reportedly ensured that the Modi issue, despite Vajpayee's public statement on 13 June 2004, was kept out of the agenda of the national executive meeting held nine days later in Mumbai. Instead, Vajpayee was forced to settle for a discussion in the smaller and more discreet forum of the party's parliamentary board and, in the end, gave his consent to the board's decision that there would be no change of leadership in Gujarat 'at this juncture'. Thus ended the last ever attempt by the former prime minister to make an example of someone who is now the party's prime ministerial candidate. Long before he infamously forced fellow RSS pracharak Sanjay Joshi out of all posts in the BJP in 2012, Modi had repeatedly trumped Vajpayee within the party.

In Advani's memoirs, there is an interesting footnote to Modi's triumph. Although he wrote an entire chapter in the book on the 2004 debacle and the subsequent 'turmoil in the party', Advani glossed over Vajpayee's renewed attempt during that period to get rid of Modi. None of the six causes listed by Advani for the BJP's defeat tallied with the one highlighted by Vajpayee, namely, Modi's handling of the 2002 carnage. On the contrary, Advani portrayed Modi as a leader who had been 'viciously, consistently and persistently maligned'. Little could he have imagined the turn of events in 2013, when he was himself seen as a maligner of Modi. It followed Advani's abortive attempt to resign from party positions protesting Modi's elevation as chairman of the BJP's campaign committee for the next Lok Sabha elections. He even boycotted the parliamentary board meeting on 13 September 2013 when it declared Modi as the BJP's prime ministerial candidate for the 2014 Lok Sabha election.

The dramatic growth in Modi's clout over the decade since Godhra, in which he won three successive assembly elections for his party in Gujarat, was in no small measure due to the very nature of his response to that arson. Modi became a legend as Godhra turned into an opportunity for the saffron brigade to unleash Hindutva with a virulence never seen before. This ideology of unifying Hindus against Muslims found expression, as discussed later in this book, in his statements and actions, especially on the crucial days of 27 and 28 February 2002. He debunked the anti-VHP narrative that had first been acknowledged by Vajpayee and Advani within hours of the train tragedy. That helped him generate enough support in the party to survive repeated attempts by Vajpayee to unseat him. More importantly, the script rewritten by Modi also served as the basis for his exoneration in subsequent inquiries and investigations.

3

The Myth of 'Justice for All'

The 'Gujarat model', a byword for development. Who hasn't heard about it? In fact, of the three elections in which he led his party in the state, Narendra Modi is said to have won the second and third—in 2007 and 2012—on the strength of his much-touted Gujarat model. The first electoral victory, pulled off within months of the carnage in 2002, had little to do though with economic growth. But there was a Gujarat model at work in that election too. And it was about justice—or whatever could pass off for it—in carnage cases. In the run-up to the December 2002 poll, the electorate got to see early glimpses of this undeclared Gujarat model of justice.

On the face of it, the model seemed to have derived from the innocuous principle of speedy justice. Consider the speed with which the first trial court judgment in a case of mass murder related to the Gujarat carnage was delivered. The judgment pertained to one of the last major massacres in the post-Godhra violence, that of seventy Muslims fleeing in two vans from their village, Kidiad, in Sabarkantha district on 2 March 2002. The 'Hindutva' mobs caught up with the vans at two different spots, about 10 kilometres apart. Though the case was rendered more complex by the fact that the killings had been executed around the same time in two distant places, yet it was investigated, tried and decided in seven months flat. The trial court judgment in the case came on 11 October 2002. From the outcome, however, it seemed to have been more a case of hasty justice than a speedy one. For all the nine accused persons who had been tried were acquitted.

Worse, this was no isolated instance of hasty justice. Two more cases, relating to the killing of about forty Muslims in Pandarwada in Panchmahal district, were decided shortly thereafter, again in October 2002. In a hat-trick of sorts, these cases too collapsed as all the twenty-one persons implicated in them were acquitted. The complete failure of the prosecution in all the three cases decided in October 2002 belied a common explanation for the high rate of impunity in India. The impunity is generally attributed to delays in investigation and legal proceedings. This is especially so in communal violence cases, where there could be a political angle and the accused persons would be several and often strangers to victims. The delays in such cases make it that much harder for witnesses, including victims, to recognize assailants.

Though there were several ingredients to the Gujarat model of justice, one key element was a misuse of the then newly introduced fast-track courts, an initiative of the Central government across the country. The misuse lay in achieving speed at the expense of justice, thereby defeating the objective of the fast-track courts. It showed that the stress was more on clearing the docket and generating impressive statistics on the disposal of cases. The imbalance between speed and justice was by no means unintentional. Despite the speed, the survivors of the Kidiad massacre case, for instance, failed to identify the accused persons produced in the court. Clearly, the speed of the trial had been offset by another common factor plaguing communal violence cases: faultily recorded testimonies. Many of the testimonies recorded by the police in, for instance, the 1984 carnage cases were judicially acknowledged to have been at odds with the versions actually given by witnesses. The police were even found to have steered clear of crucial witnesses who could have clinched the prosecution's case.

The trial court's verdict in the Kidiad case showed that the Gujarat police had followed the precedent set by the Delhi police in subverting evidence. The innovation of the Gujarat model lay in pressing for a hurried trial even when the investigation was far from complete. From the police's own admission in the charge-sheet, only nine of the eighteen accused persons had been arrested while the rest had been declared as absconders. Worse, even the nine who had undergone trial were found by the court to have been helped by the police to get off the hook. In his October 2002 verdict, trial judge Viral Desai indicated at least two major omissions on the part of the police. One, they had failed to conduct further investigation despite repeated requests by victims. Two, they had refused to implicate the assailants actually named by witnesses.

Such was the judgment, and it was historically significant as Kidiad was the first communal violence case to have been tried under a 'Hindutva' dispensation. Despite its avowed policy of 'justice for all, appeasement of none', the BJP showed no promise of faring any better than the Congress party in dealing with the wall of impunity surrounding communal violence cases. It seemed to have only introduced another layer of hypocrisy in the legal system. If the Congress party, the avowed champion of secularism, had gained notoriety for being 'opportunistically' communal, the BJP had less reason to be defensive as it was anyway known to be 'ideologically' communal. When its motto of 'justice for all, appeasement of none' was put to test in the

Kidiad case, it turned out that Muslims were denied justice and Hindus appeased. The farce played out by the Modi regime vindicated George Orwell's insight into modern politics: 'Political language is designed to make lies sound truthful and murder respectable, and to give an appearance of solidity to pure wind.'

Modi, in an interview to Reuters in 2013, infamously likened his reaction to the carnage to the pain felt on a puppy being run over by a car. In the Kidiad case, it would, however, seem that, with the police themselves at the steering wheel, the puppy was run over more than once. The first time was when, on the third day of the post-Godhra violence, Muslims in Kidiad were forced to flee their homes, as the police had failed to provide them security. The second time was when those Muslims had been allowed to be chased for kilometers at a stretch before they were intercepted and slaughtered on the streets. The third time was when the police, brushing aside the pleas of victims, initiated the trial with deliberately faulty and incomplete evidence. The fourth time the puppy was run over was after the case had inevitably become a casualty of rapid-fire justice.

The timing of the October 2002 judgment, though, could not have been any better for one of the acquitted persons, Kalubhai Maliwad. It allowed him to contest as a BJP candidate and win the assembly election within two months of his acquittal. Equally convenient for Maliwad was the police's failure to address any of the lacunae pointed out by the verdict. Nor did the prosecution bother to go through the motions of filing an appeal against the acquittals.

The last instance of brazenness displayed in the Kidiad case came to light a whole year later, in the Supreme Court, when its amicus curiae, Harish Salve, gave an account of the state's failure to file appeals against acquittals in riot cases. In an affidavit filed before the Supreme Court in December 2003, the Gujarat government came up with an array of excuses for its lapses, but the one cited in the context of the Kidiad case stood out. Stretching credulity, the state government claimed that it had learnt of the acquittals in the Kidiad case only after it had received a notice from the Supreme Court, over a year after the verdict. It blamed its ignorance on the two special prosecutors it had appointed for the riot cases in the Panchmahal district, where the massacre had taken place. The government claimed that in the cases handled by these two prosecutors, 'there was no reporting, much less intimation, about the acquittals to the legal department'.

If its claim of ignorance was not an attempt to pull wool over the Supreme Court's eyes, then the least it meant was that the systems put in place by the Gujarat government for dealing with cases of carnage were woefully inadequate. Consistent with its claim of having been unaware of the Kidiad acquittals for an entire year, the government filed an appeal against them before the Gujarat high court that very month, December 2003. After the high court ordered a further investigation, the police filed a charge-sheet against twenty-three new accused persons. The case still fell through the cracks, as most of the witnesses turned hostile during the fresh trial.

The shambolic course of the Kidiad case served as a cautionary tale for the high-profile Best Bakery case, where the Supreme Court ordered the retrial to be held outside Gujarat. In any event, the subversion of justice in Kidiad vindicated the concerns first raised by the National Human Rights Commission (NHRC). In the immediate aftermath of the carnage, the NHRC made a dramatic intervention when a team led by its chairman, former Chief Justice of India J.S. Verma, visited Gujarat during 19-22 March 2002. The visit was followed on 1 April by the publication of 'urgent recommendations', which were accompanied by a 'confidential report' to the state government. One of the issues flagged by the NHRC was in response to the widespread allegation that 'FIRs have been poorly or wrongly recorded and that investigations are being "influenced" by extraneous considerations or players'. As a corollary, it listed five major carnage cases to be entrusted to the CBI for independent investigation (Kidiad, surprisingly, did not figure among them). In a rather unrepentant response on 12 April 2002, the state government said that the police investigation 'cannot be discredited, cannot be put into disrepute and its fairness questioned merely on the basis of hostile propaganda'. Denying that its findings against the police were based on unsubstantiated information, the NHRC reiterated them in its final report on 31 May 2002. Given the hostility displayed by the Modi regime to its proposals, the NHRC said that the Centre could transfer those critical cases to the CBI, if need be, under the emergency powers conferred by Article 355 of the Constitution.

Simultaneously, having waited in vain for two months for the state government's reply to the confidential annexure, the NHRC put its contents in the public domain. The confidential note bristled with investigative leads as it turned out to be a bare account of all the allegations made before the NHRC during its visit to Gujarat. Thus, this material brought out by the NHRC along with its 'substantive recommendations' on the Gujarat carnage, constituted the first-ever indictment of the Narendra Modi regime by a statutory body. That Justice Verma was the moving spirit behind the indictment was, however, rich in irony. This was because, in his earlier avatar as Supreme Court judge, he had controversially ruled in 1995 that 'Hindutva' as such could not be 'equated with narrow fundamentalist Hindu religious bigotry'. Having derived much political mileage from it, the BJP must have been bewildered to see the author of the same 'Hindutva' verdict driving the NHRC, seven years later, to intervene so forcefully in Gujarat.

Be that as it may, the NHRC's intervention could not save the rule of law from the impact of the Gujarat model of justice. In retrospect, the NHRC should perhaps have put in place a mechanism to monitor the implementation of its recommendations. In the absence of such a safeguard, the very first verdict that came in October 2002 proved to be a disaster for the prosecution. The Kidiad verdict set off a trend of acquittals in the Gujarat riot cases. Worse, many other riot cases fell by the wayside even before they had reached the trial stage. Of the 4,252 carnage cases booked in the state, the magistrates accepted closure reports filed by the Gujarat police in as many as 2,215 of them. Clearly, the lesson from the Kidiad acquittals and other such setbacks to human rights was that the NHRC needed to push the envelope further.

The impetus for the next push for justice came on 27 June 2003, when a fast-track court in Vadodara pronounced its verdict in the Best Bakery case, involving the murder of fourteen persons in Vadodara. In keeping with the pattern established by the Kidiad and Pandarwada cases, all the twenty-one accused persons in this case were acquitted. The verdict, however, made big news as Best Bakery was among the five select cases that had been recommended by the NHRC for CBI investigation. The apparent cause for the collapse of this high-profile case was that crucial witnesses—the baker's daughter and complainant, Zahira Sheikh, and other family members—had turned hostile. Much to the dismay of human rights defenders, the Sheikhs had declared during the trial that they were unable to identify any of the accused persons. Nowhere in his twenty-four-page verdict did trial judge H.U. Mahida consider the possibility of witnesses turning hostile under duress or inducement. Instead, he made out that he was helpless in the face of such retractions. Reason: under the judicial system 'bequeathed by the British', the courts went 'entirely by the evidence on record' . From there, he took a leap, defining the judiciary in purely mechanistic terms. 'The courts are,' Mahida said, 'truly speaking, evidence courts and not courts of justice.'

Ten days after the trial court verdict, Zahira Sheikh created a sensation by declaring that she had retracted her testimony under duress. Sitting next to human rights activist Teesta Setalvad, eighteen-year-old Zahira Sheikh addressed a press conference on 7 July 2003 alleging that a BJP legislator, Madhu Srivastava, had intimidated her and her family into retracting the statements they had made to the police. Four days later, she appeared before the NHRC reiterating her charge of intimidation of witnesses and seeking its help to reopen the case. Zahira's exposure of the circumstances in which she had been forced to retract her statement hit home.

After all, it reinforced the apprehensions already raised by the Justice Verma-led NHRC in its report of 31 May 2002. Under its new chairman, former chief justice of India A.S. Anand, the NHRC decided to intervene in the Best Bakery case. The intervention was unusual, in that the NHRC did not just seek to be impleaded as a party but it also bypassed the regular appeal process, due to the exceptional circumstances of the case. The NHRC took the 'miscarriage of justice' in the Best Bakery case as a reflection of the environment prevailing in the whole of Gujarat. Accordingly, it filed a special leave petition (SLP) before the Supreme Court, seeking a reinvestigation of the Best Bakery case by the CBI and its retrial outside Gujarat.

By approaching the Supreme Court directly, the statutory body ran the risk of appearing to have no confidence in the Gujarat high court. But then, given the nature of the remedies sought by it (transferring the case to another state), the NHRC was apparently convinced that it had no option but to take this radical step. The suggestion clearly was that the extreme situation in Gujarat had called for an extreme solution. This in turn upset Modi so much that it apparently affected his sense of propriety.

Before the Supreme Court could begin hearing the NHRC's petition, Modi dragged the office of the president of India into the dispute. He made a public display of his lack of remorse, in an open letter to President A.P.J. Abdul Kalam. Without taking names, the letter, dated 5 August 2003, launched an attack on the NHRC, accusing it of falling prey to the 'propaganda' of 'vested interests'. This letter is of historical importance as much for its timing as for its petulance. Wary of the threat posed by the NHRC's petition, Modi was more brazen than ever before about his ultra-nationalist notion that demands for justice for carnage victims should be sacrificed at the altar of issues such as development, security and federal democracy. It was an exposition, as it were, of his unstated Gujarat model of justice. He began by pointing out that the average growth rate fixed by the Planning Commission for the country in the then five-year plan was 8 per cent while the corresponding figure envisaged by the same body for Gujarat was 10.2 per cent. 'This fact is a clear indication of the nation's confidence in Gujarat and its leading role in the country's progress,' Modi said, leading up to the insinuation that there was an ulterior motive to the allegations of human rights violations made against the state. This was how his argument went: 'Vested interests are trying to obstruct the path of progress. They are identifying stray incidents and exaggerating them with the sole objective of slowing the pace of development.' Whether the collapse of the Best Bakery case was a stray incident or symptomatic of a larger systemic subversion, Modi's attempt to pit the campaign for justice against the progress of the state was presented as a self-evident premise.

Equally axiomatic was his postulate that justice conflicted with democracy. For, he said that 'such activities raise serious doubts about the intentions of such groups which cannot even accept a constitutional elected democratic government'. Lamenting 'the situation facing those who cherish democratic values', Modi added:

> Our country has a federal structure and this federal polity has to ensure that the Centre and the States, judiciary and the legislature work in harmonious environment. Nothing can be more harmful to democracy than the efforts of some groups to weaken the collective strength of the democratic institutions.

The reference to 'the collective strength' in the given context betrayed an attempt to equate democracy with majoritarian rule, in which all its institutions would, like ministers in a cabinet, assume collective responsibility. It was as if his conception of democracy had no use for the scheme of checks and balances or the independence of the judiciary. There was even less space in it for vigilance by civil society. Modi deplored the fact that 'such self-appointed and so-called champions of human rights groups do not even hesitate to point fingers, with the help of a section of media, at institutions like the judiciary in the state'.

In a tacit reference to the bypassing of the Gujarat high court by the NHRC in the Best Bakery case, Modi said: 'It is more disturbing that some national-level institutions are also carried away by propaganda.' Resorting to the ultimate right-wing argument, Modi raised the bogey of security to discredit human rights concerns. He made out that the NHRC's alleged folly needed 'serious attention because Gujarat being a border State has a strategic importance for the Nation's security'.

Promising that his state would help usher in 'an era of security, justice and prosperity', Modi alleged that the Gujarat carnage had been singled out. 'Group clashes occur at times and Gujarat is no exception. When group clashes and communal riots occur in many parts of the country, why is there such focus on Gujarat? When group clashes have attained alarming proportion in other states, why have the above champions not been so active?'

In reality, for some years before or after the 2002 carnage, there was no communal violence anywhere comparable to it, in scale or intensity. Modi's attempt, in his 2003 letter to the president, to equate the Gujarat carnage with minor incidents was a clear sign of desperation. He also overlooked the fact that similar campaigns had been conducted against the perpetrators of the 1984 massacre of Sikhs in Delhi and the 1992-93 Hindu-Muslim riots in Bombay, despite the electoral mandates the parties allegedly involved in the violence had received.

The operative part of Modi's letter seeking to halt the NHRC in its tracks was a request to President Kalam 'to direct compilation of details of all major incidents of group clashes and communal riots in the country since Independence'. He wanted the data on the number of riot cases registered, charge-sheeted, withdrawn, or resulting in acquittals to be compiled state-wise and year-wise and placed in the public domain. He believed that the data would vindicate him. 'Facts on record will unveil the truth,' Modi said, 'thereby exposing the vested interests that have targeted not only Gujarat, but have tried to weaken the democratic fabric and reputed institutions of the country.'

Significantly, Modi called for such a statistical comparison at a time when Gujarat did not have a single conviction to show for the 2002 carnage. The intent of the proposed study could only have been to establish that impunity was the norm in communal violence cases. It was also a roundabout way of showing that the record of the Congress party regimes over the years was even worse. Modi could well be right about the duplicity of the rival party that professed to be secular and inclusive. He could be equally justified in suggesting, however tacitly, that for the 1984 carnage, Congress leaders, beginning with Prime Minister Rajiv Gandhi, had got away lightly for their complicity. If such comparisons had lulled him into believing that his regime could get away as lightly for the 2002 carnage, Modi overlooked a vital change: the evolution of the institutions of democracy and the rule of law since the days of the 1984 massacre.

Emboldened by the unprecedented mandate it had received from the electorate in the wake of the anti-Sikh pogrom, the Rajiv Gandhi government blocked Parliament from holding any discussion on it, even after a commission of inquiry report had been tabled in 1987. In contrast, Vajpayee's coalition government was forced to allow both Houses to discuss the Gujarat carnage, under the non-voting as well as voting clauses, even before the corresponding commission of inquiry had begun its proceedings. Similarly, the Supreme Court's activism was too nascent in 1984 to have responded with the kind of alacrity and vigour it displayed in the case of the 2002 violence. In 1984, judicial activism was not yet ready to take on politically motivated crimes. There was also no support then in the form of the NHRC because it came into existence only in October 1993, and Gujarat was indeed the first major outbreak of communal violence witnessed by this watchdog body.

Therefore, the NHRC's petition in 2003 served as a test case of whether the Supreme Court would be able to apply its much vaunted judicial activism to communal violence. The Supreme Court did take on the challenge, even if its activism unfolded incrementally or in a carefully calibrated manner. Despite sharing the NHRC's concerns over the collapse of the Best Bakery trial, a bench headed by the chief justice of India, V.N. Khare, did not right away adopt any of the radical remedies proposed by it. Instead, the Supreme Court first gave an opportunity to the criminal justice system in Gujarat to take corrective action on its own. Understandable, given that just a day after Modi's letter to the president on 5 August, the prosecution filed an appeal before the Gujarat high court against the Best Bakery acquittals.

However, on seeing the contents of the appeal that had been filed before the high court, the Supreme Court trashed it as 'a complete eyewash' and lashed out at the Modi government for shielding the culprits in the Best Bakery case. In his widely reported verbal observations, Justice Khare had a dig at Modi, making an oblique reference to Prime Minister Vajpayee's advice to him during the riots on 'rajdharma' as also Modi's own notion of democracy in his open letter to President Kalam. 'Where is the rajdharma of the government? You should quit if you cannot prosecute the guilty. Democracy does not mean you will not prosecute anyone,' Justice Khare said on 12 September 2003, while directing the state's chief secretary and director general of police (DGP) to appear in person to account for their conduct.

When the two top officers of Gujarat appeared before it a week later, the Supreme Court grilled them on the issue of intimidation of witnesses. Neither Chief Secretary P.K. Laheri nor DGP K. Chakravarthi could offer a modicum of justification for their failure to intervene and provide protection to witnesses during the Best Bakery trial. The nub of the matter was that when such a large number of them had turned hostile, should it not have raised a reasonable suspicion that the witnesses were being threatened? The Supreme Court order of 19 September 2003 reproduced the entire interrogation of the two officers. They were in effect cornered into making two vital admissions: that the witnesses, rather than being declared hostile, should have been re-examined by the prosecution and that the appeal filed by the government in the high court ought to have sought a retrial.

The errors of omission and commission exposed by the Supreme Court proceedings left the Gujarat government with no option but to amend its appeal before the high court in the Best Bakery case. The revised appeal incorporated a specific prayer for retrial. Khare's tongue-lashing on Best Bakery appeared to have had a salutary effect on other riot cases too. For two months later came the first-ever conviction in a 2002 carnage case. On 24 November 2003, Nadiad sessions judge C.K. Rane convicted twelve persons for hacking fourteen Muslims to death in Ghodasar village in Kheda district. All the twelve convicted persons were sentenced to life. It is another matter that about eight years later, on 22 April 2012, the Gujarat high court reversed the conviction of all the accused in the Ghodasar case. Curiously, in the Best Bakery case, the Supreme Court's intervention had made little difference to the outcome of the appeal before the Gujarat high court. On 26 December 2003, a high court bench headed by Justice B.J. Sethna rejected the retrial plea as it upheld all the acquittals in the case.

Obliquely attacking the NHRC's petition to the Supreme Court, the Gujarat high court verdict in the Best Bakery case said that the trial court had 'not committed any irregularity or illegality, much less manifest illegality resulting into the miscarriage of justice'. It also questioned the motives of those seeking a retrial. Echoing the allegations made in Modi's letter to Kalam, the high court said:

> There are some persons, [who] for their petty benefits, [are] trying to add fuel to the fire, which is already extinguished, and keep the situation tense. They do not know the great harm they are causing to the state and the nation. One should not cut the branch on which [one] sits. The nation will suffer if Gujarat is made to suffer.

From the tone and substance of this verdict, it seemed that the disconnect between the high court and the Supreme Court could not have been greater. However, Zahira Sheikh's appeal in the Supreme Court against the high court verdict in the Best Bakery case led to one of the most stirring instances of judicial activism. Tearing apart the high court verdict, the bench, comprising Justice Doraiswamy Raju and Justice Arijit Pasayat, followed up forcefully on the warnings that had been issued by Justice Khare's bench on the NHRC's petition. Upholding Zahira Sheikh's appeal, the verdict, written by Justice Pasayat, not only ordered a retrial of the Best Bakery case but also directed that it be held outside Gujarat. The path-breaking verdict, delivered on 12 April 2004, could not have come at a worse time for the BJP-led NDA. The judgment cast a shadow on the NDA's 'India Shining' campaign in the Lok Sabha election, which was just a few days away. It could well have been one of the reasons why Vajpayee, soon after the election, blamed Modi for his defeat.

While ordering the retrial in the jurisdiction of the Bombay high court, the apex court pointed out that even the Gujarat high court verdict had acknowledged that the police investigation in the Best Bakery case was 'dishonest and faulty'. It also expunged the strictures passed by the high court on the NHRC and activist Teesta Setalvad. The best remembered line from the Supreme Court verdict is its scathing indictment of the Modi regime: 'The modern-day Neros were looking elsewhere when innocent children and helpless women were burning, and probably deliberating how the perpetrators can be protected.'

The breakthrough made by the Supreme Court's Best Bakery verdict was the culmination of all the spadework done by Justices Verma and Anand, as successive chiefs of the NHRC, and Justice Khare, as apex court chief. Justice Pasayat's judgment proved to be a game-changer in more ways than one. It did not just retrieve the Best Bakery case. Setting a precedent, the principles affirmed by the verdict raised the bar of accountability for major cases relating to the Gujarat carnage.

The radical experiment of holding the retrial of the Best Bakery case in Mumbai was not without its share of hiccups. Despite all the trouble taken by the Supreme Court to ensure a fair trial in Mumbai, the Sheikh family again turned hostile. This time Zahira Sheikh, in fact, gave advance notice of her retraction. On 3 November 2004, she held a press conference in Vadodara, accusing Setalvad of holding her hostage. Accordingly, on 21 December 2004, Zahira Sheikh deposed in the Mumbai court claiming that, as she was in hiding, she could not see any of the rioters who had attacked the bakery on the night of 1 March 2002. If prosecutor Manjula Rao could still salvage the case, it was because she had for the first time produced the four bakery workers who had been injured in the attack and had been held back by the Gujarat police in the Vadodara trial.

Their depositions clinched the case in the face of the fresh rash of retractions by the Sheikh family members. Equally crucial was the unusual safeguard provided by the Supreme Court of having the public prosecutor appointed from Maharashtra in consultation with the victims. Where the Supreme Court seemed to have erred was in entrusting the task of further investigation to the same Gujarat police. As the Gujarat police did not bother to take a fresh look at it, the Best Bakery case remained hampered by the shortcomings in their own original investigation. In February 2006, the Mumbai trial court convicted nine of the seventeen persons arraigned before it and awarded a life sentence to each of the convicted persons. Thus, for a massacre that had taken place in Vadodara, justice finally came in Mumbai. This was not exactly the kind of national integration that India's founding fathers had envisaged!

In a further irony, while those who had induced her to make the latest U-turn got away with their crime, victim Zahira Sheikh ended up suffering all over again as part of the justice rendered on her complaint. A month after the Mumbai trial court verdict, the Supreme Court, besides directing the tax authorities to probe her assets, imposed a one-year jail term on her on the charge of committing contempt. Six years later, in July 2012, while deciding the appeals filed by the nine persons convicted in the retrial, the Mumbai high court acquitted five of them because of the infirmities in the Gujarat police investigation. Thus, for the massacre of fourteen persons in the Best Bakery case, four persons from the mob were finally convicted. This ensued from the Supreme Court's decision eight years earlier to entrust the further investigation to the same Gujarat police.

The need to let an independent agency take a fresh look at the investigation was recognized subsequently, in another Gujarat carnage case. Given the costs involved, both material and institutional, the Best Bakery remedy of holding a retrial outside the state could not possibly have been made a general policy. Yet, barely two years after the Best Bakery retrial, the Supreme Court-Mumbai combination was instrumental in undoing another shocking cover-up. The gangrape of Bilkis Bano and the slaughter of fourteen of her family, including her three-year-old daughter, was another case to have been transferred out of Gujarat. This one did not even get to the stage of trial in Gujarat as a magistrate in Dahod district in March 2003 accepted a closure report filed by the police. The police nipped the case in the bud even after Bilkis Bano's plight had been flagged in the confidential report the NHRC had given the state government during Verma's tenure.

The closure of the case prompted the NHRC to display another remarkable instance of institutional continuity under Anand. Besides helping Bilkis Bano move the Supreme Court, the NHRC persuaded senior advocate Harish Salve to represent her. The Gujarat government responded immediately by ordering a further investigation by its crime branch. There was no change of heart; it was obviously a bid to pre-empt any Supreme Court action on her petition. The new investigators were no more sensitive than the old ones. For instance, they reportedly summoned Bilkis Bano in the middle of the night to inspect the scene of crime. In December 2003, the Supreme Court handed over the investigation of the Bilkis Bano case to the CBI, which operates under the administrative control of the Central government.

The safeguard of entrusting the investigation to an agency insulated from the Gujarat government did turn the tide. While exhuming human remains from a mass grave where members of Bilkis Bano's family had been buried, the CBI discovered 60 kilograms of salt that had been used to hasten the disintegration of the bodies. Besides rounding up the twelve rioters named by Bilkis Bano, the CBI arrested a couple of police officials for their alleged collusion. Three months after the Best Bakery case had been shifted to Mumbai for a retrial, the Supreme Court in

August 2004 transferred the trial of Bilkis Bano's case to the same city. After she identified in the court the twelve men involved in raping her and killing her daughter and other members of her family, Bilkis Bano, in a remarkable display of fortitude, withstood twenty days of relentless cross-examination.

At the end of it all, the Mumbai trial court, in January 2008, awarded life sentences to eleven of the twelve accused rioters (the twelfth one had died during the trial). However, among the six accused police officials, only one was convicted. Assistant Sub-Inspector Somabhai Gori was sentenced to imprisonment for three years for recording a distorted and truncated version of Bilkis Bano's complaint. Two government doctors were let off on the charge of fudging the post-mortem reports of the victims. The solitary conviction among the eight state actors implicated in the case meant that the trial court did not uphold the charge of conspiracy to cover up the crime and shield the guilty. The verdict was nonetheless a milestone because it was a rare, if not the first ever, instance of a policeman being convicted in a communal violence case, and also of rioters being convicted on the charge of rape.

The varied strategies evolved to retrieve the Best Bakery and Bilkis Bano cases paved the way for more innovations in other cases. In the light of the partisan role betrayed by the Gujarat police in the Best Bakery and Bilkis Bano cases, the Supreme Court stayed the trial of nine select cases, including Godhra ('the original sin') and the two big massacres in Ahmedabad: Naroda Patiya (ninety-six killings) and Gulberg Society (sixty-nine killings). The stay order passed in November 2003 was meant to prevent the police from damaging these cases too. It was an interim measure adopted by the apex court at the instance of the NHRC as well as Citizens for Justice and Peace (CJP), the NGO led by Teesta Setalvad. The nine cases placed under the Supreme Court's scanner included four of the five originally shortlisted by the NHRC. The fifth case, Best Bakery, was already being monitored separately by the Supreme Court.

Another critical input for the Supreme Court was from its amicus curiae Harish Salve, who was earlier solicitor general for the Vajpayee government. His contribution lay in highlighting various forms of collusion between the Modi regime and the accused persons in the nine cases under the scanner. He lent his weight, for instance, to the allegation made by the CJP that many of the public prosecutors appointed by the Modi regime in the trial of the post-Godhra riot cases were from the very organization that had been complicit in the violence. Chetan Shah was an egregious example, having been appointed a public prosecutor in the Gulberg Society case although he was an office-bearer in the VHP and had appeared for several of the accused on bail applications in that very case. Even after some of the public prosecutors, including Chetan Shah, had been replaced, Salve pitched for an institutional arrangement to ensure that any future appointment would be in consultation with the Gujarat high court. He also highlighted the bias shown by the Gujarat police during the prolonged stay on the trial of those nine cases: While they filed over a dozen charge-sheets against Muslims in the Godhra case, they froze all investigation into the post-Godhra cases involving Hindu accused. In a similar pattern of discrimination, they allowed most of the accused in the post-Godhra cases to be released quickly on bail, although, as Salve said in a note submitted in March 2006, 'the status of the accused in the Godhra case is to the contrary'.

Such disturbing developments in those nine cases underscored the urgency of taking the investigation out of the hands of the Gujarat police. But then, having stayed the trial of those cases way back in November 2003, while dealing with the Best Bakery case, the Supreme Court took over four years to decide on who should carry out the further investigation. For much of that long interregnum, the Supreme Court, somewhat uncharacteristically, kept adjourning the hearings of the NHRC application about those nine cases, without making any progress. Repeated pleas from the CJP to expedite the matter evoked no response. In retrospect, it would appear that the Supreme Court was biding time, waiting for the outcome of the CBI-probed Bilkis Bano case in order to determine its strategy for the batch of nine cases.

It was only after the CBI had secured convictions in the Bilkis Bano case in January 2008 that the Supreme Court figured out its strategy. The more radical experiment in the Bilkis Bano case (namely, changing the investigating agency and shifting the trial out of Gujarat) was more successful than the one in Best Bakery (where only the trial had been shifted out of Gujarat). The Supreme Court contemplated adopting the innovations in the Bilkis Bano case as the template for the nine stayed cases. In February 2008, within a month of the Bilkis Bano convictions, the Manmohan Singh government filed an affidavit before the Supreme Court saying 'it would have no objection to the investigation of the cases by the CBI and transfer outside the state of Gujarat, if so desired'. The affidavit was in reponse to a query from the Supreme Court asking whether the Centre was agreeable to both options.

However, on 26 March 2008, the bench, headed by Justice Pasayat, adopted neither of the options. Instead, it came up with a third option: namely, to set up a special investigation team (SIT), with a mix of three serving police officers from Gujarat and two retired ones from outside the state. The rationale seemed to be that local members would bring the advantage of familiarity with the subject matter of investigation while non-local members would help insulate the SIT from local pressures. In an apparent bid to achieve such balance, a non-local member, former CBI director R.K. Raghavan, was appointed as the SIT chairman. Another inbuilt safeguard was the stipulation that the SIT would periodically report its progress to the Supreme Court on the further investigation of the nine cases. This was derived from the concept of 'continuing mandamus' introduced by Justice Verma while monitoring CBI investigations against political leaders in the 1990s in the Jain Hawala case.

Despite the aura of the Supreme Court mandate and safeguard of its monitoring, the SIT did not prove to be independent enough. Among the nine cases referred to it originally, this deficiency was most evident in the Godhra train burning case, where the accused were all Muslims. The SIT toed the Gujarat police line on Godhra, unmindful of its glaring infirmities, as discussed in Chapter 1 of the book. Why did the Supreme Court, in the first place, prefer setting up the SIT over the Bilkis Bano approach of entrusting the investigation to the CBI? This was perhaps because, by the time the Bilkis Bano convictions came in January 2008, the situation had become more complicated. The change of regime at the Centre in 2004, with the Congress-led UPA taking over from the BJP-led NDA, had introduced a federal sensitivity. Post-2004, the transfer of a Gujarat carnage case to the CBI was fraught with the risk of political interference. The Supreme Court could appear to have placed Modi, however unwittingly, at the mercy of the Congress party ruling at the Centre. Although it had obtained the Centre's go-ahead just a month earlier for CBI investigation, the bench, headed by Justice Pasayat, steered clear of explaining in its 26 March 2008 order as to why it had eventually preferred the SIT option. All it instead said was that 'considering the sensitive nature of the cases involved', the appointment of the SIT was 'warranted'.

Whatever the advantages of the SIT mechanism, they were neutralized by its flawed composition, whether of local or non-local members. Just how unsuitable was the choice of Raghavan as the SIT chairman is revealed in Chapter 7 of this book. Justice Pasayat's bench was perhaps unaware of the serious questions that had remained unresolved about Raghavan, rendering him unsuitable for any fiduciary responsibility of such high order. The flawed composition was anyway acknowledged by the Supreme Court in April 2010, when it was forced to drop two of the three local members originally appointed to the SIT. Geeta Johri and Shivanand Jha, both serving IPS officers of the Gujarat cadre, were dropped two years after their appointment because their continuance in the SIT had become untenable. Johri had been pulled up by the Supreme Court for concealing evidence in a fake encounter case in which the Gujarat police had allegedly gunned down gangster Sohrabuddin Sheikh. The problem with Jha was that he had himself come under the scanner of the SIT after a complaint lodged by a victim of the Gulberg Society massacre, Zakia Jafri, against the Modi regime had been referred to it in April 2009.

The last of the three original members of the SIT from the Gujarat police, Ashish Bhatia, survived the purge although he probably deserved as much to be replaced. For victims filed affidavits before the Supreme Court accusing the SIT of colluding with the accused in the Gulberg Society and Naroda cases, both of which were being supervised by Bhatia. Things came to a head in February 2010, when the SIT's special public prosecutor in the Gulberg Society case, R.K. Shah, quit the post in a huff citing reasons which corroborated the grievances of the

victims against Bhatia and his subordinates. In his resignation
letter, Shah cited specific instances which showed just how
reluctant the SIT was during the trial to provide him the material
that could have helped him bring the best evidence out of each
of the prosecution witnesses. It was precisely when Shah was in
the thick of examining important witnesses such as M.K. Tandon
and P.B. Gondia, senior police officers who had jurisdiction
over both Gulberg Society and Naroda during the carnage, that
the SIT chose to hand him over their previous statements to the
police. Needless to add, it was too late for Shah to make much
use of that material in putting his questions. The last time the
SIT made such a pretence of briefing its prosecutor was on
17 February 2010, about a week before Shah's resignation. It
was again while he was examing a witness in the courtroom that
the SIT sprang 'many' witness statements on Shah, although
these had been recorded by it over the previous year.

Shah was so disturbed by the cavalier manner in which the
trial was being conducted that, in his resignation letter, he did
not spare even B.U. Joshi, the judge who had been presiding
over it. 'The attitude of the learned judge towards the witnesses,
particularly victims-eyewitnesses, has by and large remained
hostile. He browbeats them or threatens them or taunts them.
He does not allow witnesses to go to the dock for the purpose of
identification.' Shah's letter was placed before the Supreme
Court as it was anyway monitoring the progress of the nine
cases taken up by it. The Supreme Court's immediate reaction
was to take Shah's letter as a warning signal about the integrity
of the investigating agency created by it. The bench, headed by
Justice D.K. Jain, hit the pause button in all the nine cases
handled by the SIT. Even as they were allowed to carry on with
the trial, the bench directed the courts concerned not to deliver
a final judgment in any of the nine cases for the time being. Six

months later, the Supreme Court vacated the stay in all the cases except Gulberg Society. After another six months, the stay was vacated in the Gulberg Society case, too. This was because Joshi had been replaced by another judge in February 2011.

It took a whole year to move Joshi out because the action had to be taken through the Gujarat high court. Surprisingly, no such corrective action was taken against Bhatia, although Shah's letter had alleged that both the trial court and the SIT were trying to suppress state complicity in the Gulberg Society massacre. Bhatia's survival in the SIT despite the stink raised by Shah's letter indicated the limitations of the Supreme Court's monitoring in protecting the credibility of the investigation. It also presaged the mixed results that the SIT has had despite the Supreme Court's monitoring.

More than any of the nine cases originally entrusted to it, the Jafri complaint was an acid test for the SIT's independence and impartiality, as this one was about allegations against Modi himself and a larger conspiracy behind the riots. However, the abrupt termination of the Supreme Court monitoring of the Jafri complaint in September 2011 (as explained in Chapter 5), helped the SIT get away with somersaults in its fact-finding on political complicity. There were vital and unexplained differences between its report to the Supreme Court in May 2010 and its closure report to an Ahmedabad magistrate in February 2012, five months after the termination of the monitoring. While the 2010 report, submitted by a non-local member, A.K. Malhotra, made some serious observations against Modi, the 2012 report, submitted by the SIT's local police officer Himanshu Shukla, was cleansed of all traces of such adverse findings. The blanket exoneration of Modi and his regime, including officials and political supporters, betrayed a laboured attempt on the SIT's part to exploit every loophole in law and downplay all the inconvenient evidence.

Take the cursory manner in which the SIT dealt with the implications of the Best Bakery and Bilkis Bano cases. Though the gravamen of Jafri's complaint was that the post-Godhra violence had been state-sponsored, the SIT did not make a pretence of considering whether the burial, in the first instance, of the Best Bakery and Bilkis Bano cases could have been part of a larger conspiracy to cover up the evidence. Instead, all it did was to recount the way in which each of those cases had been salvaged by the Supreme Court, and all that was only to come to a barren conclusion: 'In view of the aforesaid position in both these cases, it was not possible for the SIT to interfere in these matters.' It was silent on why it did not draw any adverse inference against the Modi government for its handling of the Best Bakery and Bilikis Bano cases. Instead, passing the buck to the Supreme Court, the SIT proposed a committee to fix responsibility on officers in the light of the various judgments and make recommendations to the government 'for further necessary action'.

Despite such unsavoury controversies, and despite all the evidence that had been frittered away in the process, the SIT was able to secure convictions not just in the Godhra case against Muslims but also in post-Godhra cases against Hindus. This was testimony to the impact that the Supreme Court's Best Bakery verdict had in restoring the criminal justice system in Gujarat. The ignominy of the retrial held outside Gujarat drove home the message to all concerned that the 2002 communal violence cases would not be allowed to go the way of the cases related to the 1984 and 1992-93 riots. The message was reinforced by the Bilkis Bano case, in which the Supreme Court took even the investigation out of the control of the Modi government. It was against the backdrop of such repeated shaming of the Modi government in those two cases that the Supreme Court, in fact, came up with the SIT as an answer to the challenge of dealing with even more heinous cases. With the Supreme Court breathing down its neck, the SIT revived the investigation into those post-Godhra cases and filed supplementary charge-sheets arraigning some of the accused persons who had been overlooked or shielded by the Gujarat police. The most dramatic example was the arrest in 2009 of a minister in the Modi government, Maya Kodnani, who was eventually convicted in the Naroda Patiya case three years later.

No less critical were the pains taken by the Supreme Court in combating systematic intimidation of witnesses, as highlighted by its Best Bakery verdict. It put in place elaborate security arrangements for scores of witnesses in the monitored cases. This was in fact the condition on which the bench, headed by Justice Pasayat, in its 1 May 2009 order, allowed the trials in the nine major cases to resume after a five-year stay. The protection was for 'ensuring a sense of confidence in the minds of the victims and their relatives, and to ensure that witnesses depose freely and fearlessly before the court'. The bench provided three forms of witness protection, depending upon the nature and gravity of threat faced by the person concerned. The SIT was empowered to take a call on two of those forms: first, ensuring safe passage to witnesses to and from the court precincts and, second, providing security to witnesses even at their homes. The third form, applicable to extreme instances of intimidation, entailed relocation of such witnesses outside the state with the help of the Centre.

As witnesses had complained of intimidation from Gujarat police personnel as much as from rioters, the Supreme Court specifically entrusted all duties of witness protection to Central paramilitary forces. Thus, the protection provided by the Central

Industrial Security Force (CISF) played a critical role in ensuring that none of the post-Godhra cases monitored by the Supreme Court saw a repeat of the farce that had played out in the first instance in the Best Bakery case. The leap made in terms of providing witness protection by neutral security forces in a state affected by communal violence is potentially the most enduring gain for human rights.

Such legal innovations, whether ad hoc or systemic, can all be traced to the big breakthrough made by the Supreme Court in its 2004 Best Bakery judgment. While the innovations underlined the potential of the Supreme Court to take on unforeseen situations, the role played by the individuals at the helm could not be discounted. It was perhaps no coincidence that Justice Pasayat was a common factor to at least four vital decisions made by the Supreme Court. He followed his Best Bakery verdict (directing a retrial outside Gujarat) with orders setting up the quasi-independent SIT to deal with nine major carnage cases, allowing their trials to take place with Central police protection for witnesses, and referring Jafri's complaint against the Modi regime to the SIT. The last two decisions came days before his retirement on 10 May 2009. From a theme recurring in his orders, Pasayat appeared to have been driven by a deep abhorrence of bigotry: 'Religious fanatics really do not belong to any religion. They are no better than terrorists who kill innocent people for no rhyme or reason.'

His idea of equating Hindu religious fanatics (often mistaken for nationalists) with terrorists (widely accepted as traitors) must have confounded those who had been dubbed by Pasayat as 'modern-day Neros'. It was also reminiscent of Swami Vivekananda's lament in his famous Chicago address: 'Sectarianism, bigotry, and its horrible descendant, fanaticism, have long possessed this beautiful earth. They have filled the earth with violence, drenched it often and often with human blood, destroyed civilization and sent whole nations to despair.'

The orders passed by Pasayat and his predecessor Khare, in their pursuit to break the impunity surrounding communal violence, were in the best tradition of judicial activism in India. Their impact could be gauged from, for instance, the angry letter that Modi shot off to President Kalam in 2003 protesting against the NHRC's initiative in the Best Bakery case. Modi had then asked for a compilation of data to show that the collapse of the Best Bakery case in the Vadodara court conformed to the pattern of impunity in communal violence cases right since Independence. Digging in its heels, the apex court thwarted Modi's attempt to justify the cover-up of the 2002 carnage on the basis of past injustices. It chipped away at the notion that communal violence, for the social sanction enjoyed by it, was immune to legal sanctions.

No less significant has been the unravelling of the Hindutva ideology. The miscarriages of justice that had taken place in Gujarat before the Supreme Court's shock treatment in the Best Bakery and Bilkis Bano cases showed that the BJP rule, left to itself, was nowhere near living up to its much trumpeted slogan of 'justice for all'. If anything, the unstated Gujarat model of justice employed this slogan to brazen out its systematic discrimination against Muslims.

4

So Obvious But Ignored

The siege began within 24 hours of the Godhra tragedy. The mob surrounding Gulberg Society, a Muslim pocket in the jurisdiction of the Meghaninagar police station, a predominantly Hindu neighbourhood of Ahmedabad, began to gather from as early as 7 am. Over the next eight hours or so, the mob grew to an estimated strength of over 10,000. It also became progressively more violent. What had begun as slogan-shouting and stone-pelting escalated to arson, rape and murder. Most of the residents of this small cluster of bungalows and apartments gravitated to the house of former Congress MP Ehsan Jafri, perceived as he was as the most influential among them. Jafri made numerous SOS calls from his landline to, among others, police officials and Congress leaders. Around 11.30 am, the joint commissioner of Ahmedabad police, M.K. Tandon, visited Gulberg Society and dispersed the crowd with the help of a 'striking force' which lobbed teargas shells. Tandon left shortly thereafter for Naroda Patiya along with his striking force. The mob targeting Gulberg Society regrouped in no time. Taking refuge in the plea that they were outnumbered, the fifteen policemen deployed near Gulberg Society did little in the face of the mob's aggression.

According to the case made out by the police, the situation went out of control only when the seventy-three-year-old Jafri opened fire in the afternoon. By the time Tandon returned around 4 pm, it was all over, and Jafri was among the sixty-nine persons who had been murdered in Gulberg Society.

The same day, the death toll in the neighbouring Naroda area was even higher, exceeding 100. The major massacres there were at Naroda Patiya, which was barely five kilometres from Gulberg Society, and Naroda Gam, which was another five kilometres further. The VHP leader, Jaydeep Patel, who had been formally given custody of fifty-four of the fifty-eight charred bodies at Godhra the previous night, was from this part of Ahmedabad. He and the local BJP MLA, Maya Kodnani, were seen by victims to be instigating mobs in the Naroda area. The massacre took place against the backdrop of a massive funeral procession in which ten of the bodies brought from Godhra were being taken from Ramola, near Naroda, to Hatkeshwar crematorium on the morning of 28 February. Curfew was imposed in the Naroda police station area by about 12.30 pm, following Tandon's feedback from the spot to Ahmedabad commissioner P.C. Pande. The formal proclamation of the curfew did little to stop the bloodshed in the working-class neighbourhood of Naroda.

Much has been made of the fact that Gujarat 2002 was the first-ever instance of communal violence to have played out in the age of 24x7 news channels. The dramatic footage of fresh scenes of devastation did bring out the poignancy and savagery of communal violence more vividly than ever before. However, something vital was missing in all that high-pitched coverage. Although the media did videograph mobs indulging in violence, there was apparently no record capturing live any of the major massacres in Ahmedabad. At any rate, no such evidence was ever produced on Gulberg Society, although the siege had stretched over several hours in Chamanpura, not very far from commercial hubs of Ahmedabad. Therefore, when Chief Minister Narendra Modi declared the following day that the Gulberg Society massacre was the mob's 'reaction' to Jafri's 'action' of firing, TV channels were able to play no footage to confirm or contradict his claim. The only means of verification available to them was to show victims giving a conflicting version of Jafri's death: that it was the culmination of the prolonged siege as the mob, disregarding his entreaties to spare women, dragged Jafri out, paraded him naked, dismembered his body, and set him on fire.

For all their enterprise and combativeness, TV journalists seemed to have missed out on the live action, the actual violence. One possible explanation was that, just as the police claimed in their defence, the media had underestimated the situation in Gulberg Society and Naroda Patiya/Naroda Gam, which were not traditionally prone to communal disturbances. Whatever the reason for the media's omission, the absence of such video records of those two major massacres was, however, compensated by another form of scientific evidence. This one did not require any conscious effort; the evidence was automatically generated. This was because, just as it was the first major communal conflagration under the gaze of multiple TV channels, the 2002 carnage was also the first to occur after the introduction of mobile phones in India. Mobile phones, for their sheer convenience, were used extensively by panic-stricken members of the targeted community as well as by scattered bands of marauding rioters. It transpired that mobile calls were made by rioters to keep in touch not only with each other but also with police officers and political leaders.

Inherent to the mobile phone technology was the

automatically generated call detail record (CDR). This would show who had called whom and where the two parties had been located during each call. Indeed, it was just the kind of evidence that could have helped the police nail culprits, irrespective of whether they had been seen on the spot or remained behind the scenes. This method of investigation should have been all the more obvious to the Gujarat police because their counterparts in Delhi had, barely two months prior to Godhra, tapped into the CDR to make arrests in connection with the terror attack on Parliament.

The elephant in the room, the CDR evidence, was a measure of how much the rule of law seemed to have been subverted by the Narendra Modi government. For weeks on end, the Gujarat police could not be bothered to collect the CDR evidence. Fortunately, someone from within the police establishment did finally wake up to the treasure trove of evidence that was just waiting to be unearthed. The crime branch in Ahmedabad entrusted with the Gulberg Society and Naroda Patiya/Naroda Gam cases approached the mobile phone companies, before the CDR data related to the crucial days of the carnage had been erased. The irony, however, is that even after the CDR data had been gathered after much delay, the Gujarat police never actually used it in any of the cases. Such was the extent of negligence on Modi's watch; the chief minister was all the more accountable for it as he had throughout retained the home portfolio which oversees the police.

The CDR and its cover-up would have probably remained unnoticed but for a fortuitous development. The fall of the BJP-led coalition government in the 2004 Lok Sabha election prompted Modi to widen the ambit of the Justice G. T. Nanavati Commission inquiring into the 2002 carnage. It was a bid to pre-empt the Manmohan Singh government from instituting a parallel inquiry on aspects not already covered by the terms of reference of the commission. Thus, a notification issued by the Gujarat government on 20 July 2004 expressly authorized the Nanavati Commission to inquire into the 'role and conduct of the then Chief Minister and/or any other Minister(s) in his Council of Ministers, Police Officers, other individuals and organizations' in the Godhra and post-Godhra events. The widened scope of the inquiry, however, had an unintended consequence. It prompted a CBI officer, Rahul Sharma, to resurrect the CDR evidence. It was he who had, in his earlier avatar as a Gujarat police officer, been instrumental in collecting the mobile phone data in 2002. What gave him an opportunity to bring it up two years later was the summons he received from the Nanavati Commission shortly after the expansion of its ambit. During his deposition on 30 October 2004, it was only natural for Sharma to tell the commission about the data he had gathered on all the mobile calls made in Ahmedabad at the height of the violence. If the very mention of such priceless evidence wasn't a sufficient bombshell, Sharma produced copies of the CD containing that data. Thus came to light what has proved to be by far the most revealing, and irrefutable, evidence about the Gujarat carnage.

The revelation raised a serious question about the bona fides of the Modi government: why were the Gujarat police sitting on the mobile phone data despite all its potential to help establish a rioter's presence at the scene of violence or trace a conspirator who had remained unseen? The answer lay in the adverse circumstances in which this crucial evidence came to be gathered by Sharma, who was not even posted in Ahmedabad when the Gulberg and Naroda massacres had taken place. In fact, as superintendent of police (SP) of the Bhavnagar district, in the peninsular region of Saurashtra, Sharma was among the few district police chiefs who had responded vigorously to the violence in their territories and had apparently paid for it by being transferred even while the state was in the grip of the riots.

His professionalism was put to test right at the outset when he had asked for reinforcements to strengthen the 180-strong police force he had at his disposal. According to his testimony, the state police chief, K. Chakravarthi, told him not to expect much help as 'the bureaucracy had been completely neutralized'. Unfazed, Sharma came up with an imaginative way of preventing his policemen from being similarly neutralized. In order to enforce curfew, he ordered them not only 'to use maximum force while dealing with violent mobs' but also to open fire 'whenever necessary'. This was followed by a caveat: 'if anybody asked for reinforcements without resorting to firing, they would be suspended right away'. The caveat served to ensure that, irrespective of the resources available with them, the policemen in Bhavnagar consistently took on the rioters.

His single greatest achievement in Bhavnagar was an operation in which he averted what could easily have been the worst massacre in the state. On the afternoon of 2 March a mob tried to set fire to a madrassa, a residential Muslim school sheltering about 400 students, located on the outskirts of Bhavnagar city. The mob dispersed after a few of the miscreants had been injured in the police firing. The same evening, after Sharma had left for a meeting, the mob mounted a fresh attack on the madrassa. The police again opened fire, this time leading to fatalities. Meanwhile, as Sharma tried rushing back to the trouble spot, 'I found that the mob was in a systematic manner trying to block my way to the madrassa as it had thrown burning logs and tyres on the road.' Convinced as he was that the attacks had been 'organized', Sharma shifted the madrassa children to a mosque inside the city, in a convoy escorted by a striking force. Ironically, BJP leader L.K. Advani, in his autobiography published in 2008, claimed credit for the success of this very rescue operation. Advani said that it was because he had called up Modi and his partymen in Bhavnagar that the police were effective in saving the Muslims who had been staying in the madrassa.

Advani's endorsement in 2008 of the handling of the madrassa incident was, however, at variance with the feedback Sharma had received in 2002 from Gujarat's minister of state for home, Gordhan Zadafia. 'He told me that while I had done a good job at Bhavnagar, the ratio of deaths as a result of police firing was not proper. What I understood thereby was that he was complaining that more Hindus than Muslims had died due to police firing in Bhavnagar. I told him that the ratio depended on the situations where the police had resorted to firing.' This phone conversation, according to Sharma, took place on 16 March. A week later, he found himself transferred out of Bhavnagar. It followed a spat he had with local BJP leaders and his superior officers on their demand that twenty-one miscreants who had been arrested on 23 March for an attack on a mosque be released. Within 24 hours, Sharma received orders transferring him to a post with little field responsibilities: deputy commissioner of police (DCP) in Ahmedabad's control room. This adversity, however, turned into an opportunity. It was in his new post that Sharma providentially came into contact with the Gulberg Society and Naroda Patiya cases. On 7 May, Ahmedabad's commissioner of police, P.C. Pande, asked him to assist the crime branch in the investigations of those two cases.

This was when Sharma, an electrical engineer from IIT Kanpur and a law graduate, came up with the long overdue idea of collecting mobile phone data. The impetus, he said, was the allegations of complicity made by witnesses against political leaders and police officers. His proposal to crime branch chief A.K. Surolia was that before taking action against any leader or officer named by witnesses, the police should, as a precautionary measure, verify the allegations with the scientific evidence that would be available in the CDR of their mobile phones. Accordingly, Sharma drafted a letter which was issued by the crime branch under the signature of a junior officer of the crime branch, S.S. Chudasama, who was engaged directly with the Gulberg Society and Naroda Patiya cases. The letter was addressed to AT&T (now Idea) and CelForce (now Vodafone), which were then the two mobile phone service providers in Ahmedabad. Within a week, Sharma himself went to the office of AT&T and collected the required information, which was given in the Text format. Before handing over the AT&T CD to Chudasama as case property, Sharma copied its data on his personal computer at home. As he told the Supreme Court-appointed SIT in 2009, 'This copying was required to be done if the data from the two mobile phone companies were to be analysed together.'

CelForce, however, took longer to provide its data. And it came in the format of MS Access, a database management system of which Sharma then had no knowledge. He, therefore, enlisted the help of K.J. Chandana from the computer section in the Ahmedabad police headquarters. There were some glitches with the data, which could be rectified only after Chandana had visited the CelForce office a few times. When CelForce eventually sent the information in the required form, Sharma did not receive it through Chandana. Instead, P.P. Pandey, who had by then succeeded Surolia as crime branch chief, passed on the CDs to Sharma. In a covering letter, P.P. Pandey cautioned that as the CDs had been prepared under Sharma's instructions, he alone should analyse the data.

As a prelude to such analysis, Rahul Sharma copied the CelForce data on his personal computer where he had already stored the AT&T data. The CDR of the two service providers encompassed over five lakh calls made or received in Ahmedabad from 25 February to 4 March 2002. He could not, however, merge and analyse the data at that stage for two reasons. One, of course, was his unfamiliarity with MS Access. The other reason was that shortly after obtaining the CelForce data, Sharma received fresh transfer orders in the first week of July, this time to go to Surat as commandant of the reserve police.

Pressed as he was for time, he asked Chandana to deliver the CDs personally to the crime branch chief. Chandana did not, however, find Pandey in his office the two times he visited it. Then, on the second last day of his tenure in Ahmedabad, Sharma took back the CDs from Chandana and asked a rider from the control room to hand them over to Pandey. According to Sharma, the rider succeeded in meeting Pandey and reported to Sharma that he had delivered the CDs as instructed. It was not the most ideal way of dealing with what was part of the most important evidence of the Gujarat carnage. Sharma did not receive any acknowledgement from Pandey or his office for the delivery of those CelForce CDs. Sharma later later told the SIT that he could not not send the CDs through a formal letter as his PA was on leave at that time. The gap in the paper work gave the Modi government plenty of room for plausible deniability when the CDR data became public two years later. Before he left for his posting at Surat in July 2002, Sharma took Chandana's help to 'zip' the files of the CDR on his computer's hard disk in order to compress the data of both AT&T and Celforce into a single CD.

It was copies of this CD that were given by him at the earliest opportunity to the Justice Nanavati Commission on 30 October 2004. He had by then learnt the basics of MS Access, having joined the CBI at Gandhinagar on central deputation. Three weeks after his testimony before the Nanavati Commission, *The Indian Express* ran a series of stories analysing the damning implications of his CD. The series began on 21 November, just a day before Sharma was due to appear before another inquiry body. This was the Justice U.C. Banerjee Committee, which had been appointed by the Manmohan Singh government to probe the railway safety lapses in the Godhra incident. The appointment of this committee was just the sort of Central interference that the Gujarat government had hoped to avert when it had expanded the ambit of the Nanavati Commission following the change of government in New Delhi.

As the Banerjee Committee summoned him to appear before it with all the evidence he had in his possession, Sharma again produced a copy of the CD containing mobile phone records. The Banerjee Committee in turn gave a copy of that CD to advocate Mukul Sinha, who had asked for it on behalf of his NGO called Jan Sangharsh Manch. It was not out of place for the Bannerjee Committee to look into the CD because, as Sharma told the SIT, CelForce had also furnished data on mobile phones operating from Godhra, although that had not been sought. The upshot of it all was that the mobile phone evidence of the Gujarat carnage became officially public. This enabled lawyers, activists and victims to cite the data from Sharma's CD while pressing for action against influential persons such as Maya Kodnani, Jaydeep Patel, and senior police officers in carnage cases. In the case of Kodnani and Patel, for instance, the CD lent credence to the testimonies of witnesses that those two had been present in the Naroda area around the time of the violence. The affidavits prompted amicus curiae Harish Salve to take due note of the CD in a note he submitted to the Supreme Court on 20 March 2006. Given the 'apprehension of bias' raised by the CD, Salve argued that it needed to be examined by 'some agency other than those against whom the allegations are directed'. Thus, the CD added impetus to the demand that the nine cases that had been shortlisted by the Supreme Court, including Naroda Patiya and Naroda Gaam massacres, be referred to an agency independent of the Gujarat police.

The trial of those nine cases had already been stayed by the Supreme Court in November 2003 because of the dubious role that the Gujarat police had been found to have played in the Best Bakery and Bilkis Bano cases. The CD exposed the Gujarat police further, not only in terms of the the damning evidence it brought out regarding the nexus between the rioters and police officers, but also for the failure of the police to include the mobile phone evidence in their investigations. It was only after the SIT had been constituted by the Supreme Court in March 2008 that Rahul Sharma's CD finally become a part of the evidence under investigation. Given the circumstances in which it had been appointed, the SIT had no option other than to take cognizance of the CD. At any rate, it could not have ignored the glaring evidence that had already become public against Maya Kodnani and Jaydeep Patel in the Naroda massacres. As Kodnani had by then become a minister in Modi's government, the SIT's handling of the mobile phone evidence against her tested the independence of the Supreme Court-appointed body.

Thus it was that almost seven years after the carnage, Kodnani and Patel found themselves implicated in the Naroda massacres. While Patel was implicated in the Naroda Gaam case, Kodnani was implicated in both Naroda Patiya and Naroda Gaam cases. Their implication was thanks to the discrepancies between their testimonies to SIT in December 2008 and what their phone call records suggested about their movements on 28 February 2002. Even so, in deference to their clout and stature, the SIT treated them with kid gloves when it came to arresting them. Rather than straightaway picking them up, the SIT served notices at their residences on 26 January 2009, asking them to depose before it three days later. When they did not turn up on the due date, the SIT gave them an extension of two days. Then, when they again did a no-show, the SIT could not help acknowledging that the minister and the VHP leader had gone underground. It was an awkward situation created by the SIT's reluctance, despite its mixed composition, to exercise the normal option of arresting the two persons accused of murder. In a bid to save face, the SIT declared them absconders on 2 February. Three days later, both leaders resurfaced after obtaining anticipatory bail from a sessions court.

The arrests finally took place almost two months later, on 27 March 2009, after the Gujarat high court had cancelled the anticipatory bail. The same day, Kodnani, who was minister for women and child development, resigned from the Modi government. It was a hard-fought moral victory for those who believed in a secular India, coming as it did four years after Congress leader Jagdish Tytler had resigned from the Central government for his alleged complicity in the 1984 Delhi carnage. Tytler's exit followed an indictment by a judicial inquiry conducted, incidentally, by the same retired Supreme Court judge who is probing the Gujarat carnage, G.T. Nanavati. Since her assembly constituency of Naroda suffered the highest death toll in the 2002 carnage, Kodnani is also comparable to the deceased Congress minister, H.K.L. Bhagat, whose parliamentary constituency of East Delhi had seen the largest number of killings in the 1984 carnage. During the trial stage, both had suffered the ignominy of being arrested, however briefly, for allegedly instigating violence in their respective constituencies. The massive electoral victories they had notched up before their much-delayed arrests, despite all the evidence against them in the public domain, puts a question mark on the quality of democracy in India. Kodnani was elected for the first time to the assembly in 1998 with an impressive margin of 75,000. Then, in the December 2002 election held in the wake of the carnage, her margin increased to 1.10 lakh votes in the face of the allegations levelled against her by riot victims. And in the 2007 election, by when Rahul Sharma's CD uncovering evidence of her alleged complicty in the Naroda Patiya and Naroda Gam cases had become public, Kodnani increased her margin further to 1.80 lakh votes, the highest in the state.

From the viewpoint of fact-finding, what was significant was that the high court, while cancelling Kodnani's anticipatory bail on 27 March 2009, recalled the Supreme Court's perspective equating rioters with terrorists. Referring to the order that had constituted the SIT a year earlier, Justice D.H. Waghela of the high court said: 'Religious fanatics really do not belong to any religion. They are no better than terrorists who kill innocent people for no rhyme or reason.' No less significant was the high court's confirmation of the Modi regime's long record of reluctance to act against Kodnani and Jaydeep Patel. Rejecting their argument that they were being implicated for the first time after so many years by the SIT, the high court pointed to 'the state of affairs in which names of prominent persons like the respondents were clearly alleged to have been omitted from their (witnesses') statements by the investigating officer' in the aftermath of the carnage. 'No less than six witnesses have mentioned the names of the respondents in the year 2002 itself,' the high court added. Of course, the cancellation of the bail was also determined by a prima facie appreciation of the mobile phone evidence contributed by Rahul Sharma. The high court said that Kodnani's call data showed that she 'could have been in Naroda area for about 40 minutes in the morning' and for some more time 'in the afternoon'.

When Zakia Jafri's complaint was referred to the SIT a month after Kodnani's arrest, it opened up the prospect of holding to account the police officials who had for years sat on Rahul Sharma's CD. After all, one of the thirty-two allegations gleaned by the SIT from Jafri's complaint was: 'The CD regarding telephone calls by BJP leaders and police officers during riots was not probed into by the investigating officers of the Naroda Patia and Gulberg Society cases.' The issue was so framed by the SIT that it gave itself the elbow room to probe the police neglect of the mobile phone evidence only from the time Sharma had produced his CD before the Nanavati Commission on 30 October 2004. Therefore, no questions, however relevant or fundamental, were asked about why the Gujarat police had, in the first two-and-a-half years, never used that very obvious scientific evidence in any of the carnage cases. Similarly, no probe was conducted on how the Ahmedabad crime branch had buried the original CDs of the two mobile service providers returned separately by Sharma in 2002.

Instead, taking advantage of the deficiencies in the paperwork on the CD, the Gujarat government denied the existence of any mobile phone evidence in the police records. It turned the tables by initiating disciplinary proceedings against Rahul Sharma in 2011. It was a classic example of a whistleblower being hounded by a rattled and vindictive government. It issued a charge-sheet against him on four counts: collecting the CDR data without authorization, copying the data from the original CDs to his personal computer without authorization, not informing the investigating officer about the copies of the CDs in his possession, and submitting them to the Nanavati Commission without prior permission. The objection to the submission of the CDs to the Nanavati Commission, however, worked to Sharma's advantage. This is because the law forbids action against witnesses for any deposition before a commission of inquiry. The legal premise for it is that witnesses would otherwise feel inhibited about aiding the process of fact-finding. In April 2012, the Central Administrative Tribunal (CAT) stayed the proceedings against Sharma, pointing out that the government's admitted position was that it had learnt of the CDs only from his deposition before the Nanavati Commission.

As blatant as the government's vindictive action against Sharma was the selective manner in which the SIT blamed only junior officers for not taking cognizance of his CDs, after Sharma had produced them before the Nanavati Commission. Given the media splash over the sudden appearance of the mobile phone evidence, no police officer from Ahmedabad could have feigned ignorance about it. Much less so the crime branch dealing with the big massacres of Ahmedabad: Naroda Patiya/Gam and Gulberg Society. Even so, the crime branch neither sought Sharma's CD nor fished out the original CDs from its own records. Could this apathy have been because the police had already dismissed the allegations against Kodnani in writing in 2002? Alternatively, was the crime branch under political or other extraneous pressure to bury its head in the sand? Whatever the reason, it was clear that the crime branch had deliberately not pursued the mobile phone evidence, from 30 October 2004 (when Sharma produced his CD) to 26 March 2008 (when the SIT took over the investigation of the Gulberg and Naroda cases). Mercifully, the SIT did find this omission to be culpable. But when it came to apportioning blame, the SIT's gaze did not go beyond two junior officers who had directly dealt with the investigations. It balked at examining the omissions on the part of the supervisory officers and beyond. The SIT failed to pursue this line of investigation despite its potential to uncover any high-level conspiracy to hush up the mobile phone evidence.

It took a great deal of disingenuity on the SIT's part to justify its selective approach. It first questioned Tarun Barot, who was then the police inspector in the crime branch entrusted with the Naroda Gam case, in which eleven Muslims had been killed. His blithe explanation for not approaching Sharma to get the call details was that he was not aware of the CDs that had been produced by Sharma before the two judicial inquiry bodies. Barot admitted at the same time that he had come across a news report suggesting, on the basis of mobile phone records, that Maya Kodnani and Jaydeep Patel were located in the Naroda area at the time of the massacre on 28 February 2002. Barot claimed that on the basis of this news item he had summoned Kodnani and Patel, to question them about their location on the fateful day. The two admitted nothing beyond their presence at Sola Civil Hospital, where most of the bodies of those burnt alive in the Godhra tragedy had been brought. As they denied their presence in the Naroda area around the time of the killings, Barot felt he could take no action against them in the absence of any evidence contradicting their claims.

The SIT, however, rejected Barot's defence for his inaction. 'The plea put forward by Barot is not convincing inasmuch as the news about the production of the CDs . . . had appeared in almost all the newspapers and, therefore, it is difficult to believe that Barot did not come to know about it.' Holding that it appeared to be 'an intentional lapse' on Barot's part, the SIT said that his conduct warranted 'major penalty departmental proceedings against him'.

The SIT recommended similar departmental action against G.L. Singhal, who was the investigating officer of the two bigger cases related to Gulberg Society and Naroda Patiya, where the official death toll was sixty-nine and ninety-six, respectively. Unlike Barot, Singhal admitted to the SIT that he had been aware about the production of the CD before the Nanavati Commission. However, like Barot, Singhal too claimed to have interrogated Kodnani and Patel about their whereabouts without bothering to procure their call details. Despite such flagrant dereliction in their investigations, the SIT's final report added that 'no criminal offence is made out' against either Singhal or Barot.

The SIT's reading of the law to limit the culpability of the two investigating officers to departmental action might be arguable. But the same can hardly be said about its presumption that the culpability, whether departmental or criminal, could be limited to these two junior officers. How could the SIT have condoned the equally glaring negligence on the part of the supervisory officers, including crime branch chief P.P. Pandey? After all, Pandey was the very officer who had forwarded the CelForce data to Sharma in 2002 asking him in writing to analyse it. Besides, he was also the officer to whom Sharma had reportedly returned the original CDs of CelForce when he had been suddenly transferred out of Ahmedabad. Pandey was still the crime branch chief when Sharma produced his CD two years later before the Nanavati Commission. The news stories that followed on Sharma's CD should have alerted him more than anyone else because of his past association with the issue.

If the SIT could still avoid questioning Pandey about his failure to pursue the mobile phone evidence, it was thanks partly to an omission on the part of the complainant Zakia Jafri. Although her complaint provided a list of sixty-three accused persons, Pandey does not figure in it. Instead, the complaint cites Rahul Sharma as Accused No 45. This forced the complainant to clarify in the course of the SIT's inquiry that Sharma was actually a witness who had been inadvertently listed as an accused. Had she instead listed Pandey as an accused, the SIT would have been hard-pressed to absolve him for ignoring the mobile phone evidence. Indeed, Pandey would have been accountable not just for the years after Sharma had produced his CD in October 2004 but also for those preceding that. The trail of evidence could then have led to the office of Ahmedabad's police commissioner and gone further up to the home department, headed throughout that period by Narendra Modi. The SIT would then have found it that much more difficult to maintain that there was no high-level conspiracy, whether behind the post-Godhra violence or its cover-up.

Though he escaped accountability for the 2002 cover-up, the law caught up with P.P. Pandey in 2013, when he was implicated by the CBI in the 2004 Ishrat Jahan fake encounter case. Following Kodnani's precedent, Pandey went underground for over three months. It was as bizarre as the minister's disappearance, for Pandey had by then risen to the rank of the additional director general of police. It was only after he had been taken into custody on 13 August 2013 that the Modi regime suspended Pandey. Interestingly, Pandey's subordinate Singhal, another officer who had ignored the CDR evidence, was also arrested in the same fake encounter case. He went on to make big news in 2013 for giving the CBI a cache of records of the telephone conversations he had in 2009 with the then home minister, Amit Shah, and others in connection with the surveillance of a female architect at the behest of a 'Saheb'.

The story of the mobile phone evidence did not, however, end with the filing of the SIT's closure report on Jafri's complaint in February 2012. When the trial court's judgment in the Naroda Patiya case came six months later, it brought out further evidence of the SIT's reluctance to leverage Rahul Sharma's CD. This despite the fact that the judgment delivered by sessions judge Jyotsna Yagnik on 29 August 2012 proved to be path-breaking as it was, in India's long history of communal violence, the first-ever instance of a minister being convicted. Convicted for murder and conspiracy, Maya Kodnani was called the 'kingpin of the Naroda Patiya massacre' and sentenced to imprisonment for twenty-eight years. Yet, the very evidence that had served as a catalyst for her arrest—the mobile phone records—ended up being rejected by the trial court. Kodnani's conviction was instead based on the witness testimonies that had finally been recorded against her by the SIT, as an unavoidable consequence of her implication. The mobile phone records did not survive the trial because of the SIT's failure to handle that evidence with due diligence.

One glaring omission, for instance, was that the SIT did not bother to establish the elementary detail that the mobile phone connection that was being attributed to Kodnani was indeed hers or, at the least, used by her during the carnage. This omission proved fatal as the number concerned happened to be registered in the name of the BJP and not her personally. In such a situation, the SIT was required to prove that the party had in turn allotted that number to Kodnani. The corroborative evidence could have been as simple as her letterhead or her calling card or the testimony of someone who had been in touch with her on that number. In the absence of such verification, there was no way any of the call details cited to show her location in the Naroda area during the violence could have been held against her. Sure enough, the SIT's omission gave scope for Kodnani's counsel to contest the allegation that she had ever used that connection. The trial court had little option but to hold that the mobile number alleged to have been used by Kodnani did 'not stand proved beyond reasonable doubt'. The same judgment also said 'it is surprising that no investigation has been made (by the SIT) to conclude that it was used by A-37 (Kodnani)'.

The surprise expressed over the SIT's cavalier approach to the mobile phone evidence was the closest the trial court came to pointing out the SIT's lack of independence. In the larger scheme of things, this confirmed that the Supreme Court's faith in the SIT was misplaced. The saving grace, however, was that Kodnani was still convicted because of a safeguard that had been devised by the Supreme Court while vacating the stay on the trial in 2009. It was the decision to provide security to witnesses, that too by a central police force. The security emboldened them to testify in the Ahmedabad court against a minister in the Modi government. While the Supreme Court's measure to protect witnesses yielded Kodnani's conviction, the gaps in its monitoring of the investigation allowed the SIT to scuttle the mobile phone evidence. All the same, the unprecedented conviction was due as much to the breakthroughs made by Rahul Sharma in 2002, when he took the initiative of calling for mobile phone data, and in 2004, when he blew the cover on this vital evidence. Had his exposé not forced the SIT to implicate Kodnani, the question of her conviction would not have arisen.

5

Modi's Interrogation
Unasked Questions

When Narendra Modi visited the office of the SIT in Gandhinagar on 27 March 2010, it was exactly eleven months after the Supreme Court had directed it to 'look into' a criminal complaint. Modi's visit in response to an SIT summons was a milestone in accountability—at least in potential. It was the first time any chief minister was being questioned by an investigating agency for his alleged complicity in communal violence. The summons were on the complaint by Zakia Jafri, the widow of former Congress MP Ehsan Jafri, who had been killed in the first of the post Godhra massacres in 2002.

Jafri's complaint, which had been referred to it by the Supreme Court on 27 April 2009, tested the SIT's independence and integrity more than any of the nine cases that had been originally assigned to it a year earlier. Jafri's complaint called upon it to probe allegations against sixty-three influential persons, including Modi himself. The complaint named Modi as Accused No. 1 for the alleged conspiracy behind the carnage that had taken place in fourteen of Gujarat's twenty-five districts. A Supreme Court bench, headed by Justice Arijit Pasayat, authorized the SIT not only to 'look into' Jafri's complaint but also to 'take steps as required in law'. The legal steps that needed to be taken immediately were self-evident. The SIT was required to examine whether the information contained in Jafri's complaint amounted to, as Section 154 CrPC put it, 'the commission of a cognizable offence'. If so, the SIT would be obliged, under the same provision, to register a first information report (FIR), which is a statutory prelude to an actual investigation.

The SIT did conduct a probe into Jafri's complaint but it was done without fulfilling the precondition of registering an FIR. The elaborate probe, stretching over twelve months and recording the statements of 163 witnesses, took place under the guise of a 'preliminary enquiry'. Then, even after the conclusion of the so-called preliminary enquiry, the SIT was disinclined to register any FIR on Jafri's complaint. In its 12 May 2010 'enquiry report', the SIT asked the Supreme Court if it could instead conduct 'further investigation' in the existing case of Gulberg Society, where Jafri was a witness. The SIT's proposal flew in the face of Jafri's complaint, which had sought a broad-based probe into the conduct of the Modi government, encompassing all the carnage cases, rather than a narrowly-focused further investigation in any particular case. Besides, the period covered by Jafri's complaint was an extended one as it referred to, for instance, the Supreme Court's indictment of the Modi regime in 2004 in the Best Bakery and Bilkis Bano cases.

Despite the mismatch between the restricted scope of the Gulberg Society case and the wide ambit of Jafri's complaint, a Supreme Court bench, headed by Justice D.K. Jain, gave the go-ahead to the SIT's proposal. This could be because the permission for further investigation sought by the SIT was only into allegations against a junior minister, Gordhan Zadafia, and two police officers, M.K. Tandon and P.B. Gondia. Later on, though, as discussed later in this chapter, the Supreme Court extended the purview of the further investigation to the alleged complicity of Modi himself. This long-drawn-out but unusual exercise culminated on 8 February 2012 in a 'final report' to a magisterial court in Ahmedabad exonerating Modi and the rest of the accused persons of any of the criminal culpability alleged by Jafri's complaint.

Such a conclusion was predestined, if not predetermined, for a variety of reasons. Not least of those reasons was the manner in which the SIT's closure report relied implicitly on Modi's testimony. This was despite the fact that Modi's statement had been perfunctorily recorded outside the framework of CrPC. The only time he appeared before the SIT was when Jafri's complaint was still in the phase of preliminary enquiry. His statement could therefore not be recorded under Section 161 CrPC, the provision normally invoked to question any person 'supposed to be acquainted with the facts and circumstances of the case'. Had he been summoned during the 'further investigation' too, Modi would have been legally obliged to speak the truth under Section 161 CrPC. The provision stipulates that the person questioned 'shall be bound to answer truly all questions', subject to the universally recognized right against self-incrimination. That Modi was not put under such a legal obligation 'to answer truly all questions' was a curious omission. The SIT refrained from summoning Modi even as it recorded fresh statements under Section 161 of several other persons named as accused in Jafri's complaint. This led to the anomaly of the SIT's final report to the magistrate relying on the testimony given by Modi during the preliminary enquiry, which was outside the scheme of the CrPC.

When Modi's testimony was recorded, the questioning was

done by SIT member A.K. Malhotra, a retired CBI officer. What began on 27 March 2010 went on for as long as nine hours over two sessions, with the second spilling over into the wee hours of the following day. The length of the interrogation was, however, out of proportion to its intensity. Although as many as seventy-one questions were addressed to him, the transcript, bearing Modi's signature on every page, shows that Malhotra studiously refrained from challenging any of his replies, however controversial. At no point did Malhotra make the slightest effort to pin Modi down on any gaps and contradictions in his testimony. Although the questions, culled from Jafri's complaint, were extensive, the SIT refrained from asking a single follow-up question. It seemed as if Malhotra's brief was more to place Modi's defence on record rather than to ferret out any inconsistency or admission of wrongdoing. Malhotra's approach of sticking to his question script, irrespective of the answers elicited by it, helped Modi get off the hook on more than one issue. Both parties made the most of the absence of the Section 161 obligation: with Modi, it was not to 'answer truly' and with the SIT, it was not to put 'all questions'.

Take the reluctance displayed by the SIT in March 2010 to corner Modi on the terror conspiracy allegation made by him within hours of the Godhra incident. The SIT's reluctance was obvious because a year earlier the Gujarat high court had upheld a statutory review committee's recommendation that terror charges could not apply to the Godhra case. Among the reasons pointed out by the review committee headed by a retired high court judge were that the miscreants involved in the Godhra arson had not used any firearms or explosives, that they had attacked coach S-6 from only one side and that they had allowed passengers of the overcrowded coach to escape from the other side. These reasons were found convincing enough for the high court to declare in February 2009 that 'the incident in question is shocking but every shocking incident cannot be covered by a definition of a statute which defines terror'.

The high court ruling exposed Modi's attempt to magnify the Godhra arson as a terror attack. This in turn was integral to probing Jafri's charge that Modi was himself involved in the conspiracy behind the post-Godhra violence. Without bringing up the word 'terror', Malhotra did ask Modi about the basis of his allegation. But he was allowed to get away with the claim that he had never made any such allegation. In fact, Malhotra helped Modi get away with the denial by putting the question in a misplaced context. While interrogating him in a chronological sequence, Malhotra asked Modi about his Godhra allegation in the course of questions about his statement in the Gujarat assembly early in the afternoon on 27 February. This was misplaced as the allegation had actually come later in the day from Godhra. Here's how the charade played out during the recording of Modi's testimony.

> Malhotra: 'Did you declare the Godhra incident as pre-planned and that Pakistani/ISI hands were behind the Godhra incident? If so, on what basis?'
>
> Modi: 'I did not utter any such words in the assembly. Of course, the media had put some questions to me about it, but I had told [them] that nothing could be said until the investigation was completed.'

In other words, Modi admitted that on the conspiracy question, his initial reaction on the fateful day was that he would rather not comment till the police had unravelled the crime. It was a tacit acknowledgement that, as head of the state government, he could ill-afford the luxury of baseless speculation lest it provoke a law and order crisis. A logical follow-up to that could have been: How could he then abandon all caution the same evening and make the terror allegation without waiting for the police investigation to be completed? The SIT never put any such question to Modi; not even after he had made no bones about the dramatic change in his attitude to pre-judging the case during his visit to Godhra the same day. The closest Malhotra came to doing so while dealing with the Godhra visit was when he asked Modi a general question about his media interaction in that town.

Malhotra: 'Did you meet media persons at Godhra?'

Modi: 'While I was at Collectorate, Godhra, a lot of media persons had assembled there. I briefed them about the incident and informed them that the culprits would not be spared and that a compensation of Rs 2 lakhs per victim would be paid. I also appealed to [the] public through them for maintenance of peace. I also informed the media that *on the basis of facts narrated to me by the persons present on the spot as well as injured persons, the incident appeared to be a serious and preplanned conspiracy.*'
(emphasis added)

It was thus left to Modi to reconstruct on his own the allegation he had made in Godhra. The SIT did not challenge his attempt to make out that he had talked merely of conspiracy and not of terror. Modi could have been confronted with, if nothing else, the official press release issued on the evening of 27 February. On the strength of his 'spot assessment of the situation', it quoted Modi as saying that the Godhra incident was a 'preplanned inhuman collective violent act of terrorism'. The torrent of adjectives showed that he had described Godhra quite definitively as a terrorist conspiracy.

Such certitude was, however, missing eight years later when he was being questioned by the SIT. Modi claimed that all he had instead said on the day of the arson was that it was an ordinary criminal conspiracy ('serious and preplanned'), that too in a qualified manner ('appeared to be'). The sanitized account he presented to the SIT was apparently intended to convey that on the evening of 27 February 2002, he had shown due restraint in the face of extreme provocation.

In the vastly changed circumstances of 2010, Modi was wary of recalling his terror rhetoric. It was a different world in 2002 when he had reacted so stridently to the train arson. He was then tapping into the heightened fear of jehadi terror around the world in the wake of the attacks on WTC twin towers in New York and Parliament House in New Delhi. Both those major terror incidents had taken place just a few months prior to the Godhra incident. In fact, Godhra happened when George Bush's war on terror was raging on Pakistan's western border as a result of 9/11, and tens of thousands of Indian troops had been deployed on its eastern border as a result of the Parliament attack. Modi's attempt to pass off Godhra as another terror strike in such a charged environment still took a leap in logic. This is because the Godhra arson did not have any of the obvious features of terror such as RDX explosives, AK 47 rifles, or hijacked aircraft. Besides, none of the police documents generated that day in Godhra, including the FIR and the case diary, contained the slightest hint of terrorism.

The SIT's failure to pin him down on the terror issue pales in comparison to its disregard of Modi's prevarication on the post-Godhra massacres. Though his responsibility to control the attacks on Muslims was more direct, the SIT's questions turned out to be as evasive as his replies. One glaring issue was Modi's delayed response to the prolonged siege at Ahmedabad's Gulberg Society, the site of the first post-Godhra massacre. Unlike his terror allegation, this problem of delayed response though was not peculiar to Modi. It is a thread that runs through most of the flare-ups of communal violence in India, whether in remote villages or right inside big cities. The delay could stretch to hours, as it did in Ahmedabad in 2002, or more than a day, as it did in Delhi in 1984. The delay in responding proportionately is typically the gap in governance that creates room for mass crimes. The Supreme Court's intervention on Jafri's complaint provided the first-ever opportunity for an investigating agency to get to the bottom of this recurring factor in communal violence. The SIT, however, frittered away this unprecedented opportunity. The SIT was wary of questioning him on his failure to respond to the violence at Gulberg Society, although he had been in its vicinity for over two hours on 28 February. In his testimony, Modi made out that he had no clue to any of the violence at Gulberg Society, including Ehsan Jafri's murder, till he was told about it about five hours later by the police. This is how the testimony was actually recorded:

> Malhotra: Did you receive any information about an attack by a mob on Gulberg Society? If so, when and through whom? What action did you take in the matter?

> Modi: To the best of my knowledge, I was informed in the law and order review meeting held in the night about the attack on Gulberg Society in Meghaninagar area and Naroda Patiya.

What was listed as question No. 31 in Modi's testimony actually had three parts to it. The first was whether Modi had received any information about the mob attack on Gulberg Society. Modi's answer was yes. The second part was when and through whom had he received the information. Predictably, Modi indicated that he had been informed about the massacre by the police. The surprise, however, lay in the time he claimed to have been 'informed' about the massacre. Modi said that it was at the law and order meeting 'held in the night'. In a different context, while enumerating all the measures Modi had taken on 28 February, the SIT's 2012 report disclosed on page 256 that this law and order meeting had taken place in Gandhinagar at 8.30 pm. So, linking the two discrete pieces of information recorded by the SIT, this book for the first time establishes the precise time at which Modi claims to have been informed about the Gulberg Society massacre. It was 8.30 pm, a claim that strains credulity given the magnitude of the massacre which, according to the SIT's own findings, was executed right in Ahmedabad by 3.45 pm. By then, Gulberg Society had been, as the SIT report put it on page 494, 'set ablaze and lot of lives including that of Late Ehsan Jafri had been lost'.

Modi's claim to have learnt about the massacre only at the 8.30 pm meeting threw up a glaring and unexplained time lag. But the SIT neither contested his claim during the interrogation nor discussed the implications of his claim in its report. It tacitly accepted Modi's claim that he had no real time information on the prolonged Gulberg Society siege and massacre, stretching over eight hours. And even after Joint Commissioner M.K. Tandon was said to have intervened in the Gulberg Society massacre around 4 pm, Modi remained out of the loop for nearly five hours, till the news was apparently broken to him at the 8.30 pm meeting. As a corollary, insofar as the SIT was concerned, the third part of its question No. 31, asking what action Modi had taken in the matter, was rendered inconsequential. Since he somehow remained in the dark during all those crucial hours when he could have made a difference, there was no question of holding Modi to account for the Gulberg Society massacre, or so went the SIT's line of reasoning.

In reality, Modi's claim to have been ignorant about the

Gulberg Society massacre seems inconsistent with his own larger claim to have been tracking the post-Godhra violence as it unfolded. This contradiction was apparently lost on the SIT. It accepted Modi's plea of ignorance even as it meticulously listed out a series of meetings Modi had held in the days following the Godhra incident, all focused on the task of controlling violence against Muslims.

In the sequence of events reconstructed by the SIT, one such meeting was held by Modi in Gandhinagar at 1 pm on 28 February, when things were coming to a boil in Gulberg Society. Joint Commissioner Tandon had already made a brief visit to Gulberg Society around 11.30 am, when he ordered the 'striking force' accompanying him to burst tear gas shells to disperse 'a mob of around 1,000 Hindu rioters'. Further, at 12.20 pm, the police control room received a message from the Meghaninagar police station asking for reinforcements as the mob, which had regrouped at Gulberg Society and grown to 10,000-strong, was indulging in stone-pelting and arson.

How could none of these details about the escalating crisis in Gulberg Society have been brought to Modi's notice in the law and order review meeting he had at 1 pm? Modi's claim to have been unaware of the Naroda Patiya violence as well, at the end of that meeting, is even more puzzling. This is because by then, at 12.30 pm, the police had, for the first time in the context of the post-Godhra massacres, imposed a curfew in the jurisdiction of the Naroda police station. Even if it proved to be ineffective, the very imposition of the curfew signified that the administration had taken cognizance of the gravity of the situation.

Modi's general claim of ignorance sounds all the more dubious as some of his engagements on 28 February were at a venue barely three kilometers from Gulberg Society: the Circuit House Annexe in Ahmedabad's Shahibaug. He held a law and order review meeting at this venue at 4 pm, by when the massacre had been carried out at Gulberg Society and Tandon had just returned to the spot. While Modi's meeting was going on just a few kilometers away, Tandon finally ordered firing, leading to casualties among the rioters at Gulberg Society. Tandon was also engaged in the process of evacuating some 150 survivors, including women and children, from this Muslim pocket. Further, he directed Inspector K.G. Erda to 'complete the inquest promptly and send the dead bodies to hospital for post-mortem examination'.

Yet, for the next few hours, Modi was not given the slightest hint of the first big massacre in the wake of Godhra—or so went the official narrative, accepted without demur by the SIT. This, despite the SIT's own acknowledegment of a flurry of messages within the police establishment during the Gulberg Society violence. At 2.05 pm, Tandon asked for more reinforcements from the control room stating explicitly that, from the information received by him, Jafri and his neighbours had been 'surrounded by the mob'. This was followed by another urgent message at 2.14 pm, this one by the officer on the spot, Erda, saying that the mob was 'about to set fire to the entire society'. At 2.45 pm, Erda told the control room that the mob had surrounded not just the Muslims but also the police.

Besides such a chilling countdown to the massacre, the SIT report referred to a message from the highest police officer of the state, K. Chakravarthi, indicating that he was very much privy to the first major instance of post-Godhra violence playing out in Gulberg Society. The SIT also reported that it was on the instructions of the Ahmedabad police commissioner, P.C. Pande, sent at 3.16 pm, that another senior officer, P.B. Gondia, had reached Gulberg Society at 4.05 pm, shortly after Tandon's arrival.

Thus, there was an unexplained disconnect between what

the police brass were admittedly aware of and what Modi claimed to have learnt or not learnt from them in the course of that fateful day. Shortly after his law and order review meeting in the Circuit House Annexe, Modi held a press conference at the same venue from 4.30 pm to 5.45 pm, when he announced his decision to call the Army. Though it was prompted by the deteriorating situation in Ahmedabad, the decision to call the Army had nothing to do with Gulberg Society, the biggest massacre till then, as he was apparently yet to hear about it. Before leaving the Circuit House Annexe, Modi gave Doordarshan around 6 pm a recording of a customary 'appeal for peace'. It was on returning to his Gandhinagar home that Modi held the 8.30 pm meeting where he claimed to have finally heard about the mass crimes in Gulberg Society.

How could the earlier meetings, focused as they were on the escalating violence, have missed out on Gulberg Society? The best argument that could perhaps be advanced in Modi's favour was that even journalists at his 4.30 pm press conference seemed to have been oblivious to Gulberg Society. For nobody at the press conference had pointedly asked him about the first big massacre, which had just taken place a little distance away. This does suggest that as violence was breaking out across the state, journalists were as yet unaware of the enormity of the violence at Gulberg Society, including the brutality with which a former MP had been murdered there. But it is implausible to assume such ignorance on the part of someone wearing the hats of the chief minister and home minister of Gujarat. Besides being briefed at the meetings held by him through the day, Modi would have been regularly receiving 'sitreps' (situation reports) from the state police control room and the state intelligence bureau on the law and order crisis. If there was any truth to his claim to have been out of the loop till 8.30 pm, then the police brass should have been held to account by Modi himself, let alone the SIT. After all, the issue was not just their lapses in dealing with the violence; he should have been even more affronted by their failure to alert him, during the meetings and in their 'sitreps', about what was till then the worst instance of violence. At stake were not just the lives of innocent Muslims but his own self-styled image as a decisive and impartial administrator.

Since he had taken no action against the police in all the years before the SIT probe, it should have been all the more a reason for the SIT to question Modi on the wide gap in his narrative between the time of the mass killings and the time he had come to know about them. Such a gap was harder to accept in his case than that of, say, Prime Minister Rajiv Gandhi, for the corresponding situation in the 1984 carnage. While Modi was admittedly immersed in the challenge of combating the post-Godhra violence, Rajiv Gandhi had the fig leaf that he was himself in mourning during the massacres of Sikhs and that he was most of the time standing next to the body of his assassinated mother Indira Gandhi lying in state in Teen Murti Bhavan. For that matter, even Prime Minister P.V. Narasimha Rao had the excuse that the Constitution did not permit him in 1992 to take any pre-emptive action to save the Babri Masjid from being demolished by kar sevaks allegedly in collusion with the BJP government in Uttar Pradesh.

The unexplained incongruities in Modi's account would have lent credence to Zakia Jafri's allegation that he was complicit in the massacres of Muslims. So, playing it safe, the SIT refrained from confronting Modi with any of the obvious follow-up questions. This charade bore a lesson in fact-finding. The integrity of fact-finding hinged on a deceptively simple factor: the nature of the questions that have been put or not put. Despite the monitoring by the Supreme Court, the SIT got away with dodgy manoeuvres during the interrogation. This ensured that Modi never had to account for key issues such as the basis of his terror allegation on Godhra and his claim to have been unaware of the Gulberg Society massacre even as he was apparently grappling with the post-Godhra violence. It took so little to cover up the truth behind the 2002 carnage.

This fiction of fact-finding is a far cry from a stirring example of governance set early in the history of India's experiment with secularism. When Mahatma Gandhi was assassinated within six months of Independence, any irresponsible remark at that sensitive moment from those in authority could have revived the communal bloodbath seen at the time of the subcontinent's partition. When independent India's first governor-general, Lord Mountbatten, arrived at Birla House within minutes of the assassination on 30 January 1948, he heard someone in the crowd shouting that it was a Muslim who had murdered Gandhi. Mountbatten showed the presence of mind to scotch the rumour even before he learnt the identity of the killer. 'You fool, everyone knows it was a Hindu,' he shot back, in a bid to gain time for the administration to control the situation. All India Radio (AIR) deferred the announcement of Gandhi's death by over half an hour till the police confirmed that the assassin was indeed a Hindu. The decision to convey both details together helped avert attacks on Muslims. This was how the national broadcaster broke the news at 6 pm: 'Mahatma Gandhi was assassinated in New Delhi at twenty minutes past five this afternoon. His assassin was a Hindu.' Barring stray attacks on Maharashtrian Brahmins, the country remained peaceful.

By not holding Modi to the kind of standards of governance that had been set way back in 1948, the SIT belied the faith that had been reposed in it by the Supreme Court. But then, the Supreme Court too is to blame for the resultant impunity.

There were at least two reasons for this. One was its folly, however unwitting, in selecting unsuitable members for the SIT and in not being vigilant enough to see that that they carried out their responsibility with impartiality and integrity. Chapter 3 discussed the circumstances in which two of the three SIT members from the Gujarat police had been removed. More importantly, Chapter 7 of this book uncovers a controversy about R.K. Raghavan which should have kept him from being considered for the post of SIT chairman. He was himself a beneficiary of equally serious questions not being put to him about certain security lapses, which had done inestimable damage to India in a different context. The other reason for which the Supreme Court could be blamed for Modi's impunity was the failure of its much-touted safeguard of monitoring the SIT probe. Having been ordered by Justice Arijit Pasayat's bench just before his retirement in April 2009, the SIT probe into Jafri's complaint took place on the watch of its successor bench headed by Justice D.K. Jain. The monitoring done by Jain's bench proved to be ineffective, when it came to the crunch. As discussed in Chapter 3, a member supervising the Gulberg Society case was allowed to continue in the SIT even after its own prosecutor had blown the whistle on its attempts to conceal state complicity. Similarly, in Jafri's case, the Supreme Court overlooked deficiencies as glaring as the ones in the questioning of Modi. Given the reputation for independence built by the Supreme Court over the years, how did its monitoring of the probe in this critical case turn out to be such a letdown?

A key element of the monitoring was the mechanism of the amicus curiae, a senior lawyer appointed by the Supreme Court to provide independent advice to it. While the amicus curiae for nine cases originally entrusted to the SIT was senior advocate Harish Salve, the one for Jafri's complaint was senior advocate

Raju Ramachandran. From what has been disclosed of the monitoring, the voluminous reports, testimonies and documents presented by the SIT on Jafri's complaint were scrutinized not so much by the three judges on the bench as by Ramachandran. Much as he played this critical role with due independence, Ramachandran, it would appear, could have done with greater thoroughness. For someone who had been a law officer for the Vajpayee government, Ramachandran displayed remarkable independence as amicus curiae, in standing up to the SIT's resolve to exonerate Modi of all charges. At the same time, his scrutiny seemed to have been hampered by the fact that he never really stepped out of the frame set by the SIT. Ramachandran's literal interpretation of his brief might have enhanced the credibility of his reports but, in the process, he seemed to have overlooked some material evidence.

Take his failure to notice the farcical nature of the SIT's questions to Modi. Neither of his reports, which were the bedrock of the Supreme Court monitoring, made any comment on those questions. Whatever had been held back or played down by the SIT, in effect, escaped the Supreme Court monitoring, irrespective of its relevance to the subject of the probe. As a consequence of this rather blinkered approach, Ramachandran missed the import of Modi putting the imprimatur of his office on the VHP's terror allegation. For the events of 27 February, the amicus curiae reacted only to an allegation framed—and rejected—by the SIT. The allegation, made by Jafri, was that on returning from Godhra, Modi had told police officers at a closed-door meeting in his Gandhinagar residence to let Hindus give vent to their anger during the VHP-organized bandh the next day. Unlike his publicly-made terror allegation in Godhra, this one—accusing Modi of prejudicing police officers the same night—was contested.

Among the officers who admitted to have participated in the meeting, the only one who corroborated Jafri's allegation was Sanjiv Bhatt, whose very presence there was, however, disputed by others, including Modi. In its May 2010 report to the Supreme Court, the SIT held that there was 'no reliable material' available to prove the allegation against Modi.

Since appraisal of evidence depended more on credibility than arithmetic, Ramachandran disagreed with the SIT's exoneration of Modi on the allegation of secret instruction to the police. In his interim report in January 2011, Ramachandran said that Modi's alleged interference with policing warranted 'further investigation' under the CrPC, going beyond the preliminary enquiry done by the SIT. This followed the further investigation that the SIT had already conducted with the Supreme Court's permission against minister Gordhan Zadafia and police officers M.K. Tandon and P.B. Gondia. The further investigation against these three had happened before Ramachandran's appointment in November 2010 and had led to the conclusion that the evidence was insufficient to prosecute any of them. Whatever the odds stacked against it, the fresh line of investigation proposed by Ramachandran opened up the possibility of the SIT probe substantiating the allegation of a high-level political conspiracy behind the post-Godhra violence. This was especially because of his forthright observation that the further investigation should 'examine the role of Shri Modi immediately after the Godhra incident to find out if there is any culpability to the extent that a message was conveyed that the state machinery would not step in to prevent the communal riots'. Moreover, one of the reasons cited by Ramachandran's interim report for the proposed probe into the meeting was the evidence of Modi's own lackadaisical response the following day to the violence against Muslims. 'There is nothing to show that the CM intervened on 28.02.2002 when the riots were taking place. The movement of Shri Modi and the instructions given by him on 28.02.2002 would have been decisive to prove that he had taken all steps for the protection of the minorities, but this evidence is not there. Neither the CM nor his personal officials have stated what he did on 28.02.2002. Neither the top police nor bureaucrats have spoken about any decisive action by the CM.'

Thus, the recommendation for further investigation into Modi's 27 February meeting was reinforced by the incisive observation that he had not taken 'any decisive action' the next day to control the post-Godhra violence. Subsequent to Ramachandran's note, the Supreme Court directed the SIT on 15 March 2011 to give its response, adding that it could 'if necessary carry out further investigation in light of the observations made in the said note'. The SIT did carry out further investigation, this time against Modi. There was a conspicuous departure though from the earlier round of further investigation. The two officers subjected to it, Tandon and Gondia, were interrogated afresh. But when it came to the further investigation against Modi, the SIT made no effort to question him on any of the issues raised by Ramachandran. In fact, Ramachandran's observations should have impelled the SIT to issue fresh summons to Modi in 2011, making up for its omissions in the interrogation conducted the previous year. In reality, the SIT balked at calling Modi afresh even as it recorded the statements of as many as forty-eight witnesses in connection with the allegations against him. For questions that Modi alone could have answered, the SIT settled for one of his aides, officer on special duty Sanjay Bhavsar. It was on the testimonies of Bhavsar and other witnesses relating to Modi that the SIT gave its further investigation report on 24 April 2011.

Unsurprisingly, the SIT reiterated that Modi could not be faulted for anything he had done or not done during the carnage. As on the previous occasion, the Supreme Court directed Ramachandran to pore over the material presented by the SIT. In fact, it went further than the last time as it asked him not just to comment on SIT findings but also to verify them. Through its order on 5 May 2011, the Supreme Court asked the amicus curiae to 'examine the report, analyse and have his own independent assessment of the statements of the witnesses recorded by the SIT and submit his comments thereon'. Significantly, it gave him the discretion 'to interact with any of the witnesses who have been examined by the SIT, including the police officers, as he may deem fit'. Even more significantly, the Supreme Court added that if Ramachandran 'forms an opinion that on the basis of the material on record, any offence is made out against any person, he shall mention the same in his report'. Since the trigger for this further investigation was his observations against Modi, the implication of the Supreme Court order was clear: that Ramachandran was mandated to specify if any criminal case was made out against Modi.

In the event, after visiting Ahmedabad and meeting witnesses there and in Delhi, Ramachandran concluded that a case was made out against Modi, invoking provisions of hate speech. In his final report submitted on 25 July 2011, he rejected the pains taken by the SIT to rule out Bhatt's presence at Modi's meeting on the eve of the post-Godhra violence. Instead, Ramachandran held that there was 'sufficient ground for proceeding' against the chief minister. There was a sound basis to his view that Bhatt's presence at the meeting and the veracity of his allegation against Modi 'can only be decided by a court of law' and that it would 'not be correct to disbelieve the version of Shri Bhatt, at this prima facie stage'. As he argued, 'If Shri Bhatt stands the test of cross-examination, then regardless of the fact that other witnesses have not supported his statement, a court of law may return a finding that Shri Bhatt indeed was present at the meeting on 27.02.2002, and that Shri Modi did make a statement as is being alleged by Shri Bhatt.' Despite the reservations about the nine-year delay in coming out with his version and his involvement in a 'strategizing' effort, Ramachandran pointed to the absence of any 'indisputable material' establishing that Bhatt could not have been present at the controversial meeting. Proceeding on the assumption that Modi's role was 'limited to allegedly making this statement' in the meeting at his house with the officers, Ramachandran said that the offences that could be made out against him 'at this prima facie stage' related to various provisions of hate speech in the Indian Penal Code. The pointed reference to the evidence 'at this prima facie stage' left open the possibility of higher charges being framed in the course of the trial.

However tenable his attempt to base the whole case on the thin sliver of Bhatt's testimony, it need not have come to this at all. Had Ramachandran not overlooked the oddities in Modi's testimony, he could have built the case on grounds that were more substantial and irrefutable. Had he made an issue of the inflammatory terror allegation aired by Modi within hours of the arson, the SIT would have found itself on the defensive, having toed the Gujarat police line in the Godhra case. That he missed this point was clearly an opportunity loss for fact-finding. Making matters worse was Ramachandran's silence in his final report on a critical issue he had himself raised in his interim report: the absence of 'any decisive action' by Modi on 28 February 2002 when Ahmedabad had been ravaged by violence against Muslims. This was the closest Ramachandran had come to questioning Modi's controversial suggestion that even as he was engaged in saving Muslims he was oblivious the whole day to the two big massacres of Ahmedabad. All that the SIT came up with in defence of Modi was a list of the meetings he had held and the decisions he had taken, although they had apparently made little difference on the ground. In fact, on the basis of details provided by Bhavsar, the SIT added that it had taken over five days for Modi to visit Gulberg Society and other riot-hit areas in Ahmedabad because he had been 'awfully busy'. Though none of this could have been passed off as 'decisive action' by him on the first day of the post-Godhra violence, Ramachandran gave in to the SIT's explanation. He said: 'As far as the SIT's conclusion with regard to the steps taken by Shri Modi to control the riots in Ahmedabad is concerned, the same may be accepted, in the absence of any evidence to the contrary.' Ramachandran's failure to notice the 'evidence to the contrary' in Modi's interrogation was a major reason why the Supreme Court's monitoring of the investigation proved to be illusory. This was despite the fact that unlike its choice of SIT members, the Supreme Court's selection of Ramachandran as amicus curiae was beyond reproach.

In an unintended consequence, his proposal of Modi being tried purely on Bhatt's testimony seemed to have prompted the Supreme Court to end the monitoring rather abruptly, on 12 September 2011. The end was so abrupt that the Supreme Court, despite authorizing him earlier to mention 'if any offence is made out against any person', gave no indication in its order that Ramachandran had actually named Modi. Without any explanation, it also departed from the precedent set in the same case of directly handing over the amicus curiae's report to the SIT. The bench, headed by Justice Jain, instead said that as far as his second and final report was concerned, 'it will be open to the SIT to obtain (a copy) from the amicus curiae'. This meant that the SIT had the option of not seeing Ramachandran's final report at all. As a corollary, there was no question of the bench telling the SIT to take his final report into account. This was a far cry from its reaction to the interim report when it had told the SIT to make a reappraisal 'in light of the observations' made by Ramachandran. In effect, his interim report, which proposed a further inquiry against Modi, had been accorded a higher status than his final report, which said that Modi be tried for hate speech.

Such procedural inconsistencies are uncharacteristic of the Supreme Court and are indicative of a stress suffered by the system. It would appear that the judges were unsure whether they could, on the basis of Ramachandran's final report, push the SIT any further on the Modi issue. The monitoring of the investigation was itself an act of judicial activism, warranted by the exceptional nature of the case. Generally, the object of the monitoring is to ensure that the investigating agency is not prevented from proceeding against influential persons. When it came to Jafri's complaint against Modi, the judges, however, let go of the matter once they received Ramachandran's final report. They were probably wary of directing the SIT to take into account Ramachandran's proposed charges against Modi, lest their judicial activism turned into judicial overreach. The investigator is anyway supposed to take the final call on whether any charge can be filed or not. The Indian law is fundamentally different in this regard from its counterparts in the UK and US, where the prosecutor rather than the investigator takes this vital decision. If the complainant is aggrieved with the investigating agency's bid to close the case, the remedy provided by the Indian law is to let her challenge it before the magistrate who has jurisdiction over the case.

Accordingly, in its judgment of 12 September 2011, the

Supreme Court directed the SIT to submit its own final report to the Ahmedabad magistrate who has jurisdiction over the Gulberg Society case. In a safeguard to the complainant, it added that if the SIT's final report turned out to be a closure report rather than a charge-sheet, then the magistrate would have to issue a notice to Jafri and give her all the material before taking a decision. In the event, Jafri's complaint was a rare instance where the Supreme Court's monitoring of the investigation did not result in any charge-sheet at all. The experiment was, however, not entirely in vain. Jafri's protest petition against the closure report drew extensively from the wealth of material that has been generated and made public on account of the Supreme Court's monitoring of the investigation.

Whatever its legal infirmities, the SIT's closure report on Jafri's complaint has had far-reaching political implications. It served as a green signal for Modi's transition to the national stage. For all his bravado, Modi has shown signs of being aware of the narrow escape he has had in terms of fact-finding. Consider the worry he betrayed in an interview to DNA on 8 February 2009 when the bench headed by Justice Arijit Pasayat was on the verge of referring Jafri's complaint to the SIT. Factoring in the possibility of his chinks being exposed, Modi said, 'If I have intentionally made a mistake, I should not be spared and must be punished . . . But if it is unintentional, then, as I have said so many times, I am also human and I can also make mistakes. But I will never do anything with mala fide intent.' This contrasted with the chutzpah Modi displayed after the SIT had pulled off the cover-up despite the Supreme Court's monitoring. Two months after the SIT's final report had been made public, Modi gave his first interview in July 2012 and, in another first, it was to an Urdu newspaper, *Nai Duniya*. 'If any government is responsible for the riots, it should be hanged in a public square.

It should be hanged so that for the next hundred years, no ruler should attempt this. And if I am responsible, I should be hanged.' It was a tacit declaration of his triumph over India's fact-finding capacity.

The BJP thought it fit to declare Modi as its prime ministerial candidate in September 2013, days after Jafri's counsel had ended their arguments against the SIT's closure report before magistrate B.J. Ganatra. The chance taken by the BJP was vindicated by Ganatra's dismissal of Jafri's protest petition, through a 440-page order delivered on 26 December 2013. Based as it was on the facts framed by the SIT, the order upholding Modi's exoneration said nothing about the questions that had remained unasked by the SIT and unanswered by the Gujarat government. So it missed out on the unexplained incongruity of Modi's claim that he was unaware of the Gulberg Society massacre for almost five hours. Rejecting Jafri's conspiracy allegation against Modi, the magistrate's order said that he 'showed alacrity in requisitioning the Army and took necessary steps to control the situation'. Thus, Modi's decision to call in the Army at the 4 pm meeting he had held minutes after the Gulberg Society massacre was passed off as an instance of his 'alacrity'. In order to arrive at the conclusion that Modi had displayed 'alacrity', the fact-finding process studiously ignored his claim to have been unaware of the Gulberg Society massacre till his 8.30 meeting. The moral of the story is clear. When the right questions are not put, there will be neither the right evidence nor the right conclusions.

6

Shifting Bodies, Shifting Facts

The subject of the formal letter written in Gujarati on an official letterhead was: 'Regarding dispatch of dead bodies.' The dispatch in question related to the bodies of fifty-four of the fifty-eight persons killed in the Godhra train tragedy.

The four bodies that got separated were those which had been identified and claimed by the relatives of the deceased in the course of that traumatic day at the Godhra railway station. Subsequently, each of those four bodies was sent by road to the districts of Anand, Dahod, Vadodara, and Panchmahal. The rest could either not be identified due to the extent of burn injuries suffered by them or remained unclaimed as the relatives of the deceased did not turn up for over 12 hours after the carnage had sent shock waves across the country.

The letter was written on the night of 27 February 2002 by the mamlatdar (revenue officer) of Godhra, executive magistrate Mahendra Nalvaya. The communication relating to the dispatch of the fifty-four dead bodies from Godhra was addressed to Jaydeep Patel, the then joint general secretary of the Gujarat unit of the VHP. It was this organization that had mobilized the kar sevaks who apparently constituted the bulk of the casualties in the arson attack. The letter was, however, not concerned with seeking the VHP's assistance in locating the families of the deceased. In a radical departure from the norm, the letter actually authorized the VHP to take over the custody of the bodies in lieu of the families of the deceased.

For this somewhat unusual and alarming deviation, the brief letter offered little explanation. In cryptic officialese, the body of the letter simply read: 'With reference to the above (subject), with sadness it is to state that on 27/2/2002 anti-social elements set fire to the coach of a railway train at Godhra and accordingly below mentioned dead bodies in all ___ trucks being dispatched herewith, which may be accepted.'

Though the blank for the number of the trucks remained unfilled in the typed portion, the letter contained a handwritten list of five trucks with their registration numbers and a breakup of the number of bodies loaded in each.

GJ 16 T 9253 — 12
GJ 17 T 7557 — 15
GJ 17 T 7327 — 12
GJ 17 5055 — 12
GJ 17 x 3225 — 3

The list was followed by the signature of the mamlatdar. The next page carried a more detailed table, again handwritten, enumerating the identity numbers of the bodies loaded in each of the five trucks. Below the second page was a one-line scrawl that said: 'Received the dead bodies as shown above.' The receipt was signed by a certain Hasmukh T. Patel on behalf of Jaydeep Patel.

The letter requesting the VHP to accept the custody of fifty-four dead bodies from the Godhra carnage was a curio, fraught with legal and political connotations. The letter was legally untenable, irrespective of the context in which it had come into existence. The law does not permit the custody of a dead body being given to anyone other than the legal heir or guardian of the deceased person. If there was any exceptional reason to depart from the norm, the letter should have disclosed it. The absence of such an explanation reinforced the suspicion that the letter was an act of appeasement. Alternatively, that the ruling party's collaboration with the VHP had gone beyond merely supporting its call for a bandh across the state the following day. The matter-of-fact tone in which the letter requested Jaydeep Patel that the dead bodies 'may be accepted' was a measure of the extent to which the BJP government had surrendered to the VHP. Worse, the administration showed such undue deference to the VHP at a time when it had already been mobilizing kar sevaks around the country to defy the Supreme Court's status quo order on Ayodhya and had just then posed a threat to the law and order situation in Gujarat with its bandh call.

The letter remained a secret until it was discovered years later in the cache of documents submitted by the police in the Godhra case. In April 2009, it became a bone of contention in the proceedings before the Justice G.T. Nanavati Commission probing the Godhra and post-Godhra violence. The timing was propitious for at least two reasons. The first was that barely a month earlier, the Supreme Court-appointed SIT had arrested the same Jaydeep Patel in connection with a post-Godhra massacre in Ahmedabad's Naroda Gaam. Besides relying on witness statements, the SIT had arraigned Patel on the basis of a CD produced before the commission in 2004 by the whistleblower police officer, Rahul Sharma. The CD contained records of the mobile calls made in Ahmedabad and Godhra at the height of the 2002 violence. Another reason why the mamlatdar's letter gained traction seven years after it had been written was the Gujarat high court's order upholding the validity of the mobile phone evidence on the basis of which the SIT had implicated Jaydeep Patel, along with Maya Kodnani, minister in the Modi government, for the Naroda killings. One of the highlights of the data contained in Rahul Sharma's CD was the evidence of the calls—in fact, repeated calls—made by Patel on 27 and 28 February to police officers, ministers, and even to the chief minister's office. The calls made on the day of the Godhra arson were indicative of the string-pulling that might have helped the VHP leader procure the written authorization for taking custody of the bodies.

The Jan Sangharsh Manch (JSM), an NGO appearing before the commission on behalf of victims, cited the mamlatdar's letter as one of the reasons for seeking to cross-examine Narendra Modi. As the commission put it, the JSM attacked 'the manner in which (the) dead bodies of the passengers were handed over to Jaydeep Patel, an unauthorized person, under the orders of the Chief Minister and were brought to Ahmedabad'. Understandably, the JSM saw the letter as testimony to the government's complicity in helping the VHP orchestrate a massive backlash against Muslims.

In a bid to pin down the government on this unusual documentary evidence, the JSM persuaded the commission to issue a notice to the mamlatdar who had written the letter. Nalvaya responded with an affidavit on 5 September 2009, confirming that the dead bodies meant to be shifted to Ahmedabad had been 'handed over to Dr Jaydeep Patel'. He gave no explanation, however, for his peculiar letter about the dead bodies, which, in the normal course, would have remained in the custody of the police till they were claimed by the next of kin. All that Nalvaya stated in his defence was that he had written the letter on the instructions of his two immediate superiors, the district magistrate and additional district magistrate of Godhra .

Nalvaya's admission that he was instrumental in handing over the bodies to Patel threw up at least three questions. One, was the decision to dispatch the bodies the same night to Ahmedabad justified in the given circumstances? Two, was Modi himself involved in taking the controversial decision? Three, should the bodies have been handed over to the VHP, that too after it had called for a bandh the following day?

These questions were relevant to determine the charge that the Modi regime had a hand in organizing reprisals against Muslims. The Nanavati Commission as well as the SIT headed by the former CBI director, R.K. Raghavan, did deal with each of the three questions. Although both refrained from drawing any adverse inference about Modi's conduct, their reasons were altogether different as they diverged on two of the three questions. The commission and the SIT were equally convinced that there was nothing amiss with the decision to send the bodies to Ahmedabad the same night as the bodies were anyway of passengers heading towards that city. The two fact-finders, however, disagreed with each other on whether Modi had been involved in the decision. They were also at odds on whether the bodies should have been entrusted to the VHP.

The differences in their appraisal of the evidence at hand revealed the sheer subjectivity of the fact-finding done by the commission and the SIT. And that subjectivity was partly thanks to the procedure adopted by each. While the commission refused to summon Modi, the SIT had the benefit of recording his statement. Since the Supreme Court was monitoring its probe, the SIT did not have the option of giving Modi a clean chit without going through the motions of interrogating him. In fact, as described in Chapter 5, the only time Modi has ever been questioned for his alleged complicity in the post-Godhra violence was when he appeared before the SIT on 27 March

2010. It was on a complaint against the Modi regime by Zakia Jafri, widow of former Congress MP Ehsan Jafri, who had been killed along with his neighbours in Ahmedabad's Gulberg Society a day after the Godhra arson.

If Jafri's complaint pushed the SIT to summon Modi in 2010, the JSM had tried to extract a similar order from the Nanavati Commission a year earlier. While rejecting the JSM's plea for summoning Modi, the commission held on 18 September 2009 that the decision to send those bodies by trucks to Ahmedabad had been taken by 'local authorities'. On the other hand, the SIT, in its final report published in May 2012, said that the decision on the bodies had been taken 'unanimously' at a meeting held by the chief minister himself. The SIT's finding was based on the testimonies given by Modi and others who attended the meeting, which had taken place in the Godhra collectorate. The SIT's attribution of the decision to no less an authority than Modi, therefore, seemed more credible than the Nanavati Commission's laboured attempt to limit the responsibility for it to Godhra's local authorities, from the district magistrate downwards.

The commission's folly lay in more than its failure to put Modi in the witness box. No less dubious was its failure to take into account any evidence to the contrary. It overlooked the statements it had recorded of two senior officers of the state— Ashok Narayan, who was the chief bureaucrat in the home department during the riots, and P.C. Pande, who was the police commissioner of Ahmedabad at that time. They made a couple of key disclosures in their separate statements recorded in Gujarati way back in August 2004: one, that they had been apprehensive about the bodies being brought to Ahmedabad and two, that they could do nothing about the decision as it had been taken at the highest political level.

This was how Narayan described the fears he had about the VHP's intentions on the eve of the post-Godhra massacres. 'I knew that VHP members had died in the Godhra incident and that the VHP had called for a bandh the next day. The combination of these two factors raised an apprehension of law and order in my mind.' Then why did he not take any preemptive action? 'The decision to shift the dead bodies to Sola Civil Hospital had been taken at a high level,' Ashok Narayan said, adding, 'I was not at the highest level in the government. This decision to bring the bodies to (Ahmedabad's) Sola Civil Hospital was taken by the Chief Minister himself.'

P.C. Pande too made no bones about the reservations he had on the same issue. 'I have no idea why the bodies were brought that night to Ahmedabad. Nor have I tried to find out the reason. I don't know who took the decision to bring the bodies to Ahmedabad. When I came to know that nearly 58 (*sic*) dead bodies were being brought to Ahmedabad or had already been brought, I feared serious repercussions because Ahmedabad was a communally sensitive city and was in fact like a tinderbox.'

That the English word 'tinderbox' figured in Pande's testimony despite being recorded in Gujarati seemed to underscore the gravity of the situation he had apprehended. The highest-ranked police officer in Ahmedabad, however, claimed to have been helpless in the face of that imminent danger. 'The decision to bring the bodies to Ahmedabad was not taken by me. That decision, I believe, was taken at a higher level, and I did not interfere with the implementation of that decision. Whoever had taken the decision, it was not in my power to come in the way of its implementation and so I did not make any attempt to stop those bodies from entering the boundaries of Ahmedabad.'

On the whole, Pande and Narayan displayed a remarkable

degree of candour when they deposed before the Nanavati Commission in August 2004. The environment then was conducive for such candour due to a confluence of judicial and political factors: the Supreme Court's forceful intervention in the Best Bakery and Bilkis Bano cases and the fall of the BJP-led government at the Centre. The same officers, however, turned rather cautious when they deposed before the SIT repeatedly from 2009 to 2012, in vastly changed circumstances. Having led his party in 2007 to its second consecutive victory in the Gujarat elections, Modi had by then become more formidable than ever before in political terms. Even otherwise, the stakes were higher when it came to the SIT, for they were more than mere witnesses before it. Narayan and Pande figured along with Modi among the sixty-three accused persons named in Jafri's complaint. The Nanavati Commission's refusal to summon Modi in September 2009 despite their damning testimonies might also have influenced Narayan and Pande to play it safe in their statements to the SIT. And as Raghavan noted in his 'comments' to the Supreme Court in 2010 on his team's enquiry report, Narayan and Pande were among the officers who had by then been 'accommodated in post-retirement jobs and are therefore obliged not to speak against the Chief Minister or state government'.

Whatever the real cause for it, the testimonies given by Narayan and Pande before the SIT bore little resemblance to their earlier testimonies before the Nanavati Commission, whether in tone or substance. In their SIT testimonies, there was no trace of any of the misgivings they had admitted to before the Nanavati Commission over the decision to bring the bodies to Ahmedabad. Pande, for instance, avoided telling the SIT that the situation in Ahmedabad was 'like a tinderbox' when Modi had decided to bring the charred bodies from Godhra. Conveniently for Pande and Narayan, the SIT spared them the embarrassment of explaining the discrepancies in their testimonies before the two fact-finders. The irony though is that one of the thirty-two allegations framed by the SIT at the beginning of its probe, on the basis of Jafri's complaint, was about Modi's decision on the dead bodies 'as testified by Shri Ashok Narayan in his cross examination before the Nanavati Commission'. But when it came to giving a finding on that allegation, the SIT recorded the evidence of Narayan as also of Pande on a clean slate. It was as if their 2004 testimonies, dissonant as they were with Modi's decision to shift the bodies right away, had been erased from records. Had it not been so shy of holding them to their 2004 testimonies, the SIT would have found it difficult to deny that, in deciding to send the bodies to Ahmedabad on the eve of the bandh, Modi had ridden roughshod over serious law and order concerns within the government. Clearly, the monitoring of the SIT probe by the Supreme Court bench headed by Justice D.K. Jain left a lot to be desired.

One fallout of this lax monitoring was the conflicting findings by the SIT and the Nanavati Commission on the mamlatdar's letter. In the process, the key issue that remained unaddressed was: how could the government hand over the bodies to any outsider, least of all to Jaydeep Patel? Having held that the decision to send the bodies to Ahmedabad was that of local authorities in Godhra, the commission had no qualms in upholding the custody given to the VHP through the mamlatdar's letter. 'The dead bodies were of passengers who were VHP members,' it said, glossing over a range of deviations, including the fact that nineteen of the fifty-four bodies could not be identified on February 28 and had been cremated by authorities after taking their photos and DNA samples.

The commission held that the JSM had made 'an unwarranted

assumption' in alleging that the dead bodies had been handed over to Jaydeep Patel 'at the instance or under the order of the Chief Minister'. In doing so, the commission, headed by a retired Supreme Court judge, overlooked the blatant illegality of the mamlatdar's letter. It was at pains to reject any suggestion that the letter might have been issued with Modi's blessings. The commission would have us believe that though Modi happened to be in Godhra, none of the major decisions, such as sending the bodies to Ahmedabad and asking the VHP to take their custody, had been taken with his knowledge or consent.

Likewise, the SIT's demands on credulity are no fewer. Even as it conceded that Modi had been involved in the decision to send the bodies to Ahmedabad, the SIT insisted that he had nothing to do with the mamlatdar's letter drafting Patel into the operation. It came to this conclusion without ever asking him about the mamlatdar's letter in the course of its interrogation. This omission was despite Modi's claim that the bodies of the Godhra victims, contrary to the import of the letter, had remained all through in the custody of government authorities. The closest the SIT came to touching upon the mamlatdar's letter was when it asked Modi in 2010 if Patel had approached him about the dead bodies.

> SIT: Did you know Shri Jaydeep Patel, the then VHP General Secretary, and whether he met you at Godhra and made a request that he should be allowed to accompany the dead bodies to Ahmedabad?

> Modi: I know Jaydeep Patel, the then VHP General Secretary. I do not remember to have met him at Godhra. After the decision was taken to transport the dead bodies to Ahmedabad, it was the duty of the district administration to chalk out the modalities of the transportation. I do not know the details, as to how and when the dead bodies reached Ahmedabad.

However, the custody of the dead bodies remained with the district administration, police officers and the hospital authorities.

It was a carefully worded answer, aimed at conveying that he was involved only with the decision and not with the mode of its implementation. While he too avoided mentioning it, he was indirectly claiming that he had nothing to do with the letter addressed to Patel. For good measure, he added that he did not even remember to have met the VHP leader that day in Godhra. His claim that the custody of the dead bodies remained with government authorities was a perfect cue for the SIT to confront Modi with the mamlatdar's letter. He would have been hard pressed to rebut the charge of collusion, had the SIT questioned him on the import of the letter and the accompanying receipt of dead bodies signed on behalf of the VHP.

Its omission to bring up the mamlatdar's letter during Modi's interrogation did not, however, exempt the SIT from dealing with that documentary evidence in its report. For one of the express allegations made in Jafri's complaint was that it was Modi who had decided to transport the bodies immediately to Ahmedabad. Having still failed to question Modi on the mamlatdar's letter, the SIT took pains to draw the sting out of that document. In its report, the SIT upheld the chief minister's contention that throughout the transit from Godhra to Ahmedabad, the custody of the bodies had actually remained with government officials. At the same time, it could not help admitting that their custody was *de jure* with Jaydeep Patel. For it said that once the bodies had been brought to Ahmedabad's Sola Civil Hospital, 'Jaydeep Patel handed over the letter to the hospital authorities and the local police as well as the hospital authorities took charge of the dead bodies.'

This was in effect an admission that the letter addressed to

Patel had served as the link document allowing the authorities in Ahmedabad to take over the bodies brought from Godhra. The SIT could not, however, face up to an obvious implication of the letter: that on the eve of the post-Godhra violence, the Modi regime had colluded with the very group that allegedly went on to unleash the mass killings of Muslims under the cover of a bandh. The letter incriminated the Modi regime even if the custody given to the VHP was taken to be purely symbolic. The message conveyed by it in any event was ominous. It legitimized VHP's game plan of playing the martyr and whipping up a communal frenzy.

Symbolic or not, the Modi regime owed an explanation on the letter. No such explanation was sought although Patel, by the SIT's own admission, had been allegedly involved in organizing Naroda killings within hours of handing over the custody of the bodies to Sola Civil Hospital. The SIT came up with its own logic for desisting from linking the dots. It insisted that no higher-up from the Modi regime, not even Godhra's district magistrate Jayanti Ravi, was responsible for the letter issued by the mamlatdar. The letter, according to the SIT, was entirely the handiwork of the mamlatdar himself. Though Nalvaya claimed that the dead bodies had been 'handed over officially' to the VHP 'as per the instructions' given by Jayanti Ravi, the SIT placed reliance on the district magistrate's defence that she had given no such instruction and that 'Jaydeep Patel was merely to accompany the dead bodies to Ahmedabad.'

As a result, the junior official became the fall guy. While accusing Nalvaya of issuing the letter on his own, the SIT overlooked the fact that there was no alternative document on record to pass off as the actual basis for the transfer of the bodies. The letter to Patel was admittedly the only document on which the Sola Civil Hospital had taken custody of the bodies from Godhra. Going by that letter, it was the police that accompanied Patel on his authorized mission to take the bodies to Ahmedabad. The SIT, however, relied on Jayanti Ravi's assertion to the contrary, in its report to the Supreme Court in May 2010. It found that Nalvaya had 'acted in an irresponsible manner' by issuing the letter to Patel 'in token of having handed over the dead bodies, which were case property'. And for the lapse that this junior officer was found to have committed on his own, Nalvaya deserved to be dealt with 'through strong departmental action against him'. Thus, the SIT relapsed into the pattern it displayed all through its reports of limiting culpability among government officials to the lowest level possible. It could not have gone any lower than Nalvaya as his signature was there on the letter in question.

The matter would have probably rested there had it not been for the safeguard adopted by the Supreme Court of asking its amicus curiae Raju Ramachandran to give his independent opinion on the SIT's preliminary report. Ramachandran laid bare the incongruity of blaming the mamlatdar in the face of a glaring contradiction overlooked by the SIT.

The contradiction was on whether Patel and Modi met in Godhra when the two had visited it separately in the wake of the train burning. In their respective testimonies, each took pains to dispel the suspicion that there was any collusion between them. Modi told the SIT, as mentioned earlier, that though he knew Patel, 'I do not remember to have met him at Godhra.' The VHP leader was more categorical in denying that he had met Modi or any of his ministers in Godhra, although he managed to get the custody of the bodies from the local administration. In fact, Patel went to the extent of claiming that he was not even aware that Modi too was in Godhra at the same time as him. 'I did not meet Narendrabhai Modi,' he said, 'though I subsequently learnt from newspaper reports that he had visited Godhra on that day.'

But the two leaders were contradicted, however unwittingly, by district magistrate Jayanti Ravi. This was thanks to a disclosure she made about the meeting held by Modi in her office, the one he said had yielded 'a unanimous decision' that the bodies be sent the same night to Ahmedabad. Even as she concurred with the chief minister's testimony that the decision had been unanimous, Jayanti Ravi threw a spanner in the works. She said that Patel had been present at that meeting held by Modi in her office in Godhra. The SIT took due note of this admission in its 12 May 2010 report: 'Smt Jayanti Ravi has stated to SIT that in the meeting held at Collectorate, one Shri Jaydeep Patel, a VHP activist, was also present.' In a separate note signed two days later, the SIT chairman, R.K. Raghavan, went a step further in accepting Patel's presence at the meeting. While cautioning that it was 'not clear who all were present or consulted', Raghavan said, 'Apart from the district magistrate, the presence at least of Gordhan Zadafia (minister of state for home) and Jaydeep Patel, VHP activist, has been confirmed.'

The conflict between the testimonies of Modi and Patel, on one hand, and Jayanti Ravi's testimony and Raghavan's 'comments', on the other, was, however, left unresolved. This was in effect pointed out by Ramachandran in his interim report on 20 January 2011. Though he avoided referring to Modi's testimony, the import of Ramachandran's observation was clear: 'The statement of Jaydeep Patel that he did not meet Shri Narendra Modi does not inspire confidence. This has to be examined as the mamlatdar would not have handed over the dead bodies to a non-government person i.e. Jaydeep Patel until and unless somebody very high told him to do so.'

Thus, the amicus curiae clearly recommended that the SIT should find out the identity of that 'somebody very high' who had directed the mamlatdar to issue the letter handing over the dead bodies to Patel. The SIT, however, did nothing of the sort. In its final report, it slipped in a bald assertion denying that Patel had met Modi in Godhra. Under the guise of 'further investigation', the SIT tweaked its narrative of Modi's meeting in the Godhra collectorate. Listing out all those who had been present at the meeting, the SIT made out that it had been attended only by ministers, officials and legislators. The clear implication was that, contrary to Jayanti Ravi's admission and Raghavan's note, Patel was not present at the meeting. Referring to the interaction Modi had with the press after that, the SIT added for good measure: 'Jaydeep Patel, VHP leader, who was at Godhra on that day, did not meet him.' Then, in a bid to reconcile Jayanti Ravi's testimony with the disclaimers of the two leaders, the SIT's final report conceded that Patel had been present in the collectorate, though not at the meeting. This is how the SIT made the subtle distinction: 'The remaining 54 dead bodies were to be sent with police escort to Sola Civil Hospital, Ahmedabad, and Shri Jaydeep Patel, who was present at the collectorate, was to accompany these dead bodies to Ahmedabad.'

Despite such reformulation of events, there was still one more conflicting testimony, which had been given to the SIT by the seniormost police officer present at the meeting: Inspector General of Police Deepak Swaroop. As chief of the Vadodara range encompassing Godhra, Swaroop revealed that after Modi had been 'heckled by the Hindu mob in the railway yard', he 'escorted the CM safely to the Collectorate, where he met Hindu leaders and (the) media apart from (holding) discussions with the administration and police officers.' Swaroop's testimony, revealing that Modi had engaged with Hindu leaders in the collectorate, strengthened the credibility of Jayanti Ravi's admission that Patel had been present at the meeting held by Modi, where the decision on the dead bodies had been taken. Jaydeep Patel was after all the most important Hindu leader present in Godhra on that day and, by the SIT's own admission, he was even present at the collectorate when it was decided that he would 'accompany' the dead bodies to Ahmedabad.

Another indication of collusion between the Modi regime and the VHP was Patel's admission recorded in the SIT's report that he had met Jayanti Ravi between 11.30 pm and midnight, just before the departure of the convoy of trucks carrying the bodies to Ahmedabad. The SIT neither contested nor explored the implications of Patel's claim of meeting her at that late hour. Yet, it would have us believe that Jayanti Ravi was somehow unaware that the letter issued to Patel by then by the mamlatdar, her subordinate, was contrary to the decision that he would only accompany the bodies rather than take custody of them.

As if all this were not hard enough to believe, the SIT came up with a dubious explanation for playing down any link between the mamlatdar's letter and the mobile phone calls exchanged by Patel on that fateful night with minister of state for home Gordhan Zadafia. The link was evident from Rahul Sharma's CD, which, according to the SIT report, showed that after Modi had departed from Godhra, Patel and Zadafia exchanged four calls between 8 pm and 9.30 pm. All that the SIT, however, inferred from those four calls was that it was 'quite possible that Shri Gordhan Zadafia, the then MoS (Home), might have instructed the police authorities to allow Shri Jaydeep Patel to accompany the dead bodies'.

Then, what was the reason for the calls exchanged by Patel around that time with Sanjay Bhavsar, officer on special duty in the chief minister's office? The SIT's final report sidestepped the evidence of Patel's interaction with Bhavsar. This was despite an evasive affidavit filed by Bhavsar before the Nanavati Commission in January 2010 in response to the allegations levelled against him by JSM. Taking refuge in the many calls the chief minister's office had received on 27 February 2002, Bhavsar's affidavit said: 'It is quite possible that Shri Jaydeep Patel, leader of VHP, might have called me on my official/cell phone on the same day or on the subsequent dates . . . However, because of the long passage of time, I am unable to recollect the exact nature of the conversation that I had with Shri Jaydeep Patel.'

Such were the loose ends left by the SIT in its final report while discounting Ramachandran's commonsensical observation that Nalvaya 'would not have handed over the dead bodies' to Patel 'until and unless somebody very high told him to do so'. Its insistence that the mamlatdar alone was culpable for the blatant illegality of his letter hung tenuously on assertions that stretched credulity or were contradicted by its own evidence. The SIT's exoneration of Modi owed much to its reluctance to link the dots and get the big picture of Gujarat as it stood on the eve of the post-Godhra carnage: his announcement of a terror conspiracy in the train arson despite the absence of any such evidence with the police, his party's support to the bandh call given for the next day by the VHP, his decision to shift the bodies the same night to Ahmedabad despite the misgivings of senior officers and the mamlatdar's letter entrusting the bodies in Godhra to the very VHP leader who was later implicated by it for a massacre during the bandh.

Luckily for Modi, the SIT viewed his decision on the dead bodies in isolation, limiting itself to checking whether they had been brought to Ahmedabad, as alleged by Jafri, in order to parade them. The SIT relied on the word of a senior police officer, R.J. Sawani, to deny that the riots had been instigated by a massive procession in which ten of the charred bodies had been taken from a locality near Naroda called Ramol to the Hatkeshwar crematorium. It had no qualms about taking Sawani's testimony at face value despite the evidence of frequent phones calls between him and Patel on 27 and 28 February. Indeed, in this charade of fact-finding, the SIT avoided putting the right questions to the right people. Consider what it could have obtained from N.K. Barot, who was police inspector of Ahmedabad's Bapunagar police station during the carnage. In an affidavit he filed before the Nanavati Commission on 1 July 2002, this was how Barot described the situation on 28 February: 'As newspapers reported that the BJP was supporting the VHP's bandh, the impact of the bandh was total ... When the dead bodies of Hindus killed in Godhra had been brought to Ahmedabad, communal passions were inflamed and the anger of Hindus burst out. A huge number of people, young and old, started pouring out like ants in the jurisdiction of the Bapunagar police station in order to collect in mobs and give vent to their anger.' This junior police officer's graphic account in 2002 of the reactions to the dead bodies tallied with the apprehensions admitted to in 2004 by commissioner Pande and additional chief secretary Narayan.

Not surprisingly, the SIT, led by Raghavan, had little use for any such incriminating evidence. In its final report, the same Pande and Narayan come out sounding as officers who had never an iota of doubt over the efficacy of Modi's decision on the bodies. Why, the final report glossed over Raghavan's own written endorsement of the SIT's 2010 finding that Patel had been present at the meeting held by Modi prior to the issuance of the mamlatdar's letter. Those who read only its 2012 report would have no clue as to how much the SIT had watered down its facts.

The wealth of evidence disregarded by it includes a tell-tale disclosure by Jaydeep Patel of the drama he witnessed in the Sola Civil Hospital after he had handed over the mamlatdar's letter to the authorities there. It is reminiscent of senior police officer Deepak Swaroop's revelation about the heckling that Modi had faced in the Godhra railway station the previous evening before he pacified those Hindu hotheads with his terror plot declaration. Emboldened perhaps by Modi's capitulation, the Hindu right displayed more belligerence the next morning in Ahmedabad, at the hospital where the bodies had been brought from Godhra. Two BJP legislators, who went on to become ministers in the Modi government, were physically attacked by Hindu hotheads. As Patel told the SIT, 'Amit Shah, the then MLA, Sarkhej, and Dr Mayaben Kodnani came to Sola Civil Hospital and the mob thrashed them between 1100 and 1130 hours for their inability to protect Hindu kar sevaks.' In her testimony to the SIT, Kodnani confirmed the attack even if she put it more mildly: she and Amit Shah had been 'surrounded by a big crowd, who were shouting hostile slogans' and that when they had became 'aggressive', the two MLAs were 'escorted' out of the hospital by the police. Such pressure from the Hindutva constituency might have prompted Kodnani to rush to Naroda shortly thereafter and instigate the mobs for which she, along with Patel, was implicated by the SIT years later. Many more bodies thus piled up, this time mostly of Muslims. Yet, while probing Jafri's allegation of a larger conspiracy behind the post-Godhra massacres, the SIT baulked at making the connections.

7

When the Investigator Himself Is Indicted

It was long before he was pulled out of retirement by the Supreme Court in 2008 and appointed as chairman of the SIT for Gujarat carnage cases. It was long before even the Godhra violence took place in 2002. It was in fact way back in 1991 when R.K. Raghavan was 'overall in charge of security' at an election meeting. As an inspector general of police in Tamil Nadu, Raghavan had barely entered the last decade of his government service when he was entrusted with the task of ensuring security at a meeting in Sriperumbudur, near Madras (now Chennai). The meeting on 21 May 1991 was due to be addressed by the former prime minister, Rajiv Gandhi, who was at the time the most threatened person in the country.

Rajiv Gandhi's convoy arrived at 10.10 pm at the venue, which was an open ground with temporary structures. Raghavan left it to one of his subordinates to receive the VIP and escort him to the dais. Some of the police officials kept vigil over the separate queues of men and women, who were waiting in the 'sterile zone' to offer Rajiv Gandhi garlands, towels or shawls. As Rajiv walked in the sterile zone towards the stage, Raghavan, in his own words, 'followed him at a distance of about ten feet to maintain an overview of the VIP and his immediate surroundings'. The immediate surroundings included a ring of police personnel providing proximate security.

Turning to the left of the red carpet laid out for him, Rajiv Gandhi went close to the general enclosure and engaged with the crowd across the barricade. Later, he moved to the right of the carpet and started receiving offerings from those who had lined up. 'After presenting their towels, the first two persons in the line-up were trying to follow the VIP,' Raghavan said. 'I pushed them away.' This was the last clear memory he had of doing his bit to protect the VIP.

For, 'immediately thereafter', Raghavan 'turned around for a few moments to order a police officer standing close by to rearrange the convoy for the return journey'. He had no explanation, however, for why he got distracted by an issue that could well have waited. The immediate situation was far from secure as Rajiv Gandhi was being mobbed, although the sterile zone was supposed to be accessible only to the few who had been cleared. However, if he still took his eyes off Rajiv to get the convoy readied for the return journey, it must have been a wee bit longer than the 'few moments' admitted by him.

Reason: the next time he saw Rajiv in that meeting, the leader was lying dead on the red carpet. Raghavan said as much in a sixteen-page affidavit filed by him on 14 August 1991 before the Justice J. S. Verma Commission probing the security lapses that had led to Rajiv Gandhi's assassination. Sriperumbudur changed the course of India's history, no less than the way Godhra did a decade later. The Grand Old Party hasn't since found another leader who could be both a vote-catcher and prime minister.

A lot happened during the crucial moments Raghavan claimed

to have turned his back to Rajiv Gandhi. Take the account given by the chief of the CBI team that had investigated Rajiv Gandhi's murder. In his 2004 book, *Triumph of Truth*, D.R. Kaarthikeyan said a Congress party member, after presenting his shawl to Rajiv Gandhi, posed for a photograph, 'all the while holding him with both hands!' Once he finished with the queue of about twenty men, Rajiv Gandhi reached the women's line. After being greeted by a few women Congress party workers, Rajiv Gandhi was detained by a teenager, Kokila, who read out a poem to him. It was then that a 'suicide bomber' blasted herself, right in front of the leader. Kaarthikeyan added, 'This was about ten minutes after Rajiv Gandhi had stepped out of his bullet-proof car.'

Thus, a good part of what happened to Rajiv Gandhi during the ten minutes he was alive at the Sriperumbudur venue was apparently missed by Raghavan, thanks to his diversion from the task at hand. As a corollary, he disclaimed any personal knowledge of how Rajiv Gandhi had come to be killed on his watch. His affidavit filled the gap in his personal knowledge with second-hand information. It pertained to a fatal slip-up that allowed the human bomb, Dhanu, an activist of the dreaded Liberation Tigers of Tamil Eelam (Eelam), to gain access to the protected person. The entire account of these crucial circumstances was put within parenthesis, attributing it to the information Raghavan had gathered from woman sub-inspector (SI) E. Anusuya, who had lost a couple of fingers in the blast.

The parenthetical message was shocking, as it suggested that Rajiv Gandhi himself was to blame for the security lapse that had led to his murder. Quoting Anusuya, Raghavan insinuated—in fact, alleged—that the security arrangement had been breached when Rajiv Gandhi had 'beckoned' to a group standing behind a police cordon on the right of the red carpet. He added that Rajiv

Gandhi, making matters worse, had not allowed Anusuya to block women of that group, including Dhanu, from reaching him.

These were Raghavan's exact words, complete with the parenthesis: '(Meanwhile, as I learnt later from Woman SI Anasuya, the VIP had beckoned to the crowd behind the rostrum that was rushing towards him and was being held back by the police cordon. The VIP signalled to the police to allow them to come near him. I also learnt that when the women in this crowd rushed towards the VIP and surrounded him, Woman SI Anasuya pushed them back. Noticing this, the VIP patted her and said "Relax".)'

While Raghavan still apparently had his back to Rajiv Gandhi, busy making arrangements for his return journey, the calamity struck. 'Within seconds, I heard a loud explosion,' he said. 'Startled at this, I quickly turned towards the rostrum and saw a flash in the air at about 7 to 8 feet from the ground. This flash lasted a few seconds. Following this, there was commotion and disorder.' So all he admitted to have seen of the assassination that took place on his watch was just the flash that followed the explosion. 'It took a few moments for me to realize that a bomb had exploded at the scene.' So it was again 'a few moments'. This time, though, it was understandable that Raghavan took some time to gather his wits and take charge of the scene of crime, where eighteen people, including Rajiv Gandhi and nine police officials, had suddenly been killed by the impact of the RDX explosion.

Notwithstanding the police fatalities, there was clearly a failure in preventing the suicide bomber, carrying hundreds of metal pellets under her dress, from accessing Rajiv Gandhi in the sterile zone. This was sought to be explained away through the 'beckoning' theory. Dhanu could apparently pull off the assassination because of the unforeseen help she had received from her target. The attempt to blame the security lapses on Rajiv Gandhi went on to become more blatant.

In his carefully-worded affidavit, Raghavan made out that the recklessness Anusuya had allegedly noticed in Rajiv Gandhi on the fateful night was part of a pattern that the deceased leader had displayed over a period. Under the sub-heading, 'VIP's changed style of campaigning,' Raghavan referred to press reports saying that 'he had switched over to minimum security and started mingling freely with crowds' after he had stepped down as prime minister in 1989. This change in Rajiv Gandhi's attitude had allowed his party members, according to Raghavan, to adopt a cavalier approach to his security needs. 'The mental framework of the VIP could have had its own impact on the organizers of Congress Party functions, encouraging them to indulge in a certain laxity with regard to basic security precautions. This was very much in evidence in Sriperumbudur.'

Having traced the security lapses to Rajiv Gandhi's 'mental framework', Raghavan dropped all pretence of the caution he had displayed in his initial reference to Anusuya's testimony. Despite his disclaimer of any personal knowledge of the manner in which Rajiv Gandhi had been killed, Raghavan had no qualms in passing off the 'beckoning' theory as an established fact in the course of the same affidavit. 'The final critical breach of the police cordon occurred when the protected person himself beckoned an uncleared group of people who were being held back by the police cordon,' Raghavan asserted. 'Had this cordon and, later, the woman SI been allowed to perform their duties of preventing the critical breach in the human cordon placed by the police between the protected person and the people milling around near the rostrum, the life of the VIP could have been saved.'

Thus, the 'beckoning' theory, which had been slipped in as a parenthetical observation, on the basis of Anusuya's disclosure, transformed into a certitude, on the basis of 'Rajiv Gandhi's changed attitude to personal security'. In turn, it served as the basis for Raghavan's exculpatory claim: that while Rajiv Gandhi and his party members contributed to security lapses, the police led by him did their best in the circumstances. 'In sum,' as his affidavit put it, 'I submit that there was no lapse on the part of the police personnel present at the Sriperumbudur public meeting venue in providing security to the VIP.'

But then, how could Raghavan have absolved himself and his subordinates of any responsibility when his 'beckoning' theory itself was premised on a security lapse committed by the police? The very reason for the formation of the police cordon on the right side of red carpet area, according to his affidavit, was the failure of the organizers to provide a barricade over there. How could the same police cordon have allowed Dhanu to enter the sterile zone? Their attempt to blame the breach on Rajiv Gandhi betrayed their own cavalier attitude in apparently yielding to his thoughtless signal. The police had no option but to admit their security lapse to that extent. But even that was attributed, conveniently, to a dead police officer. The chief of the local district police, Superintendent of Police (SP) T.K.S. Mohammed Iqbal, was the seniormost officer to have died in the blast. It was made out that Rajiv Gandhi's beckoning was followed quickly by a direction from Iqbal telling the police cordon to let Dhanu and others get into the sterile zone.

This devious attack on the deceased SP was made through an affidavit filed by the junior official who had been in charge of the police cordon, Sub-inspector K. Ulaganathan. In keeping with the beckoning theory, Ulaganathan said that when a group of women were pushing the police cordon to let them enter the sterile zone, 'the VVIP noticed and waved his hand signalling to allow them.' And then he passed the buck to Iqbal: 'The Superintendent of Police also waved his hand directing us to allow them. The party people thus joined the line of garlanders.'

Needless to add, Anusuya too filed an affidavit before the Verma Commission, in consonance with the information that Raghavan claimed to have obtained from her. In Anusuya's account, Rajiv Gandhi betrayed irresponsibility twice over— once in beckoning uncleared persons and then in restraining her from blocking Dhanu, when the killer was on the verge of reaching the target. Among Raghavan's senior subordinates, the additional superintendent of police (Addl SP), V. Ramakrishnan, echoed the beckoning theory. He was the officer who had received Rajiv Gandhi on his arrival at the venue. Curiously, Ramakrishnan did not talk of any gesticulation by Rajiv Gandhi in his first affidavit, which was filed the very day Raghavan came up with the beckoning theory in his. In the event, Ramakrishnan referred to the beckoning theory only after the commission had asked him to file an additional affidavit, responding to specific questions. One of the questions put by the commission was: 'Can you pinpoint the reasons or the failures which culminated in the assassination of Rajiv Gandhi?' It was in response to this question that Ramakrishnan fell in line in his additional affidavit in September 1991.

The cumulative claim of the affidavits filed by Raghavan and his subordinates at Sriperumbudur was unmistakable: the suicide bomber could strike because Rajiv Gandhi, besides encouraging his party members to be lax on security, had committed the suicidal mistake—or the 'final critical breach'—of directing the police to let her get close to him. Rajiv died simply because, it would seem, he hadn't let the police do their job. Raghavan and his colleagues could not have come up with a more self-serving spin, deflecting blame from security personnel to the very VIP they were meant to protect.

Whatever the truth of their claim, this twist to Rajiv Gandhi's assassination warranted not just a judicial scrutiny but a public debate. None of the affidavits touting the beckoning theory was, however, discussed in the public domain. Nor were Raghavan and his subordinates held to account for their counter allegations against Rajiv Gandhi, which were inherent to the beckoning theory. This omission was despite the mandate given to the Verma Commission to determine 'whether there were lapses or dereliction of duty on the part of any of the individuals responsible for his security'. Since he was the highest-ranking 'individual' responsible for security at Sriperumbudur, Raghavan's personal explanation for the murder should have been of utmost significance to the inquiry. The commission was, however, opaque about Raghavan's propagation of the beckoning theory, both during the inquiry and in the discussion and findings in its report. Raghavan's affidavit was buried in the mountain of affidavits and statements contained in the second volume of the report which, unlike the first volume, was not circulated in the public. Even the few who were privy to the affidavit, whether in the government or in the Congress party, avoided making an issue of it.

As a result, the story set forth by Raghavan and his subordinates, about how exactly Dhanu had gained access to Rajiv Gandhi, is being published here for the first time, that too in a book on fact-finding on the Gujarat carnage. The connection is more than the coincidence that the subject of inquiry for the security lapses in Rajiv Gandhi's assassination went on to be entrusted with fact-finding on whether Narendra Modi had committed any wrong in his handling of the Gujarat carnage. Had the fact-finding on the 1991 incident not been so opaque,

Raghavan was unlikely to have been chosen to supervise the probe into the 2002 violence. Adding to the irony was the further coincidence that Verma too had done a fact-finding report on Gujarat. In his own post-retirement avatar as chairman of the National Human Rights Commission (NHRC), Verma was the first statutory authority to have indicted the Modi regime, after touring Gujarat in the immediate aftermath of the carnage. As it turned out, Raghavan as SIT chief would contradict Verma on the Modi regime's accountability, in what was a stark example of a shoddy fact-finding on one subject paving the way for an even more shoddy fact-finding on another subject. For all his reputation as an independent judge, Verma declined to go on record when the author of this book had asked him about his opacity on the most shocking part of Raghavan's affidavit on the Sriperumbudur tragedy.

Verma had much to answer for in this regard. Consider the manner in which the Verma Commission let Raghavan off the hook, even as he was apparently indicted. Owing to the sensitivity of the subject, the commission's proceedings in 1991–92 were open only on half the days—on thirty-seven out of seventy-four days by its own admission. On the remaining thirty-seven days, the sittings were held in camera, either partially or completely. Raghavan was, of course, among the key officers to have been questioned in camera. Besides, a lot of the official documentation submitted to the commission by officers was kept confidential, for security reasons. The shroud of secrecy ensured that the press never quite wised up to the 'beckoning theory', whether in its pristine form in Raghavan's affidavit or on the basis of his cross-examination on it. During the year-long inquiry, there were enough barriers, systemic or otherwise, to prevent the press from getting the import of his defence.

Luckily for Raghavan, his bid to take refuge in the beckoning theory went unnoticed even after the commission had submitted its findings in the 291-page first volume of its report in June 1992. This was despite its repeated references to the beckoning theory. Giving cogent reasons, the commission even rejected the beckoning theory. It observed that 'the theory of beckoning is quite improbable'. In other words, Justice Verma disbelieved Raghavan's testimony on the critical issue of how exactly Dhanu had accessed Rajiv Gandhi. Raghavan got away with it because the report, strangely enough, did not ascribe the beckoning theory to him, personally. Even the extracts of his cross-examination, reproduced in the report, steered clear of this audacious aspect of his defence. The references to the beckoning theory were essentially in the context of arguments and counter arguments presented by various lawyers.

The arguments in favour of it were, of course, made by senior advocate C.S. Vaidyanathan, who represented almost all the Tamil Nadu police officers, including Raghavan. Vaidyanathan was quoted as saying that 'some women broke the police cordon behind this queue and gatecrashed on being beckoned by Rajiv Gandhi to come near; and this is how the human bomb also managed to reach near Rajiv Gandhi'. Interestingly, as a good defence counsel who would cover all flanks, Vaidyanathan added before the commission that the 'other possibility . . . is that the human bomb came in the motorcade'. Either way, the thrust of Vaidyanathan's argument was that Dhanu had made 'a last-minute entry in the proximate sensitive area'. The publication of the beckoning theory as one of the two alternative arguments made it seem all the more as a matter of legal strategy of the police force than as a defence claimed by the top officer in his affidavit.

The counter arguments too, as cited in the Verma report, made no reference to Raghavan. They were from senior advocates M.N. Krishnamani, who appeared for the local organizers of the meeting, and Kapil Sibal, who represented the Tamil Nadu unit of the Congress party. Contending that Dhanu had joined the queue of cleared persons prior to Rajiv Gandhi's arrival, Krishnamani said that 'the human bomb had sneaked into the queue and not gatecrashed'. Sibal, who is now a minister in the Manmohan Singh government, contradicted the beckoning theory by referring to photographs taken by Haribabu, a deceased member of the assassin squad. Sibal alleged that the photographs, allegedly shot for LTTE chief V. Prabhakaran's consumption, made two significant revelations: that Dhanu had been present in the sterile zone 'much before the arrival of Rajiv Gandhi' and that the police had 'ample time to check and frisk the people present in that area'.

The ten photographs found in Haribabu's camera were indeed the most irrefutable evidence of the laxity in the security arrangements at the Sriperumbudur meeting. In particular, the first and the ninth photographs, which showed Dhanu's presence in the sterile zone. The first photograph showed Dhanu and Sivarasan, the leader of the assassin squad, standing in the company of the teenager, Kokila, in the sterile zone well before Rajiv Gandhi's arrival. The ninth photograph, taken seconds before Rajiv Gandhi's murder, again showed Dhanu right next to Kokila. It undermined the beckoning theory as it showed no signs of gate-crashing either: While Anusuya stood to the leader's right with a smiling face and Rajiv held the shoulder of Kokila standing to his left, Dhanu could be seen approaching him from just behind Kokila, a direction opposite to Anusuya. Appreciating the evidentiary value of these photographs, the commission said that Dhanu's presence appeared 'normal like that of any other person near Rajiv Gandhi before the bomb blast' and that she could not have been there unless 'her entry to that place was either expressly permitted or remained unobstructed for any reason'.

Having given such a sinister interpretation to her photographs, the commission could not but have rejected the beckoning theory. To begin with, it pointed to the evidence that the lighting behind the dais was so 'inadequate' that 'unauthorized persons could without any difficulty remain in that area and then sneak in close to Rajiv Gandhi when he arrived'. Many of the people in that grey area, who were 'not checked or frisked', were unaffected by the police cordon as they were already within it, in the immediate vicinity of the dais. The report quoted Raghavan as estimating that the police cordon had been formed 'at a distance of 25 to 30 ft behind the dais to check infiltration of people who had collected near the palmyrah trees at a distance of about 60 ft behind the dais and had refused to leave'.

Raghavan's admission of the distances involved, coupled with the deficient lighting, made it hard for the commission to accept his beckoning theory. Referring to the six photographs of Rajiv Gandhi shot by Haribabu (including the last one in which Dhanu too figured), the commission said that they 'show enough people around him and close to him at all times, to exclude the possibility of Rajiv Gandhi being able to see clearly through that crowd to a distance of about 30 ft across the police cordon, if any, to be able to beckon them from there'. The conclusion was ironic as the commission used Raghavan's own testimony to demolish the beckoning theory, without, however, letting out that he was himself its proponent.

Apart from the improbability of Rajiv Gandhi being able to see the people standing beyond the police cordon, the commission pointed out the flaw in the logic of the defence presented by Vaidyanathan. It said, 'even if Rajiv Gandhi so beckoned some people at that distance, which is extremely unlikely, the police cordon was not meant to give in and to give way to those women'. Likewise, although the scenario of some people having gatecrashed was 'inconsistent with what is seen in the photographs', the police should have in that case been all the 'more vigilant' about those who had allegedly breached the cordon.

In short, the beckoning theory was exposed for what it was: a ruse to hide police lapses. Its rejection undermined the credibility of Raghavan's testimony—at any rate, the credibility of his affidavit. But then, the commission showed no inclination to go wherever the inquiry took it. The reluctance was evident from its failure to disclose an elementary detail: that the beckoning theory had come from Raghavan's affidavit and oral testimony. The commission instead passed it off as just another argument made by the counsel for police officers. Had Verma not obfuscated the origin of the beckoning theory, Raghavan's career would have probably never recovered from its dismissal. The commission could attribute this controversial claim to Vaidyanathan without any repercussions to him—a lawyer has the licence to go to any lengths to defend his client. But then, since its mandate was about determining the lapses of 'individuals responsible' for Rajiv Gandhi's security, the Verma Commission should not have shirked from uncovering the dubiousness of Raghavan's defence.

Raghavan's defence was also contradicted by the deputy inspector general of police (DIG), S.P. Mathur. Next only to Raghavan in rank among those present at the Sriperumbudur meeting, Mathur happened to be one officer from that lot who was not represented by Vaidyanathan before the commission. This was a likely reason why his testimony did not fit into the concerted effort to suggest that Dhanu had gatecrashed at the last moment, aided and abetted by Rajiv Gandhi. Yet, of all the extracts of depositions published in the report, his turned out to be the only one dealing with questions on the beckoning theory. More importantly, Mathur was shown to have actually debunked it. The report quoted Mathur as saying that he 'did not see Rajiv Gandhi beckon to any member of the public'. His testimony was out of sync with Raghavan's story even on Anusuya's attempt to block Dhanu, after she had been let into the sterile zone allegedly at Rajiv Gandhi's instance. Mathur simply said: 'I do not recall having seen any policemen or policewomen pushing back the people.'

Since it anyway withheld Raghavan's association with the beckoning theory, the commission gave no hint that Mathur had contradicted the testimony given by the senior officer. Mathur's deviation, however, might have been because of an accident of circumstances. Though he happened to be standing close to Rajiv Gandhi at the fateful moment and had even suffered injuries in the blast, Mathur had little personal stake in downplaying the police's lapses at Sriperumbudur. For unlike Raghavan and other proponents of the beckoning theory, he had not been involved in the security arrangements at the venue. He had been specially tasked by Raghavan to escort Rajiv Gandhi from the Madras airport to the Sriperumbudur meeting.

Little wonder then that Mathur was not among the three police officers indicted by the Verma Commission from the 300 police personnel present at the venue. Though Raghavan could not escape indictment, it was mainly on a technicality, since he happened to be the overall in charge of security at the meeting. All that the commission gave was a generic finding to the effect that Raghavan and the other two officers who had worked under his supervision were responsible for 'the proximate cause for the assassination'. It was their failure to adhere to 'the prescribed standard' that allowed the human bomb to gain access to Rajiv Gandhi. The shadow of the beckoning theory did not fall on Raghavan.

The abstract nature of the indictment understated the magnitude of the lapses borne out by the evidence. If Dhanu had not gatecrashed at the last moment, did it not imply that she had already joined the queue from within the sterile zone? Just the first photograph taken by Haribabu, more than an hour before Rajiv Gandhi's arrival, was enough to bear out that possibility. Particularly because it showed Dhanu standing in the sterile area in the company of three women who died in the blast: Kokila, her mother Latha Kannan and police constable P.C. Chandra.

This meant that Dhanu had remained undetected for long although she was not authorized to enter the sterile zone; although she carried a belt bomb that could have easily been spotted by a metal detector; and although she wore a salwar kameez, an unusual dress those days in a small town of Tamil Nadu. Damaging as it was, Raghavan's affidavit steered clear of Haribabu's first photograph. After all, it lent itself to a range of adverse inferences against those responsible for security at Sriperumbudur. One such inference was drawn by the commission itself when, combining the first photograph with the one taken seconds before the blast, it said that 'her entry to that place was either expressly permitted or remained unobstructed for any reason'. But then, when it came finally to indicting Raghavan, the commission did not cite any of this photographic evidence against him.

Another damning evidence, which could well have confirmed that Dhanu had been waiting for Rajiv Gandhi in the red carpet area with a mix of cleared and uncleared persons, was a video film that had been shot at the venue on the fateful night. Commissioned by the local organizers of the meeting, the video film captured a lot of the drama that preceded Rajiv Gandhi's murder. The evidentiary value of this video film was underscored by a 'secret' document placed before the commission by India's top spy organization, the Intelligence Bureau (IB).

Dated 22 May 1991, the day after the assassination, it was a letter in which the IB chief, M.K. Narayanan, gave his assessment to Prime Minister Chandra Shekhar. This high-level communication conceded that despite the barricading and police cordon, unauthorized persons had 'easy access to the sterilized zone' at the Sriperumbudur venue. More importantly, it disclosed that the IB was trying to find out when exactly 'the lady'—as he referred to Dhanu, whose identity was yet to be discovered—had joined the queue of persons cleared to greet Rajiv Gandhi with garlands or shawls. Narayanan said: 'It has not yet been possible to establish whether the lady made her way into the sterilized area once Shri Rajiv Gandhi approached or whether she had previously managed to stand in line as one of those offering salutations to Shri Rajiv Gandhi.'

In other words, long before the Verma Commission was set up, long before Raghavan conjured up the beckoning theory, Narayanan had hit the nail on the head. He had pointed out that the challenge of fact-finding was to establish whether Dhanu had joined the queue of cleared persons before or after Rajiv Gandhi's arrival. The answer to this question would in turn determine, among other things, the level of culpability on the part of Raghavan and other police officers at Sriperumbudur. Their culpability would be greater if Dhanu had been found to have been waiting in the sterile zone in the run-up to Rajiv Gandhi's arrival. This was precisely the reason why Raghavan took pains to establish that Dhanu had entered the sterile zone only after Rajiv Gandhi's arrival, and that too because of the VIP's recklessness. Ironically, even as it rejected Raghavan's defence, the Verma Commission refrained from giving a finding on the issue that had been framed so presciently by Narayanan within a day of the assassination.

Remarkably, Narayanan had displayed such insight on 22 May 1991, a whole day before Haribabu's photographs were developed by the Tamil Nadu forensic sciences department. Though her torso had been blown off by the belt bomb and her head and limbs had been scattered at a distance, Narayanan found that the salwar kameez worn by the killer was 'an unusual dress for this part', suggesting that 'she had used this mode of dress to conceal the explosives on her person'. Besides the crime scene evidence, Narayanan's letter relied on the video cassette. The visuals in it were apparently so promising that Narayanan thought it fit to bring them to the notice of the prime minister, as a possible breakthrough on the killer. The letter ended on a highly expectant note: 'Video pictures of this part of the meeting are presently being scanned to try and IDENTIFY THE LADY.'

The last three words, written in capital letters by Narayanan, conveyed clearly that Dhanu was visible in the video. The message was startling, given that the public to date never got to see any visual of Dhanu in Sriperumbudur, other than those two Haribabu's photographs in which she had figured. Yet, according to the spy chief's letter, those video pictures could reveal not only her identity but also whether she had joined the queue in the sterile zone before or after Rajiv Gandhi's arrival. This suggested that the video segment, shot around the time of Haribabu's ninth photograph, captured the last few seconds of Dhanu and Rajiv Gandhi. Thus, it had the potential of nailing or validating Raghavan's beckoning theory.

But when the video cassette was screened before the commission, this was the very segment that had gone blank. As the commission put it, 'It is indeed extraordinary that the video cassettes of May 21, 1991 appear blurred in the crucial portion soon after showing arrival of Rajiv Gandhi at the venue and presentation of a few shawls and towels to him before the bomb blast.' In another reference to the video evidence produced by the CBI, which investigated the murder case, the commission said that 'nothing could be seen a little after the scene of Rajiv Gandhi moving along the red carpet towards the dais.'

Clearly, the video tape seemed to have been compromised, considering the feedback Narayanan had given of it in the immediate aftermath of the assassination. The commission did note the difference. 'It is of some significance' that Narayanan's letter had said that the video was being scanned to try and identify the 'lady'. This showed that originally 'there were available video pictures of that part of the meeting which could reveal the identification of the suspected human bomb'.

Since no such video pictures were, however, 'made available' to it, the commission pointed out 'this unusual feature' to Kaarthikeyan, head of the CBI team. To any reasonable person, this unusual feature of video pictures being withheld by police authorities should have aroused a suspicion of a cover-up of the security lapses. The Verma Commission, however, went out of its way to dispel that logical suspicion. Passing the buck to the CBI, the commission made out that the apparent loss of those images in IB's custody might be related more to the conspiracy behind the murder than to the security lapses that had led to it. Its stated reason for referring the matter to the CBI: 'It may have greater significance for investigation of the crime even though to the commission it amounts to absence of some useful evidence alone.'

In his follow-up response, Kaarthikeyan told the commission that 'action had been taken to have these video cassettes examined by foreign scientific experts to find out whether they had been tampered (with) to obliterate any part of the video recording of significance'. The mystery, however, remained unresolved as the CBI never disclosed the outcome of the probe into the video tape. In its final sitting, Kaarthikeyan informed the commission that the findings of the foreign experts were still 'awaited'. The commission said that 'except for recording this fact', it did not propose to 'say anything further in this connection'. Thus was buried the prospect of ever finding out what exactly the videotape had shown of Dhanu in the crucial seconds before the blast and who had tampered with that vital evidence and for what reason. Having minimized the relevance of the video tampering to the inquiry into security lapses, the commission refrained from exercising even the obvious option of calling Narayanan to explain the admission he had made of Dhanu's presence in the videotape, and the outcome of IB's attempt to ascertain when exactly she had joined the queue in the red carpet area.

The enormity of the Verma Commission's failure in New Delhi to appreciate the video evidence became evident once the trial court in Madras began its proceedings in the Rajiv Gandhi assassination case. For, the CBI shed its silence in the trial court on whether Dhanu had been originally visible in the video cassette. It produced a witness who testified to having seen Dhanu in the video, however briefly, when it had been played the day after she had blown herself. Witness Selvam had been associated with the shooting of the video and had seen it when it had been played again and again on May 22, 1991 in the house of studio owner Sambaiah. According to Selvam, the video cassette showed Dhanu 'sneaking into the ladies crowd which surrounded Rajiv Gandhi and came closer to him'. He claimed, however, that the part showing Dhanu had got blurred because of 'repeated playing'.

In an intriguing twist, Selvam claimed in his deposition that it was only the following morning, on 23 May 1991, that the police seized the tape from Sambaiah. This sequence did not, however, match with Narayanan's letter, which had been written on 22 May 1991. Since the IB was already scanning the video on 22 May to identify the human bomb, it put a question mark over the claim made by Selvam, as a CBI witness, that the only copy of the cassette had been in Sambaiah's possession the whole of that day and had got blurred in that crucial part because of repeated playing.

Since the beckoning theory had been discredited by the Verma Commission, there was no echo of it during the trial against those allegedly involved in the LTTE conspiracy to kill Rajiv Gandhi. Among the witnesses deposing before the trial court, even Raghavan did not dwell on the beckoning theory. Or so it would seem from the 1,656-page judgment delivered in January 1998. Though it was not about security lapses and only about the conspiracy behind the murder, the verdict came as a repudiation, however obliquely, of the beckoning theory. None of the independent witnesses produced by the CBI vouched for either of its essential ingredients: that Rajiv Gandhi had beckoned to women outside the sterile zone and that they had breached a police cordon to access him.

On the contrary, the trial court judgment cited ample witnesses testifying to a great deal of disorder within the sterile zone, during the long wait for Rajiv Gandhi's appearance. About Dhanu in particular, some deposed to have seen her in the queue of cleared persons before Rajiv Gandhi's arrival while others said that she had sneaked into the group of cleared women after he had come. Either way, she seemed to have moved seamlessly across different parts of the sterile zone, without any of the drama conjured up by the beckoning theory. In any event, while narrating the sequence of the crime, the trial court 'clearly established' that Haribabu's first photograph of Dhanu had been taken 'between 8.30 pm and 9.00 pm' (one to one-and-a-half-hours before the blast), and that too 'on the left side of the dais' (the area where the assassination had taken place).

In May 1999, seven years after the assassination, the Supreme Court upheld these trial court findings, which showed the performance of the Tamil Nadu police in a poor light. It was, however, no setback to Raghavan, personally. For he had by then more than recovered from the indictment suffered in 1992 at the hands of the Verma Commission. In fact, in January 1999, four months before the apex court verdict in the Rajiv Gandhi case, Raghavan had been appointed as chief of the CBI, the very organization that had probed the assassination as well as the video tampering. Fortuitously, he was the first to be appointed to that coveted post under a selection system introduced by a Supreme Court verdict of Justice Verma, in the corruption-related Jain Hawala case.

What helped Raghavan get over the Sriperumbudur disaster was, however, more than just the Verma Commission's disregard for the body of evidence against him. It was also because the commission had left it to the Tamil Nadu government to delineate individual culpability. The commission's excuse for not going beyond the obvious in its indictment was the collusion among police officers. It said that Raghavan and his colleagues had put up a 'common defence denying any lapse of the police force'. As a corollary, they made 'no attempt to show the individual responsibility inter se amongst them'. Claiming that the commission was therefore 'not in a position to further determine the responsibility of individual officers of the police force', Verma said: 'This exercise has to be performed departmentally.'

Thus, in Verma's conception of his statutory powers, the police strategy of putting up a common defence was enough to thwart the inquiry. This betrayed his poor estimation of the commission of inquiry as an instrument for finding facts. Unmindful of the independence only a judge is guaranteed, Justice Verma claimed that the responsibility of individual officers could be 'better examined' in departmental action as 'they would not suffer from the constraint of being bound by a common stand of denying the responsibility of the police force as a whole'. He did not explain though how he had expected the Tamil Nadu government to muster the will to take action against its own senior police officers.

Sure enough, in the absence of a specific finding against any of the officers, nothing came of Verma's pro forma recommendation for follow-up action. Though the indicted officers, including Raghavan, had been served notices by their disciplinary authority, all of them were let off, just on the basis of their own explanations. This information, to be sure, is unavailable in the public domain. The author of this book gathered it from Vaidyanathan, who had represented Raghavan before the commission. The revelation implies that the Tamil Nadu government did not even go through the motions of a full-fledged inquiry. Thanks to the opacity of the departmental process, it is anybody's guess whether Raghavan's exoneration was based on his beckoning theory or he had taken a new line of defence for his security lapses.

One factor that was most likely to have been held in his

favour in the departmental process was the praise he had received from the Verma Commission, as a caveat to his indictment. Whatever his responsibility for security lapses, the commission recorded its 'appreciation' of Raghavan's role 'immediately after the bomb blast'. Although he was left only with Ramakrishnan among senior police officers to manage the aftermath, 'this duty he performed admirably remaining at the scene till the next day'. Raghavan was found to have helped 'preserve available evidence of the crime and this is how Haribabu's camera with the photos he had taken became available'. The commission held that Raghavan's contribution to the discovery of this vital evidence 'has to be kept in view while determining the price he has to pay for his failure in the lapse of the police force'.

On the face of it, this proposition of citing the recovery of the camera as a mitigating circumstance might seem fair. Except that Raghavan himself did not make—or dare make—any such claim about the camera in his affidavit, lest he be exposed to searching questions about the photographs recovered from it. The affidavit was couched in general terms. 'I cordoned off the scene of crime so that it was not disturbed before its examination by scientific experts. This way I was able to preserve valuable clues.' Nowhere did Raghavan's affidavit say a word about the camera. The commission in effect gave him the benefit of something he had himself never claimed, even as it glossed over his attempt to get off the hook with his beckoning theory.

Not only did the commission abandon a sense of proportion, it also overlooked the procedural violations committed by Raghavan in his handling of the camera. Besides fearing questions about Haribabu's photographs, Raghavan had a legal reason too for his reticence on the camera in his affidavit. As he admitted there, he was supposed to preserve the sanctity of all crime scene evidence till the arrival of the forensic team. By the time they arrived in the morning, Raghavan had, however, pre-empted them by directing a couple of police personnel to take the film-based camera to a local studio. But the one that they specially got opened at that unearthly hour did not have the facility to develop the colour film found in the camera. At their instance, the studio owner cut the exposed portion of the film and packed it separately. The vital film remained thereafter in the possession of a police photographer from Kanchipuram, K. Varadarajan, as he searched for a studio with the requisite facility.

Thanks to such extra-legal consequences of Raghavan's instructions, the duly empowered forensic team, led by P. Chandra Sekharan, could not find the camera at the scene of crime the morning after the assassination. In his book, *The First Human Bomb*, Chandra Sekharan said he had looked specially for the camera as he had seen it lying intact in one of the photographs published in that day's newspapers. 'Basic crime scene ethics dictates that barring the removal of an injured human being, the crime scene is left undisturbed for the forensic officers to "read" the scene in its unaltered state,' he wrote, adding, 'I could only guess that someone had filched it for a lark, without knowing the evidentiary value of its contents.'

Chandra Sekharan was left guessing because Raghavan had not done the necessary paperwork—recording of a seizure memo—before allowing that vital piece of evidence from being taken away from the scene of crime. As a result, even the crime branch, which took over the investigation on 22 May, was unaware that the film was in Varadarajan's possession. Since markets were shut in Tamil Nadu due to the assassination, Varadarajan could not find anybody to develop the colour film, the whole of 22 May and even the first half of 23 May. This was how Varadarajan finally took it to the Tamil Nadu Forensic Sciences Laboratory and Chandra Sekharan came to see

Haribabu's photographs late in the evening on 23 May. The delayed surfacing of evidence prompted him to make a sarcastic remark in his book: "Removal of the camera from the scene was a gross violation of basic crime scene ethics—and my last guess would have been that a law enforcement officer would have been responsible!"

Having examined Dhanu's severed head, Chandra Sekharan immediately recognized her in Haribabu's first photograph. In his excitement to break the news about this discovery, he shared the photograph at that late hour with *The Hindu*. This was how the investigators themselves came to see Dhanu's photograph, for the first time, when *The Hindu* published it on 24 May. 'The photograph published by *The Hindu* before we or the Crime Branch had access to the photographs, and even before the CBI registered the case, did create some consternation among the investigators,' Kaarthikeyan confessed, in his book.

Such was the abnormal outcome of a chain of events triggered by Raghavan's bid to shortcircuit the legal method of dealing with the scene of crime. Fortunately, his post-assassination lapse, unlike the ones committed earlier, did not have any disastrous consequences. Nevertheless, he needed to be asked if the abortive attempt to get the film processed in a local studio had been driven by a desperate hope to find some evidence that could divert attention from his lapses. Far from raising such questions, the Verma Commission made out that Raghavan had upheld the rule of law, for the manner in which he had dealt with Haribabu's camera. Equally ironic was the reprieve he received for the very camera that had photographs exposing his security lapses.

With the dramatic resurrection of his career in January 1999, Raghavan played the camera card again, this time to get a pat from the Supreme Court itself. The hearings before the Supreme

Court in the Rajiv Gandhi case were still on at the time of his appointment. The three members of the bench that had heard the case delivered three different judgments. Though all of them upheld the CBI's version of events at Sriperumbudur, which undermined the beckoning theory, one of the members, Justice D.P. Wadhwa, thought it fit to offer 'a word of praise' for Raghavan. It was an out-of-the-blue reference to Raghavan; in fact, the one and only reference in the three judgments delivered in the case. So Justice Wadhwa had to give a brief introduction of Raghavan before coming to the praise.

'He was on duty,' the judgment said, 'at the time the crime was committed at Sriperumbudur.' Since the person in question was the overall in-charge of security at the meeting, this observation would seem to be a prelude to holding him accountable for the assassination. In reality, Justice Wadhwa focused entirely on Raghavan's reaction to the blast, as though he had nothing to do with the security lapses leading to it. 'He immediately realized the gravity of the situation,' Justice Wadhwa wrote. 'He stayed on at the scene of crime, organized relief and ensured that material evidence was not tampered with.' And then came the apparent clincher: 'It was he who found the camera on the body of Haribabu which provided a breakthrough in the case.'

This testimonial to Raghavan, at the fag end of Wadhwa's verdict, was a measure of the clout wielded by the office of the CBI director. The praise for Raghavan seemed to have been inserted without any thought to the damning finding about his lapses in the same judgment. As it happened, Wadhwa was more categorical than any other judge in holding that Dhanu had been waiting in the queue in the red carpet area before Rajiv Gandhi's arrival. Wadhwa's finding was somewhat inaccurate too as he mixed up the first and ninth photographs of Haribabu while summing up the sequence of events. 'About 9.30 pm there was announcement that all persons who were waiting to garland and greet Rajiv Gandhi might make a queue near the carpet. Dhanu was standing between the mother (Latha Kannan) and daughter (Kokila). After some time, announcement was made that Rajiv Gandhi was coming. Thereafter Rajiv Gandhi arrived. Subha and Nalini (other members of the assassin squad) got up from the ladies enclosure and moved away. Subha was holding the hand of Nalini and was nervous. There was a loud explosion. Dhanu exploded herself.'

Be that as it may, the Supreme Court's imprimatur on his departmental exoneration made it possible for Raghavan to be trusted with his post-retirement assignment on Gujarat. Thus, in a quirk of history, Raghavan ended up playing a profound role in the fates of the central figures in both the 1984 and 2002 carnages. While Rajiv Gandhi was killed on his watch in 1991, Narendra Modi was exonerated by him in 2012, when the SIT headed by him filed a closure report on riot victim Zakia Jafri's complaint. Between the two events involving Raghavan came the resurrection of his career under the Atal Bihari Vajpayee government. All this background could well be an underlying explanation for a proclivity betrayed by Raghavan in his latest avatar. It was the tendency to cover up inconvenient truths about the Modi regime, despite the responsibility of steering an investigation entrusted to him by the highest court of the land.

8

Symptoms of Fact-fudging

'You took two armoured cars with you?'
    'Yes.'
'Those cars had machine guns?'
    'Yes.'
'And when you took them you meant to use the machine guns against the crowd, did you?'
    'If necessary. If the necessity arose, and I was attacked, or anything else like that, I presume I would have used them.'
'When you arrived there you were not able to take the armoured cars in because the passage was too narrow?'
    'Yes.'
'Supposing the passage was sufficient to allow the armoured cars to go in, would you have opened fire with the machine guns?'
    'I think, probably, yes.'
'In that case the casualties would have been very much higher?'
    'Yes.'
'And you did not open fire with the machine guns simply by the accident of the armoured cars not being able to get in?'
    'I have answered you. I have said that if they had been there the probability is that I would have opened fire with them.'

'With the machine guns straight?'

'With the machine guns.'

'I take it that your idea in taking that action was to strike terror?'

'Call it what you like. I was going to punish them. My idea from the military point of view was to make a wide impression.'

'To strike terror not only in the city of Amritsar, but throughout the Punjab?'

'Yes, throughout the Punjab. I wanted to reduce their morale; the morale of the rebels.'

'Did it occur to you that by adopting this method of "frightfulness"—excuse the term—you were really doing a great disservice to the British Raj by driving discontent deep?'

'I did not like the idea of doing it, but I also realized that it was the only means of saving life and that any reasonable man with justice in his mind would realize that I had done the right thing; it was a merciful though horrible act and they ought to be thankful to me for doing it. I thought I would be doing a jolly lot of good and they would realize that they were not to be wicked.'

There were indeed some 'reasonable' people in India—and a lot more perhaps in Britain—who thought that General Reginald Dyer had done 'a jolly lot of good' to the Raj, with the bloodbath he had ordered at Jallianwala Bagh on 13 April 1919. Just as much as equally 'reasonable' voters in Gujarat, over eighty years later, might have thought that Narendra Modi had done a jolly lot of good to independent India for the manner in which he had handled the Godhra and post-Godhra violence.

This sharp exchange on Jallianwala Bagh, which took place in Lahore on 19 November 1919, was part of a detailed and rigorous cross examination of Dyer. It was before an eight-member committee headed by Lord William Hunter, former solicitor general in Scotland. Though set up by the colonial regime with a notoriously tyrannical record, the inquiry was rigorous. So much so that it exposed Dyer, the bearer of the most embarrassing secret of the Raj, to the risk of being questioned in public, that too by Indians.

Three out of the eight members of the Hunter Committee were Indian. In the procedure adopted by the committee, all the questioning was done in turns by its eight members. Apart from the lieutenant governor of Punjab and three others, all the government functionaries, including Dyer, were grilled in public. Displaying a remarkable degree of courage and independence, the Indian members were more unsparing than their British counterparts in questioning colonial officers. The above-extracted exchange with Dyer was, in fact, a representative sample of how Indian members had risen to the challenge of fact-finding. The interrogator in this instance was Sir Chimanlal Setalvad, a lawyer from Gujarat based in Bombay.

From the British perspective, though, the line of cross examination adopted by Setalvad, to induce Dyer into making damaging admissions, was objectionable. Had the passage leading to Jallianwala Bagh not been too narrow for the armoured cars, would Dyer have taken them inside and used the machine guns mounted on them to mow down the peaceful gathering? Since he had anyway not been able to take the armoured cars inside, the general could well have declined to answer such hypothetical questions. It was foolhardy of him to have rendered his position all the more untenable by admitting to excesses that he *could* have committed, besides what he had actually committed.

On the other hand, from the Indian perspective, Setalvad acquitted himself well by building on Dyer's responses to the questions put by the two British members who had preceded him. For instance, Dyer had already admitted to Lord Hunter that although 'a good many' in the crowd might not have heard of his ban on the public meeting, he had ordered firing at Jallianwala Bagh without giving any warning. Worse, although he could have 'dispersed them perhaps even without firing', he felt it was his 'duty to go on firing until (the crowd) dispersed'.

Following up on such admissions to the two British members before him, it was but apt on Setalvad's part to probe Dyer on the two armoured cars he had been forced to leave out. In any event, not all the questions put by Setalvad were hypothetical. He helped shed light on the callousness displayed by Dyer even after the firing had left almost 400 dead and many more injured. Setalvad asked the general if he had taken any measures for the relief of the wounded. 'No, certainly not. It was not my job. But the hospitals were open and the medical officers were there. The wounded only had to apply for help.'

The exertions made by the Indian members in the process of fact-finding were by no means confined to the recording of evidence. Setalvad and his two Indian colleagues were equally assertive about the recording of conclusions. This led to irreconcilable differences. The Hunter Committee ended up giving two reports—the majority report by the five British members and the minority report by the three Indian members. Even so, both reports indicted Dyer, in no uncertain terms. While the inquiry dealt with the 1919 disturbances in Delhi, Bombay Presidency and Punjab, the difference between the two reports was only in the degree of condemnation, in so far as Jallianwala Bagh was concerned. The nuances of the condemnation by each report were acknowledged vividly in a note to London from the viceroy of India, Lord Chelmsford.

The British members' report denounced Dyer on two grounds: that he opened fire without warning and that he went on firing after the crowd had 'begun to disperse'. Though his intention to create a moral effect throughout Punjab was 'a mistaken conception of duty', the British members thought it was 'distinctly improbable that the crowd would have dispersed without being fired on'. They, however, rejected the official stand that Dyer's action had 'saved the situation in the Punjab and averted a rebellion on a scale similar to the (1857) mutiny'.

The condemnation by the Indian members was more severe as they also criticized Dyer for 'suggesting that he would have made use of machine guns if they could have been brought into action'. Further, they were appalled that even after the crowd had begun to disperse, Dyer had continued the firing 'until his ammunition was spent'. Citing Dyer's own admission, they disagreed with the opinion expressed by their British counterparts that the crowd was unlikely to have dispersed without the firing. In conclusion, the Indian members of the Hunter Committee described Dyer's conduct 'as inhuman and un-British and as having caused great disservice to British rule in India'.

Taking both reports into account, Chelmsford conceded that Dyer 'acted beyond the necessity of the case, beyond what any reasonable man could have thought to be necessary, and that he did not act with as much humanity as the case permitted'. As a result, Dyer had no option but to resign and return to England in disgrace. The punishment could have been more commensurate with the crime, had it not been for the support enjoyed by him among colonial officers in India and the right-wing opinion in Britain, which bought into his claim that the blood spilt in Jallianwala Bagh had saved the Raj. In fact, the inquiry itself could be instituted only after an indemnity law had been passed protecting Dyer and other recalcitrant officers from criminal liability. Such was the polarized environment in which the experiment of fact-finding, with members from both countries, had been conducted in the first place. Halfway through its proceedings, the Hunter Committee had also suffered the setback of being boycotted by Indian nationalists, represented by the Congress, because of the government's refusal to release Punjab leaders on bail.

Whatever its deficiencies, the Hunter Committee was a milestone in the history of fact-finding in India. Despite the differences between its British and Indian members, and despite the withdrawal of the Congress from its proceedings, the committee set benchmarks for rigour and transparency in fact-finding. The minority report, drafted by Chimanlal Setalvad, held to account even the viceroy of India, Lord Chelmsford, for imposing martial law in Punjab in the wake of Jallianwala Bagh. The native members, needless to add, faced adverse consequences for daring to embarrass the high and mighty in the colonial establishment.

Setalvad proved that he was no toady although he had been knighted by the British monarch, just a few months before the Jallianwala Bagh inquiry. He was then vice-chancellor of Bombay University. In his memoirs published in 1946, *Recollections and Reflections*, Setalvad disclosed that before the Hunter Committee had developed 'the sharp cleavage of opinion', he had accepted an offer to be a temporary judge in the Bombay high court as a prelude to being appointed as law member of the viceroy's executive council. Subsequent to the publication of the two differing reports of the Hunter Committee in 1920, Setalvad was, however, told that the verbal proposal was 'merely a casual conversation and no definite intention of offering me the law-membership had been expressed'. What did Sir Chimanlal make of it? 'I was not surprised at this change of attitude as the report of the Indian members of the Hunter Committee holding that there was no justification for the imposition of martial law and its continuance, was a serious reflection on the action of the Government of India.'

About eighty years later, his home state Gujarat seemed to have turned its back on the high standards Setalvad had set for fact-finding, in the unlikeliest of circumstances. Former Supreme Court judge G.T. Nanavati, probing the 2002 mass crimes for over a decade, could not have been more different from Setalvad in his approach to fact-finding. Adding to the pathos was the coincidence that the struggle for justice for the 2002 post-Godhra crimes has been led by Setalvad's great granddaughter, activist Teesta Setalvad.

The contrast was most evident from the fact that even as his probe dragged on for years, Nanavati never deemed it fit to issue a notice or summons to Chief Minister Narendra Modi, the central figure in the breakdown of law and order. This was despite repeated pleas by the Jan Sangharsh Manch (JSM), the main participant in the inquiry, to call Modi. His obvious reluctance to question Modi made a mockery of the whole inquiry.

This was admitted even by the Modi regime, however obliquely and inadvertently, when it specially amended the terms of reference of the Nanavati Commission in July 2004. Significantly, the amendment came two months after the BJP-led Atal Bihari Vajpayee government had been voted out at the Centre. The timing made it obvious that the amendment was in response to the political speculation that the newly installed Congress Party-led Manmohan Singh government might set up a fresh judicial inquiry into the 2002 violence. Since a parallel inquiry would be indefensible, the Centre's proposal, if any, could only have been on aspects that had not been expressly spelt out in the Nanavati Commission's mandate. In a pre-emptive move, Modi specifically brought himself and members of his regime under the purview of the Nanavati Commission. The fresh notification mandated it to probe 'the role and conduct of the then chief minister and/or any other minister(s) in his council of ministers, police officers, other individuals and organizations' in the Godhra and post-Godhra phases of violence.

In what seemed to be an even greater gesture of self-abnegation, Modi's notification also required the commission to find out whether those in power had colluded with the perpetrators of the violence (goons from the BJP, the VHP, and the Bajrang Dal). One of the new terms of references tasked the commission to look into the Modi regime's role and conduct 'in dealing with any political or nonpolitical organization which may be found to have been involved in any of the events'. This meant that if it was not found to be directly complicit in the violence, the Modi regime, depending on evidence, could still be indicted for colluding with the saffron organizations that had allegedly perpetrated the violence.

In other words, after the loss of a supportive government at the Centre in 2004, Modi offered himself to be probed on the very sort of issues that human rights defenders had been raising from the beginning. Except that it was prompted not by any change of heart but by realpolitik. The belated gesture showed that he did not suffer from the 'politically correct' illusion that a judicial inquiry was ipso facto non-partisan. Post-independence, the history of India is littered with examples of commissions of inquiry embroiled in unsavoury controversies for doing the bidding of the governments that had appointed them. Modi was therefore willing to subject himself only to a judicial inquiry that had been appointed by the Gujarat government. Having already seen its functioning for two years, Modi was evidently

counting on the unlikelihood of the Nanavati Commission
turning out to be anywhere as independent as the Hunter
Committee.

In theory, however, the Nanavati Commission should have
been more independent than the Hunter Committee. For the
Hunter Committee had been appointed purely under an
executive order, without any legal underpinning. So it was not
vested with any statutory powers. As a result, while recording
evidence, the Hunter Committee did not have the authority to
make its witnesses testify under oath. Yet, the process was taken
seriously enough to induce witnesses like Dyer to open up
before the committee. On the other hand, the Nanavati
Commission had been set up under the Commissions of Inquiry
Act 1952, which conferred on it the powers of a civil court. This
meant it could summon anybody for recording their evidence.
Passed in the early years of the Indian republic, this law was
modelled after Britain's Tribunals of Inquiry (Evidence) Act,
1921, which in turn happened to be passed shortly after the
Hunter Committee's probe.

Thus the law on fact-finding had not only been codified but
had also evolved a great deal since the days of the Hunter
Committee. This meant that even before the apparent
enlargement of its remit, there was little doubt that the Nanavati
Commission could have—and should have—called Modi to
testify before it. Its reluctance to call Modi despite the 2004
amendment shredded all pretence that the Nanavati Commission
meant to uncover the truth about the 2002 mass crimes. Its
unwillingness to let the inquiry be driven by evidence, wherever
it went, flouted the law, in letter and spirit.

Nanavati's disinclination to let Modi be questioned defeated
the object of Section 4 of the Commissions of Inquiry Act. This
is the provision laying down that the commission 'shall have the

powers of a civil court' in respect of 'summoning and enforcing the attendance of any person from any part of India and examining him on oath'. The premise for vesting the commission with such judicial powers is self-evident. Unless it was empowered to summon anybody acquainted with the facts under inquiry, the commission would not be able to fulfil its remit.

The Nanavati Commission has been equally guilty of neglecting its statutory duty to issue a notice to Modi under Section 8B of the Act. While summons can be issued under Section 4 to anybody connected with the subject matter, the duty to issue Section 8B notice applies only to those whose 'conduct' is in question or their 'reputation' is at stake. It is a safeguard complying with a principle of natural justice, the right to a fair hearing. Section 8B stipulates that the person concerned be provided 'a reasonable opportunity of being heard in the inquiry and to produce evidence in his defence'. Whether somebody was entitled to such an opportunity is, however, not a matter of discretion. The law makes it clear that the commission 'shall' give Section 8B protection 'at any stage of the inquiry' in two situations: when the commission 'considers it necessary to inquire into the conduct of any person' or when 'it is of opinion that the reputation of any person is likely to be prejudicially affected by the inquiry'.

Since Modi was chief minister as well as home minister of Gujarat during the 2002 disturbances, it was clear from the beginning that there was no way the Nanavati Commission could have avoided examining his conduct, even if it was convinced that his reputation was unlikely to be prejudicially affected by the inquiry. There was no loophole that would exempt the Nanavati Commission from issuing a Section 8B notice to Modi, sooner or later. It was duty bound to do so, simply for the reason that it had been mandated to give findings on his conduct. Its failure to discharge its statutory obligation was rendered all the more untenable by the 2004 amendment, as that notification had turned the implicit into the explicit.

Conversely, Modi could have himself, as a logical consequence of his amendment, filed an affidavit before the commission on all that he had done or not done during the riots. For in the wake of the 2004 amendment, the commission did issue a fresh public notice inviting affidavits concerning the conduct of the chief minister and others brought under the ambit of its inquiry. Modi could have responded with an affidavit, setting out his side of the story. His failure to do so did not, however, detract from the commission's onus to summon him under Section 4 while giving him the protection of Section 8B. In the event, it took neither of the steps contemplated by the law.

The deviation from the norm betrayed the commission's design to give its findings on Modi based entirely on the testimonies given by others. But then, some of the evidence that emerged during the inquiry was, on the face of it, damaging to him. Take the receipt obtained by the Godhra administration for handing over the dead bodies to the VHP, subsequent to Modi's visit. There was no way the commission could have examined this document without dealing with the allegation that the bodies had been given to the VHP with Modi's blessings. The commission still did not observe the prescribed safeguard of serving a Section 8B notice to him so that nothing was said about Modi's conduct behind his back. If Modi has not bothered about this anomaly violating his right to a fair hearing, it was a further confirmation that the widening of the commission's ambit was a cosmetic exercise. The chief minister had apparently no need for the fair-hearing safeguard.

Be that as it may, the commission gave a preview of how it would deal with allegations against Modi, without recording any evidence from him. The preview came in September 2008, in a separate report the commission submitted on the Godhra arson. The 2008 report held that there was 'absolutely no evidence' to show that Modi or any other state functionary had 'played any role in the Godhra incident'. The commission's procedural lapses were, however, of academic nature, insofar as Modi was concerned. For the 2008 report was confined to the arson that had taken place on the morning of 27 February 2002 and to the alleged conspiracy behind it. On these specific aspects, nobody had made any credible allegation against Modi. His role began essentially with his arrival at Godhra on the afternoon of 27 February. The commission still gave a finding on Modi in the 2008 report because the 2004 amendment had required the commission to probe if he had a role in the arson as well.

The danger involved in conducting the inquiry minus procedural safeguards was manifest in the case of Muslims. For the commission held that the train burning was the result of a conspiracy and that a whole lot of Muslims had been involved in it. They were all indicted without due process. None of them received Section 8B notices nor even summons to record their testimonies. The commission had no qualms in indicting Muslims on second-hand evidence. The material basis for the indictment was the testimony given before it by the Gujarat police's investigating officer, Noel Parmar, along with the 'statements and confessions of many persons' recorded by them in the criminal case then pending before a trial court. This was a far cry from the approach adopted by another fact-finding body, against the accused in the Babri Masjid demolition case. The Justice M.S. Liberhan Commission gave an elaborate hearing to ministers in the Atal Bihari Vajpayee government—L.K. Advani,

Murli Manohar Joshi and Uma Bharti—even as they were facing criminal charges from the CBI in the same context.

The Muslims indicted by the Nanavati Commission included the alleged mastermind of the conspiracy, Maulvi Umarji, and the president of the Godhra municipality, Mohammad Kalota. The credibility of their indictment, however, came under strain barely two years later. For in February 2011, the trial court dealing with the Godhra case acquitted both Umarji and Kalota, along with sixty-one others of their community. Needless to add, none of those acquittals would have taken place unless the accused persons had been given a chance during the trial to prove their innocence. Had he applied the same basic principle of fairness to his fact-finding, as required by law, Nanavati would have been spared the shame of regurgitating the police claim that the train had, for instance, been burnt on 'the directions of Maulvi Umarji'. The trial court verdict came when the Nanavati Commission had for long been putting together its report on post-Godhra incidents. Had it taken the precaution of hearing accused persons like Umarji and Kalota before making up its mind on the Godhra conspiracy, the Nanavati Commission would have probably been, like the trial court, wary of the trumped-up evidence adduced by the police.

To be sure, this was not the first time that an inquiry into a communal incident had been conducted in such a biased manner in India. A somewhat similar thing happened after the slaughter of Sikhs in Delhi in 1984. The inquiry conducted by a serving judge of the Supreme Court, Ranganath Misra, cleared top Congress party leaders, including Rajiv Gandhi, of any complicity in the carnage. Nanavati could well claim to have followed the precedent set by the the Misra Commission. For it gave its report in 1986 without issuing a summons or notice to any of the Congress leaders exonerated by it. Except that when the

Misra Commission had dispensed with due process, it was only to exonerate Congress leaders. It was precisely because the Misra report had little credibility that the Vajpayee government, responding to demands from the victim community, appointed a fresh inquiry in 2000, almost a decade after the murder of Rajiv Gandhi, the central figure in the Delhi carnage. The task of conducting the second judicial inquiry, an unprecedented development in India, was entrusted to none other than Nanavati.

Since the very purpose of the re-inquiry into the 1984 massacre was to undo the damage caused by Misra's procedural lapses, Nanavati went by the rule-book, at least on the face of it. He made sure that he issued the necessary summonses and notices to Congress stalwarts such as P.V. Narasimha Rao, Kamal Nath, H.K.L. Bhagat, Jagdish Tytler and Sajjan Kumar. It was therefore ironic that when it came to the Gujarat inquiry, the same retired judge balked at summoning or notifying Modi. This was despite the overlap of the first three years of the Gujarat inquiry with the Delhi inquiry. Yet, rather than applying to the Gujarat inquiry the standards he had adopted in the Delhi inquiry, Nanavati seemed to have taken a leaf out of Misra's unstated doctrine of arriving at predetermined findings.

Consider the cavalier manner in which the Nanavati Commission sat for three years on repeated pleas from the Jan Sangharh Manch to summon Modi. Starting in January 2006, the JSM had filed at least three applications before the commission submitted its 2008 report on Godhra. These applications drew upon a treasure trove of evidence lying with the commission ever since police officer Rahul Sharma had submitted a CD to it in October 2004 in the course of his deposition. It was on account of the extension of the inquiry earlier that year to the conduct of Modi and other high-ups that this whistleblower came forward with the CD. As related in earlier chapters, the CD contained data of the mobile phone calls that had been made in Godhra and Ahmedabad during those fateful days in 2002. Sharma had gathered the data from service providers as part of his official assignment aiding the investigations into the massacres that had taken place in Naroda Patiya and Gulberg Society. The CD came as a huge embarrassment to Modi as it lent credence to the allegation made by his detractors that those involved in the post-Godhra violence had been in touch with key police officers, bureaucrats and political leaders during the riots. Worse, it also seemed to undermine Modi's allegation that the Godhra arson was the result of a terror plot.

In its 2008 Godhra report, the Nanavati Commission could gloss over this fortuitously available phone data as the Gujarat government had questioned its evidentiary value. But the Gujarat high court subsequently upheld its validity, paving the way for the arrest of one of Modi's ministers, Mayaben Kodnani, on the basis of the CD for the massacres in the Naroda area. Citing the high court's endorsement of the CD, the JSM filed a fresh application before the Nanavati Commission in April 2009, seeking summonses for seven persons, including Modi. It cited eighteen distinct grounds for summoning Modi and subjecting him to cross examination. One of the grounds, for instance, was the terror conspiracy allegation he had made on Godhra, right on the first day. The JSM alleged that Modi had made that statement 'without any evidence whatsoever with him on that day'. As it resulted 'in deep animosity between the communities', Modi's statement, it added, raised 'serious questions about the intention of the Chief Minister to disturb the peace'.

The long pending issue of summoning Modi finally drew a response from the commission in September 2009, almost four years after the matter had first been raised. The delay did not matter though as the commission anyway rejected all the eighteen grounds cited by the JSM for questioning Modi. The reasons cited for rejecting each of those grounds confirmed the commission's anxiety to shield Modi from cross examination. Take the excuses trotted out by it for not letting Modi be questioned on the basis of his allegation of a terror conspiracy or the wisdom of making such an inflammatory statement in the circumstances.

Without citing a shred of evidence, the commission endorsed Modi's proclamation on Godhra. 'By the time the Chief Minister made the statement that it was a pre-planned act of terrorism,' the commission said, 'he had received reports from various authorities, including the collector and district magistrate of Godhra.' This bald assertion was contrary to the commission's own report on the Godhra incident. The testimonies of none of the authorities—district, police, railways—quoted extensively in his 2008 report would bear out Nanavati's claim in 2009 that they had from the beginning thought of Godhra as a pre-planned act of terrorism. There was no such suggestion even in the testimony of the collector and district magistrate of Godhra, Jayanti Ravi, who was the only one to have been named from among the 'various authorities' allegedly consulted by Modi before making his terror plot statement. In effect, the commission put its own gloss on Modi's statement, sparing him the danger of being caught out in a cross examination for overstating the Godhra crime.

All that Nanavati conceded while refusing to summon Modi was the possibility that his statement might have influenced the course of events. 'As regards the effect of the statement made,' the commission said, 'the same will be considered while appreciating the other material relating to the post Godhra incidents.' In other words, it would rather go by the testimonies given by others than put Modi in the dock, to give a finding on whether his statement on Godhra had aggravated the law and order crisis. There were clearly some questions that only Modi could have answered, in keeping with his constitutional authority and responsibility as chief minister and home minister of Gujarat.

The commission has been able to get away with its refusal to summon Modi because of the reluctance displayed by the judiciary to interfere with its discretion. There was a bit of drama though in the Supreme Court on the JSM's petition, seeking a direction that Modi be summoned before the commission. On 19 March 2012, the Supreme Court first issued notices on the petition to the commission and the Gujarat government. Four days later, it recalled the notices. After another three days, the apex court dismissed the petition saying it could not judge a report even before it had been submitted. But then, once the report on post-Godhra violence had been submitted, the tenure of the Nanavati Commission would automatically lapse and it would be too late for any corrective action.

Modi is, of course, not the first political beneficiary of such a cover-up. In fact, in India, fact-fudging is increasingly the norm, fact-finding the exception. It is time this insidious form of abuse is acknowledged as systemic subversion, committed from within the judicial fraternity. There is enough archival material on commissions of inquiry, headed by serving or retired judges, meriting a larger study on fact-fudging. Given that a commission can be legally appointed only for a 'definite matter of public importance', the costs of impunity fostered by fact-fudging are immeasurable. Fact-fudging militates against the principle of recording truth as a means of providing a sense of closure.

Besides having social repercussions, it undermines the quality of governance and democracy. Fact-fudging can be diagnosed when the commission concerned displays any of these symptoms:

- **Inordinate delay in completing the inquiry**: The Nanavati Commission gave its report on the Godhra violence after a lapse of six years. Its 2008 report indicated that it was close to submitting its report on the post-Godhra violence too. Its exact words were: 'We have now completed the scrutiny of the material in respect of the post-Godhra incidents.' When this book went to press another five years later, at the end of 2013, there was still no sign of any findings on the post-Godhra incidents. The Nanavati Commission has had a precedent in the Justice M.S. Liberhan Commission, which took seventeen years to submit its report on the Babri Masjid demolition. The delay helped the Liberhan Commission diffuse the responsibility so far and wide that its report revealed little about the conspiracy behind the demolition. Such time frames are a far cry from the speed with which the Hunter Committee submitted its report, although its mandate was to probe the 1919 disturbances spread across Delhi, Punjab and Bombay Presidency. In spite of holding hearings in far-flung cities (Delhi, Bombay, Lahore and Ahmedabad) in pre-air travel days, and in spite of questioning witnesses ranging from Dyer to Mahatma Gandhi, the Hunter Committee conducted its entire inquiry and delivered its two reports in less than five months.
- **Refusal to call key witnesses**: The highlight of the Nanavati Commission's proceedings in the last seven years has been its stonewalling of all efforts by the Jan

Sangharsh Manch to call Modi for his cross examination. The Misra Commission had similarly conducted an inquiry into the 1984 carnage without questioning Rajiv Gandhi or any other Congress leader accountable for the massacres in Delhi. In contrast, three successive chief ministers of Maharashtra—Sudhakar Naik, Sharad Pawar and Manohar Joshi—were cross examined before the Justice Srikrishna Commission, which probed the Bombay riots of 1992-93. There is such a precedent even in Gujarat. The Justice P. Jagan Mohan Reddy Commission, probing the Gujarat riots of 1969, summoned and interrogated Chief Minister Hitendrabhai Desai.

- **Bias towards the government that appointed the inquiry**: The Delhi carnage avatar of the Nanavati Commission was appointed by the Vajpayee government. So Nanavati had no hesitation in questioning and indicting rival Congress leaders for their complicity in the carnage. But in its Gujarat carnage avatar, the Nanavati Commission radically changed its approach to the issue of political complicity. Having been appointed by the Modi regime, Nanavati went out of its way to spare him the political embarrassment of being questioned for the riots. This compares poorly with the independence displayed by the Justice M.C. Chagla Commission while probing an insurance scandal in 1958. Though it had been appointed by the Nehru government, the Chagla Commission grilled and indicted its finance minister, T.T. Krishnamachari, leading to his resignation.

- **Wilful transgression of the fair-hearing clause**: In its Delhi carnage avatar, the Nanavati Commission brought new facts to light as it issued Section 8B notices to the Congress leaders named by victims and witnesses. Given its express mandate to probe the chief minister's conduct, the Nanavati Commission should have similarly issued a Section 8B notice to Narendra Modi. It issued those notices only to police officers. On the other hand, the Srikrishna Commission displayed the courage to bring Shiv Sena supremo Bal Thackeray under the Section 8B process, as a prelude to indicting him for his complicity in the Bombay riots. Caveat: The bypassing of the Section 8B process is, however, not only about shielding somebody. This is borne out by the Nanavati Commission's report on Godhra indicting Maulvi Umarji without issuing any notice to him. There is a precedent in the Liberhan Commission, which indicted nobody less than Vajpayee in the same illegal manner. In the process, Liberhan betrayed his zeal to divert attention from Advani and others directly involved in the Ayodhya campaign.

- **Incoherent reasoning for its conclusions**: The Nanavati Commission took incoherence in its reasoning to a new level. Crucial parts of its Godhra report, available since 2008 as a PDF file on the Gujarat home ministry's website, are gibberish. Large chunks of the report, running into several pages, are an orgy of typographical errors. Take the vital segment dealing with the absence of any corroboration from passengers or kar sevaks for the police's claim that Muslims had broken into Coach S-6 and set it on fire after throwing petrol from carboys. Here is a verbatim reproduction of how the Nanavati report put it: 'Ht is true that no passe~ger haq sqid that he had seen anybody antering the coach with a Carboi or so-e container filded with petrol and throwing it inside the coach. What they have said is th`t init)ally burning rags and bttles and pouches filmed with imflammable0liquid were thrjwn inside the coak` thrgugh the broken windows. Some of them had fallen on the floor and some had fallen on the seats. The burning rags would have surely started burning other things with which they had come into contact. The seats were of rexine !nd therefore the burning bags thad had vallen on the seats must have made them burn and cause rmoke. All phat(must have caused lot of confushon amongst the passengers of coach S/6 and that is pzobably the reason why there is no cleqr and complete evidence regarding how and within how much time, there$was0qo much smoke in txe coach. The cmoke had cuased breathon there or in any other part of Gujarat.' Thus the Godhra report, submitted more than six years after the institution of the inquiry, ended up obfuscating through typographical errors, perpetrated on an unheard of scale.

- **Hiding of inconvenient facts behind in-camera proceedings**: The Misra Commission, probing the 1984 carnage, earned the dubious distinction of shrouding its entire inquiry in secrecy. All the proceedings were held in camera. When it came to recording the testimonies of state functionaries, Misra came up with the perverse innovation of holding 'an in-camera inquiry within an in-camera inquiry'. Meaning, he did not then keep just the media and public out of the proceedings; he did not allow even the counsel for victims to be present, let alone being allowed to question those officials. Misra's utter disdain for transparency, at the instance of the Rajiv Gandhi regime, contrasted with the spirited resistance put up by another sitting judge of the Supreme Court, Jaganmohan Reddy, to similar pressure from another Congress government. Soon after the commencement of its inquiry into the Gujarat riots of 1969, the Reddy Commission received a letter from the Hitendrabhai Desai regime asking it to hold its sittings in private. The government claimed that its request was binding on the commission under a statutory rule. The Reddy Commission, however, put its foot down saying that private sittings would 'greatly detract from the value and confidence in the inquiry'. It went on to hold all its proceedings in public.

The saving grace with the Nanavati Commission has been that it too conducted almost all its proceedings in public. But it displayed other symptoms of engaging in fact-fudging. Take Nanavati's response when retired police officer R.B. Sreekumar sent him an affidavit in September 2011 alleging that Modi had funded a secret operation to sabotage a public interest litigation (PIL) pending in the Supreme Court. This allegation had first been made by another police officer, Sanjiv Bhatt, in an affidavit before the Supreme Court in April 2011. Just a day after Sreekumar had taken charge of the state intelligence branch during the riots on 9 April 2002, Bhatt, his subordinate in the department, allegedly took him to Modi for an urgent but undisclosed purpose. It was then that Modi allegedly told Sreekumar to give Bhatt Rs 10 lakh from the secret service fund (SSF) to 'bandobast' (manage) the PIL filed by danseuse and activist Mallika Sarabhai, seeking the Supreme Court's intervention in the riots case. Bhatt's revelation of this secret transaction after nine years prompted Sarabhai to approach the Nanavati Commission for corroboration from Sreekumar. Accordingly, in August 2011, the commission wrote to Sreekumar saying that if he had anything to say on Bhatt's allegation about Sarabhai's PIL, he 'may' file an affidavit before it. When he had responded with the affidavit on 15 September 2011, Sreekumar found himself in the witness box within a fortnight before an evidently disturbed commission. Though it was the eighth affidavit he had filed before the commission, this was the first time he had been summoned since his oral deposition seven years earlier on the first affidavit.

The special hearing on 30 September 2011 was, however, not due to any concern on the part of the commission to question Sreekumar about Modi's alleged subversion of the judicial process. Instead, as the commission's records show, it 'sought certain clarifications' from Sreekumar, in a bid to make him change one innocuous word in his affidavit and its covering letter. Nanavati made no bones about his worry that on this matter damaging to Modi, Sreekumar had put on record that he had been 'directed' by the commission to respond. Nanavati was exercised over the word 'directed' as Sreekumar, to his mind, had merely been given him an option to respond by saying that he 'may' file an affidavit. Clearly, Nanavati was anxious to set the record straight lest Modi got the impression that the commission had been overly interested in finding out whether he had interfered with the Supreme Court's functioning. At the same time, Nanavati was hobbled by the need to carry out the correction discreetly, in keeping with the dignity of his office. So, in a departure from its own norm, the commission held the hearing in camera. This book pierces the veil of secrecy, for the first time. The manner in which the commission recorded its exchange with Sreekumar, gave away the underlying purpose of fact-fudging.

> Q. In your letter forwarding your affidavit you have stated 'as directed by the Commission in its letter No . . ., I hereby submit my eighth affidavit' and we put it to you that the commission has not directed to you by the said letter to file affidavit. (He is shown letter dated 3.8.2011.)

> A. I construed the word 'may' used in that letter as a direction and therefore, I have stated so in my letter dated 15.9.2011.

Q. The Commission makes it clear to you that there is no direction from the Commission to you to file any affidavit in connection with the issue raised by Ms Mallika Sarabhai and Shri Sanjiv Bhatt. Therefore, will you like to delete the words 'as directed' from your letter dated 15.9.2011 and the words to that effect in paragraph 3 of your affidavit?

A. I do not want to delete those words either from my letter or from my affidavit.

Q. We again put it to you that it would be incorrect to say that you were directed by the Commission to file an affidavit in view of the clear language used by the Commission in its letter dated 3.8.2011?

A. As I understood that the Commission wanted to know the data and inputs regarding Ms Mallika Sarabhai's PIL, I took it as an instruction to be complied with by me. In my view, the relevant matter in my eighth affidavit has direct connection with the terms of reference made by the Government of Gujarat to the Hon'ble Commission.

Much to the commission's disappointment, Sreekumar did not yield to its repeated pleas to read 'may' as an option rather than a 'direction'. How did things come to such a pass that a former Supreme Court judge was reduced to making such requests to a witness while conducting a commission of inquiry? What facts could Nanavati be trusted to find when he seemed so anxious to be on the right side of Modi, the main subject of his inquiry? Indeed, with no sign yet of his report on the post-Godhra violence, one could well ask whether Nanavati was engaged in any fact-finding at all, as it had been dragging on for over a decade for no publicly acknowledged reason? To put things in perspective, one could also recall Modi's reference to the commission in a letter he had written to President Kalam in

August 2003, protesting against the NHRC's attempt to revive
the Best Bakery case. 'We would like to inform that a judicial
commission headed by a retired judge of the Supreme Court
has been appointed to inquire into all aspects of the communal
riots. Efforts are unfortunately being made to cast aspersions on
the commission and its work through propaganda,' Modi wrote,
adding, 'It is unfortunate that these vested interests cannot even
await the report of the judicial commission.' Ten years later,
those who were branded by Modi as 'vested interests' are still
awaiting the report of the judicial commission. On 31 December
2013, the commission received its twenty-first extension to
accomplish its task.

9

Pushing the Limits of Impunity

Trilokpuri is barely 10 kilometres from the headquarters of the Delhi police. It was about 10 am on 1 November 1984, the morning after Prime Minister Indira Gandhi had been shot dead by her own bodyguards. A huge mob, armed with iron rods, wooden sticks and kerosene tins, descended on Block 32 of Trilokpuri. Block 32 was a Sikh pocket in a crowded, rundown neighbourhood. Led by local Congress leaders Rampal Saroj and Dr Ashok Gupta, the mob targeted this block as the two bodyguards who had killed Indira Gandhi happened to be Sikhs.

In a bid to thwart the mob, Sikh residents took refuge in their gurdwara. Collectively, they kept the mob at bay, using kirpans and other small arms. When the police arrived, there was, however, no visible attempt to rescue the Sikhs. Rather than dispersing the mob, the local station house officer, Soor Veer Singh Tyagi, ordered the Sikhs to return to their homes, saying that it was his responsibility to protect them.

Fearing that they would be easy prey in their homes, the Sikhs were reluctant to leave the gurdwara. Tyagi turned aggressive and fired in the air. Frightened and confused, the Sikhs obeyed his order. Sure enough, the worst of their fears came true. They had scarcely left the gurdwara when the mob pounced on them, on the street, in their houses, everywhere. As if on cue, the police withdrew from the scene, giving the rioters a free hand to commit any crime. So much free hand that the rioters in no time barricaded all roads leading to the block so that they could carry out their rampage, unimpeded, over the next day or two.

Thus took place the biggest massacre recorded in a single locality anywhere in India, since the partition of the country. Out of the official death toll of 2,733 in the 1984 Delhi carnage, about 400 Sikhs were estimated to have been killed in and around Block 32. To put it in perspective, this was a little more than the official death toll of the 1919 Jallianwala Bagh massacre, which was 379. This was also close to the death toll in Ahmedabad during the 2002 riots, which was pegged at 442. Yes, in 1984 a single block in an east Delhi colony saw almost as many killings as the whole of Ahmedabad did in 2002.

An administrative inquiry into police delinquencies in Delhi, conducted by retired bureaucrat Kusum Lata Mittal from 1987 to 1990, indicted Tyagi and his superiors, deputy commissioner of police (DCP) Sewa Dass and additional commissioner of police (Adl CP) H.C. Jatav. The indictment was for the Trilokpuri and other massacres that took place in their respective jurisdictions during the 1984 carnage. A close scrutiny of the police records together with the affidavits of victims gave a fuller picture of the causes underlying the bloodbath. It could be traced to small meetings of Congress workers held in the vicinity early in the morning by the then MP from east Delhi, H.K.L. Bhagat. The massacre followed, with the collusion of the police. A fresh judicial inquiry into the 1984 carnage, conducted by former Supreme Court judge G.T. Nanavati from 2000 to 2005, confirmed the factors at play beyond the official narrative of public anger.

If political incitement had emboldened rioters, police complicity came as a death blow to the targeted community. Without police complicity, the bloodshed in Block 32 could not have been on such a large scale, that too right in the capital of the country. In effect, the Mittal and Nanavati reports demolished the excuse that the police had been taken by surprise or had been overwhelmed. For the Delhi police made no pretence of taking on the miscreants in Trilokpuri. The law enforcers served as accessories to the crime when they drove Sikhs out of the gurdwara. Having paved the way for the massacre, they made themselves scarce. Far from calling for reinforcements, the police connived with the Congress leaders to keep the mass crime under wraps for almost 36 hours. It was left to three journalists from *The Indian Express* group to blow the cover on Block 32, against all odds, on the evening of 2 November 1984.

The official findings on police complicity in the Block 32 massacre, however, had one unintended consequence. They nailed Rajiv Gandhi's infamous tree metaphor, which he had employed in a bid to blame the carnage on 'krodh' (intense anger) among the people. Contrary to his claim, the earth did not shake in Block 32 merely because a mighty tree had fallen. The reverberations in Trilokpuri—as elsewhere in Delhi— were unlikely to have been so devastating had the police not aided and abetted the Congress party goons.

Trilokpuri's counterpart in the Gujarat riots was Ahmedabad's Naroda Patiya. With an official death toll of ninety-six, Naroda Patiya saw the single largest massacre in 2002. While Trilokpuri is about 10 kilometres from the Delhi police commissioner's office, Naroda Patiya is less than 5 kilometres from the office of Ahmedabad's police commissioner. Bhagat's counterpart here was the local BJP legislator, Maya Kodnani, who went on to become a minister in the Modi government. Kodnani's involvement in the Naroda Patiya massacre was more visible than Bhagat's was in Trilokpuri. This was because Kodnani, unlike Bhagat, visited the scene of offence, when a huge mob had collected in front of a mosque called Nurani Masjid. Besides egging them on, she was even seen to have been distributing swords to rioters. The destruction of Nurani Masjid, subsequent to Kodnani's visit, marked the beginning of the mayhem.

Another parallel was the post facto rationalizations offered by Modi and Rajiv Gandhi. For much in the spirit of Rajiv Gandhi's tree metaphor, Modi came up with his own Newtonian twist. He tried to pass off the post-Godhra killings as a 'chain of action and reaction'. But, like with Trilokpuri, there was ample evidence in Naroda Patiya showing that there was more to the violence than the anger in the majority community (the stated reason) or, for that matter, even the incitement by leaders (the unstated reason).

The mass killings following the Godhra incident were as much facilitated by the police, in various ways. One of the more sinister ways that this happened in Naroda Patiya related to a premises serving, like in Trilokpuri, as a refuge from murderous mobs. This one though was not a place of worship; rather, it was a secure base of the police themselves. Naroda Patiya was, in fact, an unlikely location for a massacre as it was in the immediate vicinity of a 20-acre campus of State Reserve Police (SRP). The massacre was facilitated by the fact that a lot of Muslims fleeing from mobs had been denied refuge in the sprawling SRP premises.

In official records, the first inkling of this incident came in a 31 March 2002 report of the National Human Rights Commission (NHRC). The report emerged from a survey of riot-affected areas by an NHRC team led by its chairman,

Justice J.S. Verma. On the basis of its interaction with victims at the Shah-e-Alam relief camp in Ahmedabad, the NHRC reconstructed the 'atrocities' committed on 28 February 2002 at Naroda Patiya and Naroda village, which, it said, 'had borne the brunt of communal riots in Ahmedabad'. When the violence began in the morning with the mob attack on Nurani Masjid, panic-stricken Muslims rushed to the SRP quarters. But as the NHRC report said, 'When the terrorized residents went to the nearby SRP camp for shelter, they were pushed back by the jawans.'

Pushed back, when they needed to be rescued? This revelation was, however, lost in a torrent of such instances of hostility to Muslims displayed by the Gujarat police in Naroda Patiya and elsewhere during the 2002 riots. It took seven years for the special significance of the SRP episode to come on record. The trigger was an order passed by the Supreme Court on 27 April 2009 referring Zakia Jafri's complaint against the Modi regime to the SIT appointed by it. About two months later, on 11 July 2009, the SIT began recording the statement of R.B. Sreekumar, who was the chief of SRP in the whole state when the post-Godhra violence had erupted. Among his many disclosures was his inside account of how Naroda Patiya victims had been refused shelter on the fateful day in what was the headquarters of SRP's Group II.

It turned out though that not all the victims had been shooed away. About 500 Muslims who had come in the morning were allowed to enter the SRP compound. Sreekumar vouched for this humanitarian gesture because the commandant of SRP's Group II had taken his clearance for it. But then, despite Sreekumar's clearance, the many more who had rushed to the SRP gate later in the day were refused entry, some of them with fatal consequences. Though several police officials gave in to

'Hindutva' pressure across Gujarat, the conduct of the SRP commandant and his deputy in Naroda Patiya was particularly revealing. For as Sreekumar pointed out, the commandant and his deputy were themselves Muslims. This fact, for all its irony, has not been brought out so far in the public domain.

The SIT report glossed over the perfidy at the SRP gate although it warranted a close scrutiny from the viewpoint of governance. The commandant, Khurshid Ahmed, was an IPS officer of the rank of superintendent of police. Given his seniority, Ahmed ought to have resisted extraneous pressures, from within the police or otherwise. Though the SRP (unlike the local police) cannot normally intervene in a law and order situation without a specific authorization, nobody could have cavilled about a rescue act at its own gate in the exceptional circumstances of 28 February 2002. Khurshid should have had no hesitation in responding to the entreaties of victims in distress, without seeking anybody's go-ahead. Having anyway taken the precaution of checking with his superior officer and letting in those who had come in the morning, Ahmed was, as suggested by Sreekumar, even less justified in denying shelter to the victims who had arrived later at the gate.

Recalling the events of February 28, 2002, Sreekumar said that when he was in his office in Gandhinagar, he had received a call in the morning from Ahmed informing him about the 500 Muslims at the gate of the battalion headquarters seeking protection. Excerpts of his testimony to SIT:

> I telephonically instructed Ahmed to open the gates immediately and rehabilitate the refugees in the barracks which were vacant as the force had gone out for bandobast. This was followed by a fax message sent to the commandant.
> However, both Khurshid Ahmed and his deputy SP Qureshi were quite shaky and worried about accommodating

Muslim refugees. I told them that their role (would) not be questioned in this regard as they were complying with my instructions . . .

Later I came to know that in the evening, a huge group of riot-affected people had sought refuge in SRP campus but the same was refused by the commandant. However, this matter was never reported to me by the commandant. Subsequently, I learnt that some of the Muslims who (had) sought shelter in SRP campus were killed in Naroda Patiya by rioters.

The allegation made by Sreekumar against his subordinates in Naroda Patiya was, by any standards, too serious a matter to be left at that. Especially in the given context of the investigation into Jafri's complaint alleging that the post-Godhra violence was the result of a high-level conspiracy. Sreekumar's testimony at the least called for summoning of records related to the SRP camp and questioning of Ahmed and Qureshi for their versions of the episode. The obvious line of interrogation would have been to pin them down on why they had, despite the abundance of space in the SRP compound, changed their policy of providing shelter to victims from Naroda Patiya. What was the compulsion to abandon victims to their fate? When he could have done it so easily, who stopped Ahmed from saving Muslims from mob violence? If need be, the SIT could even have questioned Sreekumar further on his disclosure about the conduct of his subordinate officer.

The Supreme Court-appointed SIT, headed by former CBI director R.K. Raghavan, did not raise any of these questions, although they were deeply relevant to determining whether the Modi regime had complied with the requirements of secularism and the rule of law. The cop-out was evident from the SIT's 541-page report on Jafri's complaint submitted to an Ahmedabad magistrate in February 2012. The SIT made no secret of the pains it had taken to run down the credibility of whistleblowers who had testified against the Modi regime. But when it came to Sreekumar's testimony, the report focused on his stint as intelligence chief which began about 40 days after the Naroda Patiya massacre. Conveniently for Modi, the tell-tale behaviour of the officer in charge of the SRP campus near Naroda Patiya, a disclosure relating to Sreekumar's earlier avatar as SRP chief, fell through the cracks of the SIT probe.

The enormity of the SIT's failure to probe the SRP episode and its ramifications manifested six months later. It was thanks to a trial court judgment, delivered in August 2012, on the Naroda Patiya massacre. The much-awaited verdict proved to be historic as the thirty-two persons convicted by it included Kodnani, making it the first instance in India of a minister being punished in a communal violence case. What went relatively unnoticed was the repeated reference in the 1,969-page judgment to the SRP episode. Trial judge Jyotsna Yagnik, in effect, confirmed the grievance of victims that they had been turned away at the SRP gate. She even made clear that, barring the lucky few who had made it in the morning, many of the victims turned away at the SRP gate had been pushed into the arms of the mobs.

The judgment contained accounts of victims who had been provided shelter in the morning as also those who had been attacked and driven away by SRP personnel from the gate later in the day. It summarized those accounts as follows: 'In the SRP Quarters, the Muslims were not allowed to get in or enter inside. Hence, many were beaten while attempting to enter the SRP Quarters. However, some of the Muslims could secure their shelter at SRP which might be in the morning itself and thereafter it was prohibited.'

The judicial acknowledgement of the SRP episode indicated that its suppression in the SIT report on the Jafri complaint was quite wilful. After all, in the Jafri case, the SIT recorded Sreekumar's disclosure in 2009 and submitted its report in 2012. In the Naroda Patiya trial that took place during the intervening period, the same SIT happened to be in charge of the investigation and prosecution. Thus, the SIT was very much aware that Sreekumar's testimony in Jafri's case had been corroborated by victims in the Naroda Patiya case.

Of course, the victims who testified on the SRP episode were unaware of Ahmed's distress call to Sreekumar. Their depositions were solely on what they had themselves suffered or seen on the spot. In the process, going beyond Sreekumar's testimony in the Jafri case, the Naroda Patiya trial yielded the names of two of the SRP officials who had been directly involved in shooing away victims at the gate. While the SIT balked at dealing with the SRP episode, victims sought to implead the two identified officials as accused persons. Their charge was that the officials, K.P. Parikh and somebody referred to simply as Dataniya, had been hostile to victims rather than to miscreants. As a corollary, victims alleged that Parikh and Dataniya were part of the conspiracy hatched to kill Muslims in Naroda Patiya.

While rejecting the impleadment application, the trial court ruled that Parikh and Dataniya, the SRP officials guarding their headquarters, could not have been part of the conspiracy involving Kodnani and thirty-one others. For all the courage displayed by her in convicting the former minister, judge Jyotsna Yagnik ended up taking a rather legalistic view of the refusal to shelter victims. Her rationale was that the SRP officials were, after all, not duty-bound to throw open their premises to riot victims. On the contrary, they had been entrusted with the 'lawful duty of securing the premises of SRP Quarters'.

Placing the sanctity of the place above the safety of human lives, Yagnik reasoned that 'not allowing the outsider in the SRP premises, where they were posted for the purpose, was performance of their duty and it does not seem to be due to any bias against the witness or any victim'. As a corollary, she concluded, 'It seems that they were performing their own duty, may be with more enthusiasm and with less sensitivity but for this, it cannot be termed to be part of conspiracy.' Much as it was well-argued, Yagnik's exoneration of Parikh and Dataniya overlooked the material fact that there was an unexplained change in the SRP unit's policy on accommodating victims in their spacious premises. Having acknowledged that some of the victims had been provided shelter on the SRP campus the same morning, Yagnik should not have regarded the conduct of Parikh and Dataniya in isolation, as though they were acting of their own accord. Going by the evidence on record, she should have considered the possibility that they had at some point begun to shoo away the victims on the verbal orders of their superior officers. Whether any of the SRP officials had been involved in the conspiracy or not, the apparent change in their conception of duty did help the conspirators carry out the massacre. Yagnik's failure to think through the causality of the SRP episode resulted in impunity for police complicity.

The impunity factor was even more glaring in the case of K.K. Mysorewala, inspector from the Naroda police station directly accountable for the mass killings in its jurisdiction. The very verdict that set a benchmark for political accountability, by convicting a former minister in a case of communal violence, proved woefully inadequate when it came to police accountability. Yagnik rejected the plea of victims that Mysorewala be tried on the charge of colluding with mobs. The impunity granted to Mysorewala was more curious because none of the mitigating circumstances in the case of the SRP officials applied to him. Since Naroda Patiya fell in the jurisdiction of his police station, it was very much his duty to save Muslims from mob violence. And for his failure to discharge this statutory duty, Yagnik faulted Mysorewala on more than 40 counts. The findings listed out against Mysorewala bring out the various ways in which he had allowed the massacre to take place on his watch or engaged in a cover-up as the first investigating officer.

Significantly, one of the issues on which Mysorewala was faulted by the court was his claim that the police had fired extensively during the riots. The rejection of this claim in the context of the single largest massacre of 2002 was a blow to the Modi regime as well. For Mysorewala's exaggerated claim about the extent of police firing was actually an echo of the Modi regime's familiar response to the charge of Modi's involvement in the massacres of Muslims, including the one in Naroda Patiya. The Modi camp would reel off statistics showing that several Hindus had been killed in police firing during the riots across Gujarat. Indeed, the suggestion was that Modi had a moral edge over Rajiv Gandhi as there were hardly any instances of police firing at the mobs in the 1984 carnage.

In his statement before the SIT on Jafri's complaint, P.C. Pande, who was the commissioner of Ahmedabad during the carnage, said that in all seventeen persons had been killed in the city in police firing on 28 February 2002, the worst day of post-Godhra violence . The two big massacres that took place in Ahmedabad on that day were at Naroda Patiya and Gulberg Society. While the Gulberg Society trial has been held up as it got linked to the outcome of Jafri's complaint, the Naroda Patiya verdict in 2012 gave the first judicial take on police firing claims. So, from the seventeen claimed to have been killed in police firing in Ahmedabad, how many of them were from Naroda Patiya? Since the violence on 28 February 2002 was all about Hindus attacking Muslims the day after Godhra, what was the community-wise breakup of the casualties in police firing? Yagnik's judgment established that, contrary to the much-bandied official line, the police intervention was neither forceful nor impartial.

Under the rigour of judicial scrutiny, the police could not give any definitive figure on how many had died due to their firing in Naroda Patiya. To begin with, Mysorewala and his superior officers, assistant commissioner M.T. Rana and deputy commissioner P.B. Gondia, claimed that two persons had died in police firing—one a Hindu, another a Muslim. But then, as the court pointed out, Gondia also spoke of 'only one death in police firing', and that was of a Muslim. The police evidently gave no explanation for why one of the two who had died—or, alternatively, the only one who had died—in police firing was a Muslim. As far as the number itself was concerned, the trial court had only the police's word to go by. For the police did not bother to collect any forensic evidence to back their claims on how many had died or been injured on account of their firing in Naroda Patiya. They failed to get forensic analysis done on any of the bullets recovered from the bodies of injured or dead persons. They did not pick up any cartridges, either, from the streets as proof of police firing.

The absence of ballistic reports gave them scope to make another dodgy claim: that there was 'no private firing'. In other words, the police claimed that mobs had not used firearms at all. Had they not denied private firing, the police would have been hard pressed to explain why they had not struck at the mobs with proportionate force. This anomaly could have turned the tables on the police as there was admittedly either a solitary or no Hindu casualty at all while 'many' Muslims had been proved, through oral testimonies, to have died or been injured in firing. But then, having denied private firing, the police were hoist with their own petard: if all the firing in Naroda Patiya was indeed by the police, why did the bullets hit Muslims (victims) rather than Hindus (miscreants)?

As the trial court judgment put it, 'PW-274 (Mysorewala) clarifies that no private firing was done. But then (the) million dollar question is, if only one death of Muslim was caused on account of police firing, then the testimonies of different victims which prove and specify certain Muslim deaths and certain serious injuries to Muslim victims, should be connected with private firing. The principle of probability counsels that the only brilliant possibility is that the remaining deaths, proved to have been caused because of firing and the injuries of the victims proved to have been caused because of firing, can only be connected with private firing.'

The finding on the magnitude of private firing in Naroda Patiya showed that, like in the Trilokpuri violence of 1984, the police were in cahoots with the miscreants. The trial court held that Mysorewala's claim to have 'done lots of police firing' was 'extremely doubtful'. Though police firing as such was proved 'beyond reasonable doubt' and Gondia admitted that there was 'only one death in police firing', Yagnik accepted the testimonies of eyewitnesses saying that 'death and injuries in firing are many'. Given the inconsistencies found in the official claims about police firing in the Naroda Patiya case, none of the other statistics cited by the Modi regime in the context of the 2002 carnage could any longer be taken at face value.

While she refrained from dwelling on the big picture of 2002, Yagnik could surely have accepted the victims' application to implead Mysorewala as an accused. He had much to answer for. Take the one instance of police firing that Yagnik had unreservedly accepted. It happened at midnight when Muslims were finally being taken to safety. Victims deposed that even at that late hour there were violent attempts to stop the vehicles in which they were being transported. The few policemen escorting victims were, however, able to disperse mobs, just by bursting a teargas shell or by firing in the air. Yagnik rightly inferred that if police firing could be so effective in the night, there should have been more of it earlier in the day, when the violence had gone unchecked. 'If this is the effect of single firing, what could (have been) the effect of series of firing as per the claim of PW 274 (Mysorewala)?' she wondered.

The series claimed by Mysorewala began with the attack on Nurani Masjid in the morning. Just how far he actually was then from taking any action against miscreants, let alone firing at them, could be gauged from the kind of messages he had sent contemporaneously to the Ahmedabad police control room. 'Everything is okay. *Khairiyat hai.* There is peace and happiness in Patiya area.' This was the example cited in the judgment, bringing out the degree of his misrepresentation and, thereby, complicity. It prompted Yagnik to remark, 'It was like "when Rome was burning, Nero was playing fiddle".' Having likened him to Nero, how could the trial court still conclude that Mysorewala was not liable to any criminal action?

This was apparently because of a sign of remorse displayed by him towards the end of the day. As it happened, the bulk of the killings took place in the evening. In fact, they were concentrated in a 'U-shaped place' under a water tank located between two residential societies in Naroda Patiya. In an eerie replay of the Godhra train arson which had taken place the previous day, exactly the same number of dead bodies—fifty-eight—were found in a burnt condition in the water tank area. The court gave no finding though on whether this was a coincidence or the miscreants in Naroda Patiya had intended to kill and burn exactly the same number as Godhra's original death toll. (The fifty-ninth Godhra victim succumbed to his injuries later.)

Whatever the explanation for the escalation of the Naroda Patiya violence in the evening, the judgment pointed out that the police had stirred into action only after discovering the pile of fifty-eight bodies in the water tank area. The rescue operations mounted by Mysorewala followed as a consequence of this shock discovery. Better late than never. But was that enough to condone the police for all their errors of omission and commission earlier in the day? Would it wash away their crime of letting murderous mobs have a free run of Naroda Patiya for so many hours? Such questions relating to police impunity remained unresolved.

Mysorewala was let off even after the trial court made no bones about its suspicion of his intent. 'It has to be put on record that Mysorewala has conducted himself in most surprising and shocking manner on that day. He was not *neutral* (emphasis added).' Having elaborated on his lack of impartiality, the court said that he 'did not take even elementary and routine steps and has totally avoided to do investigation altogether'. But then, in the very next line, it added that 'in all such cases of neglect or may be inefficiency, one cannot (be) labelled to have malice or any criminality'. It was a confused mass of observations. In effect, the judge held that in the face of a mob violence, a police officer could behave in a 'most surprising and shocking manner', not be 'neutral', not take 'even elementary and routine steps' and avoid doing 'investigation altogether' and yet, believe it or not, be without a trace of 'malice or any criminality'!

This was the template of reasoning on which the change in Mysorewala's conduct, with the discovery of the fifty-eight bodies near the water tank, was virtually portrayed as an Ashoka moment. It was as if the court thought that in the course of the Naroda Patiya riots, Mysorewala transformed from 'Nero' in the morning to Ashoka in the evening. The latitude extended to Mysorewala was evocative of the credit due to the legendary warrior for waking up to the horrors of violence after his Kalinga expedition.

For the pile of bodies in the water tank area, Yagnik made conflicting observations on Mysorewala's culpability. She began by blaming Mysorewala for the conduct he had displayed before its discovery. 'He has handled (the) entire situation without exhibiting any sincerity, at least up to sunset.' And then, she went on to describe the change that had come about in him in the evening. 'Mysorewala has done his duty properly only when so many Muslims were found dead at the water tank, when he noticed that several Muslims were burnt alive at the site and when he took all of them for their treatment at Civil Hospital.' Despite his culpability for letting things come to such a pass, the court said, 'There is no hesitation to record that had he not taken timely actions, the death toll of Muslims could have been higher.' The actions he at last took in the night, after ninety-six persons in all had perished in different parts of Naroda Patiya through the day, were commended by the court as 'timely'!

The judicial approval for his 'timely actions' was followed by another leap in logic, while rejecting the victims' prayer for Mysorewala's impleadment. 'In fact, his investigation is mockery of the word "investigation", but taking a balanced view, he should not be impleaded as accused in the case.' It is unclear though whether there were any judicially manageable standards for arriving at this 'balanced view'. Does the remorse the police officer display on discovering the massacre outweigh his liability for his negligence before the crime (in taking preventive measures) and after the crime (in his investigation)?

Yagnik's idea of a 'balanced view' would not, however, seem so misplaced if Naroda Patiya were to be judged by the standards of Trilokpuri. Soor Veer Singh Tyagi, Mysorewala's counterpart, never showed any sign of remorse, although the bodies littered across Block 32 were more than six times the number found near the water tank. At no point did Tyagi make any attempt to rescue the Sikhs under attack in his jurisdiction. The killings went on through the night and the next day. Despite its crowded neighbourhood, Block 32 was cut off from the rest of Delhi because of the barricades erected by rioters all around it. Fortuitously, one of the residents escaped from the rampaging mob in the dead of the night and, after being rebuffed by the police, reached the office of a newspaper the next morning. It took three attempts for *The Indian Express* reporters to enter the scene of bloodbath in Block 32. Though booked for dereliction of duty, Tyagi was subsequently discharged on a technicality: the Delhi police had failed to take the necessary sanction from the government for his prosecution.

Insofar as the issue of police accountability was concerned, the August 2012 verdict on Naroda Patiya was in tune with the SIT report submitted six months earlier on Jafri's complaint. For the February 2012 report had already absolved Mysorewala's superiors, Deputy Commissioner P.B. Gondia and Joint Commissioner M.K. Tandon, of any criminality. This was despite the fact that both the big massacres that took place in Ahmedabad—in Naroda Patiya and Gulberg Society—fell within the domain of these two IPS officers. The SIT let off Tandon and Gondia even after the amicus curiae appointed by the

Supreme Court, senior advocate Raju Ramachandran, had recommended that they be tried on the charge of 'criminal negligence'. Defined under Section 304A of the Indian Penal Code (IPC), this is a relatively mild offence punishable with imprisonment up to two years.

The SIT, however, was not bound by the sage counsel of the amicus curiae. In its February 2012 report before an Ahmedabad magistrate, the SIT stuck by its opposition to taking any criminal action against Tandon and Gondia—not even on the charge of negligence, let alone more serious ones such as abetment or conspiracy. This was despite the SIT's own finding that 'it can be safely concluded that both these officers were negligent in their duties'. But their negligence, in the SIT's opinion, was such that it amounted only to 'professional misconduct', not criminal negligence. Their conduct was found to be 'unprofessional and unbecoming of senior police officers'. Accordingly, in its report to the Supreme Court in November 2010, the SIT recommended 'departmental action' against Tandon and Gondia. Then, in its February 2012 report, the SIT reiterated that 'it may not be viable to prosecute them for the offence under Section 304A IPC as proposed by the learned amicus curiae'.

The alternative option of departmental action mooted by the SIT was, however unwittingly, a throwback to 1984. For then, the Trilokpuri SHO Tyagi's superior officers, Deputy Commissioner Sewa Dass and Additional Commissioner H.C. Jatav, happened to be subjected to the same departmental proceedings. And they were none the worse for it. While Dass received regular promotions and was exonerated in the departmental inquiry, Jatav was restored his full pension by an administrative tribunal. Such was the impunity enjoyed by those two IPS officers despite being apparently clueless about the Trilokpuri massacre taking place in their jurisdiction over two days.

To be fair to Ahmedabad's Tandon and Gondia, they were not as disconnected with the Naroda Patiya and Gulberg massacres. They had separately visited the two trouble spots before the violence intensified. Yet, in the course of their movements to quell riots, they turned out to be in the wrong place at the right time. Despite warning signals, and despite being close enough to rush back at a short notice, neither of these senior officers was present at any point during the successive massacres. Ramachandran therefore said that the actions of Tandon and Gondia 'cannot be termed as mere failure to discharge their duties as both the officers were not present at any of these places despite the fact that they were fully aware of the possibility of loss of lives'. In his report to the Supreme Court in January 2011, the amicus curiae said: 'It appears that if these officers had been present at the spot or had taken effective steps in time, the massacres could have been avoided and lives could have been saved.'

The inference drawn by Ramachandran applied particularly to their movements in the second half of the day, when the massacres actually happened. There was little to cavil about their movements in the earlier part of the day. Tandon, for instance, visited Gulberg Society for the first time around 11.30 am, when he found 'small crowds' pelting stones. He dispersed them with the help of his 'striking force' and by bursting teargas shells. Tandon went next to Naroda Patiya around noon, when he found a great deal of tension between Hindu and Muslim crowds near Nurani Masjid, which had already been damaged. Responding to the gravity of the situation, he took the consent of commissioner P.C. Pande to declare a curfew in Naroda Patiya, by 12.30 pm. So far, so good. But then, the declaration of the curfew was no magic wand. The police had barely begun to enforce the curfew when Tandon left the vicinity of Naroda Patiya within 10 minutes. He went to the relatively peaceful Dariapur and remained there for the next three hours or so, claiming that it was a communally sensitive locality. But as the SIT report said, 'records of that period do not reveal any action taken by Tandon at any of the locations in Dariapur. Further, there is no mention of any firing done at any of the places under his orders.'

Worse, despite the alarming updates from inspector K.G. Erda on the burning of Gulberg Society and the attacks on its residents, Tandon returned to that place only at about 4 pm. By then, the massacre had already taken place, with sixty-nine persons, including former Congress MP Ehsan Jafri, dead. It was while he was engaged in shifting survivors such as Zakia Jafri that Tandon was alerted about the heap of dead bodies burning near the water tank in Naroda Patiya. This second massacre was found to have taken place sometime after 6 pm. Thus, in a cascading effect, his lapses in Gulberg Society ensured that he could do little to prevent the water tank massacre in Naroda Patiya.

Gondia's movements followed a similar pattern. He reached Naroda Patiya around 11 am and remained there for about three hours, long enough to have seen the violence spreading in the wake of the Nurani Masjid episode. This was when he had claimed to have ordered police firing, which apparently led to the death of one Hindu and one Muslim. Thereafter, at 2.20 pm, Gondia 'virtually ran away' from Naroda Patiya when the situation was 'very serious', as the SIT conceded, in one of its reports to the Supreme Court. Like his superior Tandon, Gondia ended up dealing with less critical situations in Dariapur. Worse, Gondia claimed to have somehow missed messages from Erda.

It took a call from the commissioner himself for Gondia to reach Gulberg Society at 4.05 pm, shortly after Tandon's arrival. While he was working with Tandon in the aftermath of the Gulberg Society massacre, his subordinates in Naroda Patiya, left to themselves, were overtaken by another mass murder of comparable scale.

The series of lapses by Tandon and Gondia clearly had a bearing on the number of people killed or injured in Ahmedabad. Since the SIT all the same stuck to its position that no case of criminal negligence could be made out against the two, Ramachandran framed three sharply-worded issues in his final report to the Supreme Court in July 2011:

- There is no reason for Tandon to have left the Gulberg/ Naroda area in the absence of a much greater problem elsewhere in his jurisdiction at the relevant time (i.e. around 12.40 pm).
- There is no reason for Tandon not to have rushed back to Gulberg after 2 pm, when he knew the situation was getting out of control, and the situation in the area where he was situated was not that grave. In any event, there is a complete lack of any supervision by him (of the situation in the Gulberg area between 2 pm and 3.45 pm), which prima facie shows negligence.
- There was no reason for Gondia to have left Naroda Patiya area at 2.20 pm when the situation was explosive and police firing had been resorted to, in the absence of a more critical situation somewhere else.

For all their force, Ramachandran's arguments for criminal liability cut no ice with the SIT. There was, however, more to the SIT's reluctance than just a difference of opinion with the amicus curiae. Had it accepted Ramachandran's opinion, the SIT report would have had repercussions going beyond the fate of the two individuals concerned. The process of accountability might not have stopped with Tandon and Gondia. Those in higher ranks—Ahmedabad's police commissioner P.C. Pande and Gujarat's director general of police K. Chakravarthi—might also have had something to answer for, even if the principle of command responsibility was inapplicable. The prospect of criminal liability travelling so high in the hierarchy would in turn have undermined the SIT's exoneration of the Modi regime as such. This was especially since the chief minister also happened to hold the home ministry portfolio, responsible for law and order.

The potential of Ramachandran's opinion to open a can of worms was evident from the SIT report itself. Take its disclosure of a serious contradiction between the testimonies of Tandon and Gondia on why no senior officer was present at Gulberg Society during its prolonged siege and the slaughter of its residents. Tandon claimed that, on receiving a message from inspector Erda at 2.45 pm about the escalation of the situation in Gulberg Society, he had 'directed' Gondia to reach the place 'immediately'. Gondia, however, denied having received any such message from Tandon during that entire period. When it probed this contradiction, the SIT found that Tandon had 'not been able to explain as to how this direction was given to Gondia as there is no control room message or mobile phone call to Gondia at this point of time'.

Tandon's inability to explain this contradiction opened up the possibility of his having withheld the urgent message from Gondia. Did this mean he was party to the conspiracy behind the Gulberg Society massacre? In its anxiety to rule out the lesser offence of criminal negligence, did the SIT gloss over the evidence pointing to the larger offence of criminal conspiracy? But then, adding to the mystery, the SIT claimed to have probed Tandon and Gondia from the conspiracy angle as well. In its February 2012 report, the SIT said: 'Sufficient evidence has not come on record regarding involvement of these two police officers in the conspiracy/abetment of the offences.' Its choice of words was significant. The words did not rule out the possibility of those senior officers being involved in the conspiracy behind either of the massacres. All that those words suggested was that, in the SIT's assessment, the evidence on record was insufficient to slap Tandon and Gondia with any charge. This was despite Tandon's inability, for instance, to explain why neither he nor Gondia had intervened during the Gulberg Society massacre. The incongruity of its reasoning and the latitude extended to the police brought into question the SIT's own impartiality.

The SIT showed little diligence in finding out the truth about the absence of any senior officer in Gulberg Society or Naroda Patiya during crucial periods. In a bid to counter the challenge posed by the amicus curiae on facts, the SIT came up with an argument on law. It made out that Section 304A IPC, dealing with death caused by negligence, applied only to 'an act which is the immediate cause of death and not an act or omission which can be said to be a remote cause of death'. In the SIT's view, it was therefore 'necessary to show an immediate nexus between the wrongful act of an accused and the injuries received by another'.

The SIT's undue emphasis on the 'proximate cause' implied that Gondia, for instance, could not be held liable under Section 304A. For, luckily for himself, he had left Naroda Patiya long before the water tank massacre took place. So, in the SIT's line of thinking, Gondia could not be blamed for the crimes that occurred in his absence, even if his decision to leave Naroda Patiya in the first place was questionable. This was how the SIT put its facts on Gondia, in keeping with its interpretation of criminal negligence: 'During the investigation of the case, it has been established that the incident at Naroda Patiya, in which major loss of lives took place occurred after 1800 hrs. i.e., approximately four hours after Gondia had left the spot . . . In view of this, there does not appear to be any direct nexus of these killings with Gondia, who had left the spot at about 1420 hrs.' In other words, Gondia saved his skin by keeping away from Naroda Patiya even as the situation aggravated.

The SIT's narrow interpretation of Section 304A was an outdated, textbook view on the ambit of criminal negligence. Ramachandran's opinion, on the other hand, was in tune with recent advances in law. One such advance emerged from another major catastrophe faced by India in 1984: the Bhopal gas tragedy, the largest ever industrial disaster in the world. Though the Mumbai-based chairman of Union Carbide India Limited, Keshub Mahindra, had in no way been involved in the day-to-day running of the fertiliser plant in Bhopal, he was convicted for the gas leak under the very same Section 304A. Since he was nowhere near Bhopal on the fateful night, Mahindra was even more remotely connected with the toxic gas deaths than Tandon and Gondia were with the communal killings. Though Mahindra could not be blamed for the 'proximate cause', as interpreted by the SIT, that technicality did not come in the way of his conviction in 2010 for criminal negligence.

Even otherwise, it was ironic that the SIT should have resorted to the notion of 'proximate cause' to bail out two police officers. When the SIT chairman, R.K. Raghavan, had himself been indicted for Rajiv Gandhi's assassination two decades earlier, it was because his security lapses had been found to have constituted the 'proximate cause'.

10

Hate Story

The first public meeting addressed by Rajiv Gandhi as the prime minister was an extremely sensitive moment. Held at the Boat Club in New Delhi on 19 November 1984, the meeting marked the birth anniversary of his mother and predecessor Indira Gandhi. She had been killed just twenty days earlier and her assassination had led to organized violence in which thousands of Sikhs were orphaned, widowed, injured or rendered homeless. Yet, in his entire Boat Club speech, Rajiv Gandhi did not spare a thought for—much less reach out to—those who had been harmed so grievously, to avenge his mother's murder. Instead, he came up with an infamous metaphor which justified the violence. 'Some riots took place in the country following the murder of Indiraji. We know the people were very angry and for a few days it seemed that India had been shaken. But, when a mighty tree falls, it is only natural that the earth around it does shake a little.' If he expressed any reservation at all about the carnage, it was more for strategic than human rights considerations. 'Any action taken in anger,' Rajiv Gandhi said, 'can cause harm to the country. Sometimes, by acting in anger, we only help those who want to break up the country.' With an eye on the upcoming election, he commended the mobs for ending the violence in three days, although 3,000 Sikhs had been killed by then in Delhi alone. 'But, from the way you put a stop to it, from the way India has again been brought back to the path of unity with your help, and is able to stand united together again, the world can see that India has become a genuine democracy.' In the national election held a month later, India showed itself to be a 'genuine democracy', after a fashion, as Rajiv Gandhi led his party to its highest ever tally of over 400 seats.

Come the 2002 post-Godhra massacres targeting Muslims, and the Gujarat chief minister, Narendra Modi, seemed to have emulated Rajiv Gandhi's model of 'genuine democracy'. Far from displaying any remorse over the massacres, Modi launched a series of public meetings labelled, curiously, as 'Gaurav Yatra', or honour procession. The tacit implication was that the post-Godhra killings of Muslims had somehow vindicated the honour of Hindus. The invocation of honour in this perverse sense in September 2002 was of a piece with Modi's overall strategy of portraying allegations against him as attacks on Gujarati 'asmita' or pride.

It took another nine years for him to come up with 'Sadbhavna Mission', which was Modi's belated attempt at reconciliation. It came on 17 September 2011, the day he turned sixty-one, and was within a week of the Supreme Court's decision to cease monitoring the investigation into riot victim Zakia Jafri's complaint against him. Sadbhavna Mission was part of an elaborate public relations exercise by Modi to reposition himself as a moderate in the mould of Vajpayee. Further, when the SIT's exoneration of him was upheld by a magistrate in December 2013, Modi made public 'the harrowing ordeal' he had gone through during the carnage. In a blog, he said he had been 'shaken to the core', particularly because of the allegations of complicity in 'the death and misery of my own loved ones, my Gujarati brothers and sisters'. He added: 'Can you imagine the inner turmoil and shock of being blamed for the very events that have shattered you!'

Back in 2002, it was in the course of his Gaurav Yatra that Modi delivered a controversial speech at a place called Becharaji in Mehsana district. Delivered on 9 September 2002, the Becharaji speech became a subject of fact-finding, for its attacks on the minority community. It emerged as a test case for hate speech, which is recognized around the world as an exception to free speech.

The immediate spur for the Gaurav Yatra was the decision of the Election Commission (EC) refusing to hold elections to the Gujarat assembly as early as he had wanted. Modi had, in an unusual move, got the Gujarat legislative assembly dissolved about a year ahead of schedule. The premature dissolution on 19 July 2002 was perceived as an attempt to replicate the electoral harvest reaped by Rajiv Gandhi in 1984, when the Lok Sabha polls had been held within two months of the Delhi carnage. Modi, however, seemed to have overlooked that since those dark days of 1984, the EC had evolved a great deal as a watchdog body. In the event, the Gujarat election of 2002 was held five months after the dissolution of the legislature. For after visiting Gujarat, a three-member EC team, headed by retired bureaucrat J.M. Lyngdoh, declared on 16 August that it was 'presently not in a position to conduct a free and fair election in the state'. Unsurprisingly, its decision had mainly to do with the impact of the carnage on Muslims. The EC said that the electoral rolls in Gujarat had become 'substantially defective in view of the large-scale displacement of electors in the wake of the communal riots . . . and their failure to return to their places of ordinary residence'. It also held that the law and order situation was far from 'normal as fear in the minds of large sections of the electorate, particularly in the minority community, is still a palpable reality and the riot victims would be extremely wary of going to the polling stations'. Having interacted with a cross-section of people in Gujarat, the EC cited a telling testimony, saying, 'how could the situation mend when there was not even regret for what had happened'.

There was indeed no sign of Modi feeling—or, at any rate, expressing—any regret for what had happened. On the contrary, the 40-page order incensed him so much that, at a rally held within a week near Vadodara, Modi launched a personal attack on the chief election commissioner. As *The Times of India* and *The Indian Express* reported on 23 August 2002, Modi referred to him by his full name—James Michael Lyngdoh—no less than six times. It was to emphasize his Christian religion and suggest that he was biased in favour of Italian-born Congress party president Sonia Gandhi. In a no-holds-barred language, Modi said: 'Someone asked me, has Lyngdoh come from Italy? I said we would need to ask Rajiv Gandhi. Some asked, is he a relation of Sonia Gandhi? I said, perhaps they meet in church.'

When he delivered his Becharaji speech on 9 September 2002, on the second day of the Gaurav Yatra, Modi pushed the boundaries of demagogy. This time he hit out at Muslims, the community that had borne the brunt of the communal violence. He was upset that among the grounds cited by the EC was the reluctance of victims to leave the relief camps that had sprung up in the course of the carnage. The condition of Muslims in the relief camps of Gujarat was as much a cause for concern as it was in the aftermath of the 2013 riots in Muzaffarnagar and Shamli in Uttar Pradesh under the 'secular' dispensation of Samajwadi Party's Akhilesh Yadav. The EC's order on Gujarat recorded the complaints of victims and NGOs about 'the coercion of district authorities to prematurely close the camps even while large numbers of inmates were not in a position to return to their homes'. As a result of this face-off, the activists who had run officially-recognized camps were, according to the EC, forced to 'set up makeshift camps under tents in the vicinity of the earlier camps'.

In his public reaction, Modi made no bones about his policy of shutting down relief camps. The Becharaji speech was based on the premise that relief camps had outlived their utility, since it was business as usual in Gujarat. If some camps were still in existence, it was thanks to the Congress party's 'pseudo secularism', a stock accusation of the BJP to all things inconvenient. Modi slipped in this insinuation against the relief camps while claiming that the Congress party had opposed the launch of a river water project in the Hindu holy month of Shravan. He taunted his political opponents, saying, 'Now that we have brought Narmada water into Sabarmati in the month of Shravan, you can do the same in the month of Ramadan (the holy month of Muslims) when you come to power.' Under the guise of airing ideological differences, Modi carved out an opportunity to berate Muslims even as they were still struggling to recover from the post-Godhra violence.

Worse, Modi asked rhetorical questions that ended up crossing the line between political contestation and hate speech. 'What should we do now? Should we run relief camps? Should we open child producing centres?' In other words, he made out that Muslims, playing the victimhood card, were procreating in relief camps. This insinuation, however misplaced and insensitive, fed into one of the pet peeves of the Hindutva brigade: that the population growth rate of Muslims across the country was higher than that of Hindus. Modi's tacit swipe at Muslims on the population issue was followed by a pious expression of his commitment to contraception. 'We want to achieve progress by pursuing the policy of family planning with determination,' he said. He obliquely alleged that Muslims were, however, being a hindrance, because of their ways: 'We are five and ours are twenty-five (*ame paanch, amara pachees*).' Crude and gratuitous as it was, Modi's reference was to the freedom conferred on Muslim men under their personal law to have as many as four wives. As if that were not enough, Modi again lapsed into rhetorical questions to drive home his message against Muslims. 'Can't Gujarat implement family planning? Whose inhibitions are coming in our way? Which religious sect is coming in the way?' Then, he warned that 'there is a need to teach a lesson to those people who are expanding their population'. More pointedly, he launched into a discourse on how a 'Madrassa-going child' was 'deprived of primary education' and was therefore 'a burden on Gujarat'. He also raised security concerns: 'We cannot permit merchants of death to roam freely in Gujarat.' The merchants of death he had in his mind, though, did not include any of the Hindutva goons, who had massacred Muslims just six months earlier. He made this clear by training his guns on 'those plotting to destroy Gujarat', which was a euphemism for Muslims. 'The days of somebody like Dawood Ibrahim sitting in Karachi and playing games of murder and destruction are over,' Modi added. Even as he claimed the legacy of the legendary Congress leader from Gujarat, Sardar Vallabhbhai Patel, Modi raked up the Hindutva aversion to any special treatment for minorities. 'If we raise the self-respect and morale of five crore Gujaratis, the schemes of Alis, Malis and Jamalis will not be able to do any harm to us.'

From his allusions to Ramadan, polygamy, madrassa and so on, there was no mistaking that Modi was targeting Muslims even as he steered clear of naming the community. The content was rendered more inflammatory by the context. Like Rajiv Gandhi's Boat Club speech, Modi's Becharaji speech was marked by its unapologetic insensitivity to the minority community that had suffered at the time. But thanks to the evolution of judicial activism in the intervening period, 2002 has been subjected to a greater level of accountability than 1984. So Modi has had to answer questions, however cursory, for his Becharaji speech, as it figured in Jafri's complaint. When it questioned him in March 2010, the SIT asked Modi if his remarks in the Becharaji speech—including *ame paanch, amara pachees*—referred to Muslims. Modi, however, denied the allegation. His verbatim reply to the SIT was:

> This speech does not refer to any particular community or religion. This was a political speech in which I tried to point out the increasing population of India, in as much as I stated that 'Can't Gujarat implement family planning?' My speech had been distorted by some interested elements who had misinterpreted to suit their designs. It may be mentioned here that no riots or tension took place after my election speech.

Evasive as it was, Modi's answer called for follow-up questions on the Becharaji speech. To begin with, it was not strictly an 'election speech' as the poll was yet to be announced. In the event, the poll was held three months later, in December 2002. If he still referred to it as an election speech, it was a lame attempt to play down the Gaurav Yatra, in the course of which the Becharaji speech had been delivered. The mention of the Gaurav Yatra would have made him all the more vulnerable to a slew of inconvenient questions: What exactly was the Gaurav that he was celebrating? And what was the explanation for the timing of the yatra? Why this concern in the Becharaji speech for 'the increasing population of India' when his state had just been ravaged by communal violence? How could he say that his speech 'does not refer to any particular community or religion' although it clearly and repeatedly made insinuations against what could only have been the Muslim community? Would he not be liable to the charge of hate speech even if the inflammatory remarks he had made at Becharaji did not lead to further 'riots or tension'? Without probing him on such aspects, the SIT could hardly have determined whether Modi had continued to stoke hatred against Muslims.

But, as with other vital issues about the carnage, the SIT let off Modi without asking any follow-up question on the Becharaji speech. In its report to the Supreme Court in May 2010, the SIT acquiesced to Modi's attempt to give his thinly disguised derogatory comments on Muslims the gloss of a legitimate discussion on demographics. Maintaining a semblance of balance before the Supreme Court, the SIT report conceded: 'The explanation given by Modi is unconvincing and it definitely hinted at the growing minority problem.' The finding on the Becharaji speech in the preliminary enquiry report was potentially damaging. Where it said that his explanation was 'unconvincing', the SIT seemed to agree with Jafri's allegation that his speech targeted Muslims. This was reinforced by its observation that his speech was indirectly about 'the growing minority problem'. But then, it left unsaid whether Modi had, while pitting one community against another, crossed the bounds of what he had innocuously termed as 'political speech'. The SIT's reluctance to bite the bullet on Becharaji was no surprise, given its overall approach to Modi.

The SIT's conduct became more glaring after the Supreme Court had ceased to monitor its investigation in September 2011. In the closure report given five months later to a magistrate in Ahmedabad, the SIT was stronger than before in holding that there was no prosecutable evidence against Modi on any of Jafri's allegations. Whatever ambivalent observations it had made in its 2010 report to the Supreme Court were all turned into categorical exonerations in its 2012 report to the Ahmedabad magistrate. All the allegations relating to incitement, including the Becharaji speech, fitted that pattern of change in the tonality of the findings. Specifically on the Becharaji issue, all that the SIT said in its closure report was: 'No criminality has come on record in respect of this aspect of allegation.' Thus, it was more explicit than the 2010 report in holding that there was no criminality in any of his covert attacks on Muslims in the Becharaji speech. The finding in the 2012 report could not have been more favourable to Modi, as it erased any pretence of moral indictment suggested by the earlier report.

The tame conclusion on the Becharaji speech was an anticlimax to all the drama that had taken place over it in 2002. The controversy then was triggered by a request for the transcript from the National Commission for Minorities (NCM). The letter was faxed by the NCM to the Gujarat government on 10 September 2002, a day after Modi's visit to Becharaji. The request for the 'full text' was in response to press reports on the 'inflammatory speeches made during the Gaurav Yatra'. The task of putting together the required material was, in the routine course, delegated to the chief of the state intelligence bureau (SIB), R.B. Sreekumar. But then, given the inflammatory nature of the speech, the Modi regime seemed to have had a rethink on whether the transcript should be disclosed at all. It also had reason to be worried about the record of the officer entrusted with this politically sensitive assignment. For Sreekumar was the one officer who had caused much embarrassment to the government just a month earlier, for his candour before the EC. Undermining the government's claim to have restored law and order, Sreekumar told the EC that 'an undercurrent of tension and fear was prevailing beneath the apparent normalcy in the state'. In its August 2012 order, the EC relied upon Sreekumar's assessment, among other things, for rejecting the ruling party's plea for an early election in Gujarat. The remarkable independence displayed by Sreekumar before the EC was in keeping with the grim intelligence reports he had given, since his appointment to the SIB in April 2002, on 'the subversion of the criminal justice system' in Gujarat.

Sreekumar proved to be as conscientious in his handling of the Becharaji issue. He resisted pressure from his superiors to disregard the NCM request. On the evening of 12 September 2002, the director general of police (DGP), K. Chakravarthi, told him on the phone that the bureaucratic head of the home department, additional chief secretary (ACS) Ashok Narayan, did not any longer want the transcript to be sent. The verbal order was illegal and contrary to public interest. In a situation like this, the subordinate officer is apt to acquiesce to the order, especially if there were any issues that could be used against him. Sreekumar did happen to be in a vulnerable position because a departmental charge-sheet had been pending against him since 2000. In his earlier avatar as an officer of the central Intelligence Bureau (IB), he had allegedly framed scientists in the 1994 ISRO spy case. Though he had since been awarded the president's medal for 'distinguished service' in 1998 and promoted by the Gujarat government to the rank of additional DGP in 2000, it was only later in 2005 that Sreekumar was exonerated of all ISRO-related charges following departmental proceedings.

But in the trying circumstances of 2002, his conduct did not seem to have been affected by the ISRO sword that was then hanging over his head. This was vouched for by none other than R.K. Raghavan, long before his SIT assignment. He wrote an article on Sreekumar in the 6 May 2005 issue of *Frontline* magazine headlined, 'A policeman speaks out'. From his personal knowledge of Sreekumar in the IB, Raghavan wrote: 'I have not heard anything since then that would persuade me to alter my view of him as an upright official with a strong sense of values. He is intensely religious and austere, and abstemious in his habits. His only foible is that he is blunt. Where most of us would hedge, he will speak out, and this perhaps has been his undoing in Gujarat.' Underscoring the need for police reforms, Raghavan added: 'Conformity is the order of the day, and individuals like Sreekumar are, therefore, considered freaks to be sneered at and "fixed".'

Sreekumar did show signs of being a 'freak', judging from the manner in which he responded to the Gujarat DGP's verbal instruction to withhold the information that had been sought by the NCM. In his capacity as the SIB chief, Sreekumar had already received a report from his subordinate Prabhat Patel on the inflammatory speeches delivered by Modi at Becharaji and Chanasma (in Patan district) in the course of the Gaurav Yatra. Striking a blow for the rule of law, Sreekumar did two things in the face of the DGP's underhand message. First, since a request from a statutory body such as the NCM could not be taken lightly, Sreekumar asked (or, rather, dared) Chakravarthi to give his subversive order in writing. Second, without anyway waiting for the written order, Sreekumar sent Prabhat Patel's report the same evening to Chakravarthi. This was because, as he testified before the SIT in 2009, Patel's report was 'not in response' to the NCM request. Rather, it was 'an intelligence report' on the Gaurav Yatra, written as part of the SIB's duty under the police manual to take note of any speech 'having potential to incite communal passions'.

Despite his assertiveness, Sreekumar faced a fresh dilemma the next day, on 13 September. The search for an audio or video tape of the Becharaji finally bore fruit; Prabhat Patel managed to lay his hands on an audio tape. This discovery was, however, offset by Chakravarthi's persistence with his cover-up mission. He was brazen enough to put it in writing that the NCM request for the transcript be ignored. In the process, his note to Sreekumar implicated Narayan too: 'ACS (Home) told me on 11th that we do not have to send any report in this regard.' The reference to Narayan's role was revealing as it was at odds with the claim he had made around the same time to *The Indian Express*: 'We are trying to procure the text of the speech. As soon as we get it, it will be sent to the commission.'

While recording his testimony on 12 December 2009, the SIT questioned Narayan about the document, which had been produced before it by Sreekumar. Narayan disclaimed any memory of the attempt to conceal the transcript of the Becharaji speech from NCM. 'I cannot recall as to whether I had asked DGP not to send any report in this regard,' Narayan said. When Chakravarthi's testimony was recorded four days later, he did not, however, have the option of feigning amnesia, as the notation had been handwritten and signed by himself. So, contradicting his superior, Chakravarthi confirmed to the SIT that Narayan had 'informed me that no report in this regard need be sent'. Chakravarthi's adherence to the truth in this instance was of course no act of courage. Thanks to the risk of his handwriting and signature being detected, he could not help admitting the Modi regime's complicity in the cover-up. It made little difference though to the outcome of the investigation. For the SIT report glossed over Chakravarthi's tell-tale note. But more about that later.

Long before Chakravarthi contradicted Narayan in 2009,

Sreekumar had defied both of them in 2002, putting his career on the line. Disregarding their injunction, Sreekumar sent them the Becharaji transcript on 16 September 2002. Sreekumar's defiance had more to it than his general record in 2002 of placing public interest above illegal instructions from his superiors. His decision to put the material on record was also prompted by two intervening developments that had played out in the public domain. In a damage-control exercise, the chief minister's principal secretary, P.K. Mishra, denied the existence of any documentary evidence of the Becharaji speech. Mishra told *The Indian Express* on 14 September 2002: 'Since the government has neither any tapes nor a transcript of the CM's speech, it is not in a position to send the same to the NCM.'

Yet, the lid was blown off the speech on 15 September 2002, when Star News, the leading channel of the day, ran the audio tape along with the SIB report on the Gaurav Yatra. More embarrassing than the tape itself was the SIB's vindication of media reports that the chief minister's speech was inflammatory. Quoting highlights of the Becharaji speech, the SIB report candidly concluded that Modi's 'Bhasha Shaili (language style) has wounded the religious feelings of minorities' and 'may aggravate communal tension in the state'. The government tried to issue another denial, this time to claim that the SIB had never sent any such damaging report about Modi's utterances. As Sreekumar testified before the SIT on 15 July 2009, Chakravarthi called him within hours of the telecast to inquire, at the instance of chief secretary (CS) G. Subba Rao, whether the SIB report could be denied. But Sreekumar 'emphatically' advised him to desist from such a course of action. The testimony of Chakravarthi was, however, silent on this abortive attempt to deny the SIB report. All that Chakravarthi admitted to the SIT was that, 'at the instance of either ACS (Home) or CS', he had 'contacted' Sreekumar regarding the telecast. In reality, Sreekumar's refusal to participate in the cover-up came as the last straw. On 17 September 2002, two days after the telecast, Sreekumar was abruptly transferred out of the intelligence department.

Given the manipulations made by the Modi regime in 2002 to tamp down the controversy over the Becharaji speech, it was ironic that ten years later, the SIT found 'no criminality' in any of his remarks against Muslims. Insofar as those manipulations were concerned, the SIT was silent on them in its report. This was despite questioning Modi in 2010 about some of the manipulations. Did he ask Narayan to get the SIB to deny the news about its damaging observations against Modi for his Becharaji speech? Modi simply said: 'No such instructions were given by me to ACS (Home).' Did he order Sreekumar's sudden transfer from the SIB because of his refusal to issue the denial? Modi's reply: 'The allegation levelled by Sreekumar is not correct, inasmuch as this was a routine transfer, for which the proposal had been received from the home department.' There was no follow-up question asking Modi how the transfer, close on the heels of the Star News story, could have been a 'routine' one when Sreekumar had been intelligence chief for only five months.

In an even more flagrant omission, the SIT refrained from confronting Modi with the documentary evidence supplied by Sreekumar: Chakravarthi's handwritten note seeking to hide the Becharaji text. Despite Chakravarthi's confirmation of this evidence, the SIT did not ask Modi any question about it, let alone using the document to pin him down. Though the note, written three days prior to the Star News story, disclosed that Narayan was the source of the cover-up, Modi could not have washed his hands off it. Since Modi himself held the home portfolio, with Narayan as its bureaucratic head, the SIT would have found it hard to deal with the DGP's note without drawing any adverse inference against the chief minister. The SIT's ulterior motive for going through the motions of interrogating Modi seemed to be to cherry-pick aspects where there was no documentary evidence to nail him. So, while keeping away from the documentary evidence of Narayan's attempt to conceal the transcript from the NCM, the SIT asked Modi if he had ordered the same officer to procure a denial on the Star News expose. Since the latter allegation was based purely on hearsay evidence, Modi could refute it without fear of being confronted with any document. On the other hand, Chakravarthi's note, irrefutable as it was, was suppressed not just in Modi's interrogation but also in the 541-page final report of the SIT. The suppression was despite repeated and extensive references by the SIT to Sreekumar's testimony on a wide range of issues brought out by him. As in the case of the Becharaji speech, the SIT was selective about Sreekumar's evidence on other issues too.

Besides the Becharaji speech, there was a range of official utterances and actions which had fostered a climate of impunity in 2002. On some of those instances of hate speech, the SIT could not help giving adverse findings, however mild, in its 2010 report to the Supreme Court. But, as with the Becharaji speech, the SIT did a U-turn on those adverse findings in its 2012 report to the Ahmedabad magistrate. There were also instances which, despite being admitted by Modi in his testimony, found no mention at all in the SIT report. Here's a selection of instances of the SIT letting off Modi on hate speech.

Modi's contemporaneous speeches discriminated between Hindu and Muslim culprits

When Godhra happened, Modi did not broadcast his peace appeal till the evening of the next day, by which time the post-Godhra killings had been well underway. The major massacres of Ahmedabad—at Gulberg Society, Naroda Patiya and Naroda Gam—were then peaking or had played out. Though he had rushed to Godhra within hours of the train burning on 27 February, Modi did not visit the next day—or indeed for some days—any of the places ravaged by post-Godhra violence, although three of them were right in Ahmedabad. This was because he was, as the SIT put it, 'awfully busy' holding meetings and taking decisions related to the escalating crisis. Significantly, this excuse of his having been 'awfully busy' was offered by the SIT only in its 2012 closure report. This was a far cry from the finding in its 2010 enquiry report, which said: 'Modi has admitted to visiting Godhra on February 27, 2002. He has further admitted to visiting Gulberg Society, Naroda Patiya and other riot-affected parts of Ahmedabad city only on March 5, 2002 and March 6, 2002 . . . This possibly indicates his discriminatory attitude. He went to Godhra, travelling almost 300 km in a day, but failed to go to the local areas where serious incidents of riots had taken place and a large number of Muslims were killed.' In a separate note accompanying the 2010 report, SIT chairman R.K. Raghavan added: 'Modi did not cite any specific reasons why he did not visit the affected areas in Ahmedabad city as promptly as he did in the case of the Godhra train carnage.' The markedly different finding in the 2012 report to the Ahmedabad magistrate of course superseded the feedback the SIT had given in its 2010 report to the apex court.

But then, however 'awfully busy' he might have been to visit the theatres of post-Godhra violence, the SIT conceded that

Modi happened to be nearby for over two hours on 28 February 2002. For his convoy, driving down from Gandhinagar, reached Ahmedabad's Circuit House Annexe around 4 pm. After conferring with officers of the home department, Modi held a press conference there from 4.30 pm to 5.45 pm, when the decision to call in the army was announced. It was then that at about 6 pm, at the same venue, he recorded his peace appeal for repeat broadcasts. As the SIT put it, 'At about 1800 hrs, the chief minister's appeal to public for keeping peace and to maintain law and order was recorded by Doordarshan.' And it was televised for the first time at '1855 hrs, before the regional news bulletin'. Yet, in a blog he wrote a couple of days after his testimony to the SIT in 2010, Modi claimed that 'in the *afternoon* of 28 February 2002, I had appealed publicly through Doordarshan to maintain peace' (emphasis added). Why this suggestion that the appeal had been made in the afternoon, when it had actually been recorded around 6 pm and broadcast for the first time around 7 pm? Since he took the trouble of inserting links to the text and video of the appeal in his blog, it would appear that Modi became conscious of an incongruity. The speech threatened action against Muslims involved in the Godhra crime but issued no such warning to Hindus, although they had by then caused greater havoc. Since the violence had intensified in the second half of the day, Modi might have consciously used a wide term like 'afternoon' in his blog. This could have been to convey the impression that he had recorded the message before any of the post-Godhra massacres had come to his notice.

Mercifully, the SIT report bore no such obfuscation about when exactly Modi had recorded his appeal to the public. This could be because the SIT's tack was different. It was impervious to the glaring discrimination displayed by Modi between Muslim and Hindu culprits. The SIT betrayed this attitude while rejecting amicus curiae Raju Ramachandran's proposal to prosecute Modi for hate speech for his alleged instructions to police officers at a meeting in his residence on the night of 27 February 2002. The allegation was that on the eve of the post-Godhra massacres, Modi had told the police officers to let Hindus give vent to their anger. After discarding all the reasons given by Ramachandran, the SIT said: 'Even if such allegations (against Modi) are believed for the sake of argument, mere statement of alleged words in the four walls of a room (sic) does not constitute any offence.' In other words, since Hindus at large did not hear what Modi had said against Muslims in the meeting with police officers, he could not be hauled up for fomenting communal hatred. As a corollary, there was no question of examining if there was any link between Modi's alleged instruction to let Hindus vent their anger and the mysterious failure of senior police officers to respond, for instance, to repeated alerts from the inspector dealing with Gulberg Society.

Given its curious conception of hate speech, it was no surprise that the SIT referred approvingly to Modi's 'four statements within 24 hours', over February 27 and 28, including the appeal on Doordarshan. After paraphrasing each of those four public statements focusing on Godhra, the SIT said: 'It may thus be seen that the thrust of CM's speech everywhere was that the incident was heinous, organized and that the culprits would be brought to strictest punishment.' Thus, the SIT confirmed, however unwittingly, that even after Hindus had unleashed post-Godhra violence, Modi was railing only against Muslims. The SIT said nothing about the partiality shown to Hindus in Modi's statements. Even in his Doordarshan speech, Modi's condemnation was reserved for Godhra and its culprits: 'Gujarat shall not tolerate any such incident. The culprits will get full punishment for their sins. Not only this, we will set an example that nobody, not even in his dreams, thinks of committing a heinous crime like this.' As for the post-Godhra violence, all that Modi could get himself to do was to chide Hindus mildly even as he repeatedly expressed empathy for their grief and pain. 'Violation of law is not going to help the society at anytime. I can appreciate your sentiments. But I appeal to you with folded hands, we must maintain peace and self-restraint.' Thus, much like Rajiv Gandhi's Boat Club speech, Modi's Doordarshan appeal was addressed exclusively to Hindus. While the 'us vs them' tenor was common to both speeches, Modi's was likely to have added fuel to the fire as it was made in the thick of the carnage and repeatedly broadcast through that sensitive period.

In any case, Modi's Doordarshan appeal reflected the larger pattern of bias in the official discourse in 2002. A contemporaneous report, titled 'Rights and Wrongs', brought out by the Editors Guild of India in May 2002, pointed out that the bias came through even in the way the two phases of violence had been described in official press releases during the carnage. This was the finding of its analysis of the press releases: 'The phraseology most often used for the Godhra incident was "inhuman genocide", "inhuman carnage" or "massacre" while the subsequent riots were invariably described as "disturbances", and occasionally as "violent disturbances/incidents".' The SIT ignored this inconvenient finding on discrimination even as it otherwise relied on a part of the evidence collected by the Editors Guild.

When Modi blamed Ehsan Jafri for the Gulberg Society massacre

For a controversial interview given by Modi to Zee TV on 1 March 2002, the SIT had to depend on a transcript provided in the Editors Guild report. This was because of Zee TV's failure to give a CD of the interview to the SIT, despite two reminders and a legal notice. The interview was crucial because this was where, echoing Rajiv Gandhi's big tree metaphor, Modi invoked the Newtonian logic of action and reaction. In Rajiv Gandhi's case, the problem with this formulation lay in its implication that the retaliatory killings were entirely spontaneous and that there was no collusion on the part of the government or the ruling party. There was an additional problem in Modi's case, which made his Newtonian parallel even more disquieting. It was the factor he had identified as the 'action' as opposed to the 'reaction', in the context of the Gulberg Society massacre. Modi made it clear that the 'action' he had in his mind was the alleged firing by Ehsan Jafri. Modi's spin was as insensitive to Muslims as it was contrary to due process. For even if he had fired during the prolonged siege of the Muslim pocket, the former Congress MP was legally entitled to act in self-defence. Barely a day after Ehsan Jafri had been maimed and burnt alive, Modi not only prejudged him on the firing issue but also endorsed a defence that could be taken by his killers.

The SIT did question Modi about the Zee interview while recording his testimony in 2010. But it did not refer specifically to the most controversial part of the interview: his attempt to blame Ehsan Jafri for the Gulberg Society massacre. Not surprisingly, Modi too did not attempt to justify his allegation against the murdered MP. Instead, he made out that the action-reaction theory was only an appeal for peace. 'I do not recall the exact words. But I had always appealed only and only for peace. I had tried to convey to the people to shun violence, in straight and simple language.' His claim to have been merely appealing for peace was taken with a pinch of salt even by the SIT. As with other aspects of the carnage, though, the SIT's 2010 preliminary report to the Supreme Court was more strongly worded than its 2012 final report to the Ahmedabad magistrate. What was common to both versions was this admission of the basic facts of Modi's testimony: 'Modi has clearly stated in his Zee TV interview that it was Ehsan Jafri who first fired at the violent mob and the provoked mob stormed the society and set it on fire. In this interview, he has clearly referred to Jafri's firing as "action" and the massacre that followed as "reaction".' Then, both reports also expressed a gentle difference of opinion with Modi: 'It may be clarified here that in case Ehsan Jafri fired at the mob, this could be an immediate provocation to the mob, which had assembled there to take revenge of Godhra incident from the Muslims.'

Where the two reports diverged was in the conclusion. The 2010 report indicted him—morally, if not legally. 'In spite of the fact that ghastly violent attacks had taken place on Muslims at Gulberg Society and elsewhere, the reaction of the Govt was not the type which would have been expected by anyone. The Chief Minister had tried to water down the seriousness of the situation at Gulberg Society, Naroda Patiya and other places by saying that every "action" has an equal and opposite "reaction". However this utterance by itself is not sufficient to make out a case against Modi.' Ironically, the SIT too watered down its conclusion on the Zee interview, when it gave its closure report in 2012. 'No doubt, during riots ghastly violent attacks had taken place on Muslims at Gulberg Society, Naroda Patiya and elsewhere by unruly mob, yet the alleged statements made by Modi appear to have been quoted out of context and therefore, based on these statements, no case is made against him.'

Modi's exoneration in regard to the TV interview was not only for his aspersion on Ehsan Jafri but also for the remarks he made against residents of Signal Falia, the Muslim-dominated locality near the Godhra railway station. His exact words were: '*Godhra ke is ilake ke logon ki criminal tendencies rahi hain* (the residents of this locality of Godhra have displayed criminal tendencies).' His justification for religious profiling was that those people had earlier killed lady teachers and now they had committed this heinous crime, for which the reactions were being felt. Interestingly, SIT chairman R.K. Raghavan initially found these remarks 'offensive'. In his separate note accompanying the 2010 report to the Supreme Court, Raghavan said: 'Modi's statement accusing some elements in Godhra and the neighbourhood as possessing a criminal tendency was sweeping and offensive, coming as it did from a chief minister, that too at a critical time when Hindu-Muslim tempers were running high.' Raghavan's adverse observations on the Godhra part of the Zee interview came on top of his team's equally damaging findings on the post-Godhra part. Luckily for Modi, these observations, which had been made in 2010, were excised completely from the 2012 report, without any explanation.

Gujarati newspapers which participated in Modi's hate campaign

In the post-Godhra violence, one of the key contributory factors was the inflammatory reports in the Gujarati press—especially in the two big newspapers, *Sandesh* and *Gujarat Samachar*. It was bad enough that they could not help highlighting Modi's shrill assertion that the arson was a 'one-sided attack'. They made the situation worse by coming up with their own sensational reports, with provocative headlines. The front page of *Sandesh* on 28 February, for instance, carried a story on VHP's anger, with the headline screaming: 'Avenge blood with blood.' Worse, another story made the baseless claim that fifteen Hindu girls had been dragged out of Sabarmati Express in Godhra and that the breasts of two of them had been cut off. Sandesh followed this up with an equally false story the next day claiming that the bodies of two Hindu girls abducted from Sabarmati Express had been recovered after they had been raped and burnt. The coverage of the post-Godhra violence was no less sinister. The Bhavnagar edition of *Sandesh* on 1 March actually taunted Hindus for the absence of reprisals in that area during the VHP-called bandh. An unsourced report said: 'Hindus were burnt alive in Godhra and leaders in Bhavnagar did not even throw a stone in the name of bandh. Ahmedabad, Vadodara and Rajkot partly avenged the killing of Hindus in Godhra. In the case of Bhavnagar, the gutless leaders are hiding their faces under the guise of non-violence.'

For this and other such attacks on non-violence in the land of Gandhi, *Sandesh*, *Gujarat Samachar* and fourteen other Gujarati newspapers received letters of appreciation from Modi on 18 March 2002. In identical language, Modi said to each of them that he was 'grateful' to each of the newspapers for giving its 'full support to the state government'. Without a sense of irony, he wrote: 'I am happy to note that your newspaper exercised restraint during the communal disturbances.' Needless to add, those that actually maintained moderation, whether in the Gujarati or English media, were excluded from such commendation.

Modi's rather elastic notion of 'restraint' did not inhibit the Editors Guild of India, the most influential journalistic association in the country, from naming *Sandesh* and *Gujarat Samachar* as 'notable offenders' of media freedom. In its report released on 3 May 2002, a fact-finding mission of the Editors Guild held the role of those two newspapers in particular to be 'provocative, irresponsible and blatantly violative of all accepted norms of media ethics'. The mission, comprising senior journalists B.G. Verghese, Dileep Padgaonkar and Aakar Patel, showed remarkable detachment in placing the public interest over fraternal spirit. It suggested that a high judicial officer be appointed by the government to examine those sections of the media that were 'prima facie in flagrant violation of the law and recommend what action, if any, should be taken against them'. There was of course no question of Modi accepting the proposal to act against his collaborators in the media.

As it happened, Modi's failure to act against errant newspapers was cited by Zakia Jafri as an evidence of his involvement in the conspiracy behind the carnage. But the question she framed on the issue made no reference to the Editors Guild report. Instead, it made the same point on the basis of other sources: the proposals made by three senior police officers against different media organizations. The officers were: state intelligence chief R.B. Sreekumar, Vadodara police commissioner D.D. Tuteja and Bhavnagar's district police chief Rahul Sharma. The last one sought criminal action for the report in the Bhavnagar edition of *Sandesh* taunting Hindus for letting the bandh pass off peacefully. Had the SIT been anywhere as earnest as the Editors Guild in finding facts, the proposals of the three officers could well have been used by it to expose Modi's support of the anti-Muslim slant in the bulk of the Gujarati media.

When it went through the motions of interrogating Modi in March 2010, the SIT did not even ask him why he had not granted permission to those three officers to institute criminal proceedings against errant newspapers. And when it came up with its report to the Supreme Court two months later, all that the SIT said in response to this allegation was that the government had intimated in writing that 'no action had been taken' on Sreekumar's recommendations against the print media. It gave no explanation for the inaction on Sreekumar's proposal while it was silent on the proposals made by Tuteja and Rahul Sharma. Yet, the matter was dropped even as the SIT actually upheld the allegation. Skimpy on details, the brief response ended by saying: 'The allegation, therefore, stands established.' Nothing came of this indictment though, for an unlikely reason. The amicus curiae, who was a crucial instrument of the Supreme Court's monitoring, completely missed the point of the allegation about the media coverage. Far from seeing it as another dimension of the conspiracy behind the carnage, Ramachandran made out that the target of Jafri's allegation was journalists rather than Modi. Based on this erroneous assumption, he held that the allegation, despite being 'established', could be dropped as it was too late in the day to prosecute journalists. He said: 'Action should have been taken against the media, but due to lapse of more than 8 years, it is not advisable to pursue this matter any further.' Sure enough, in its final report in 2012, the SIT took advantage of this diversion of the focus from Modi to journalists. With delightful ambiguity, the SIT concluded that 'this material is not sufficient to make out any criminal case against any of the accused persons'.

When Modi's own favourite spilled the beans

P.C. Pande was very much an establishment figure who went on to become the police chief of Gujarat. His career was unaffected by the fact that in 2002, he was the police commissioner of Ahmedabad, which was the worst affected city in Gujarat. Moreover, on 28 February, 'the worst day of the riots', Pande was, as Raghavan conceded in his note to the Supreme Court, 'mostly confined to his office, did not directly handle any field situation, and chose to be content with giving telephonic directions to his officers.' About two months later, Pande gave further proof of his tendency to shirk the responsibilities of his office. This time it was his failure to take on the VHP and it youth wing, the Bajrang Dal, which were indulging in extortion and, as spelt out in their pamphlets, mobilizing Hindus to enforce a social and economic boycott of Muslims. Instead of exercising the legal powers vested in him, Pande wrote about those violations to his superior in the home department, Ashok Narayan. Thus came into existence a letter from a key member of the Modi regime providing a chilling account of the hate mongering that was going on in Ahmedabad even 'when the situation is returning to normal'. In his letter dated 22 April 2002, Pande complained about the 'undesirable activities' of the VHP and the Bajrang Dal, which were described by him as 'organizations supporting the government'. This was how he listed out their shenanigans:

- In Ahmedabad city, activists of VHP and Bajrang Dal are extorting money from merchants, on the pretext of providing protection from the minority community. Out of helplessness, the merchants pay up but they are unhappy about it.
- VHP and Bajrang Dal activists are exerting pressure on merchants to prevent employment of members of the minority community in their areas of business. The merchants are scared of revealing this truth in public or to the police.
- There are instances in which whenever members of the minority community go for jobs in the localities of the majority community, they are intimidated and told to look for jobs in their own localities. Since this is adversely affecting their means of livelihood, members of the minority community are quite frustrated about the situation. Consequently, stray incidents of violence are taking place. VHP and Bajrang Dal activists are involved in these incidents.

- In places where properties of the minority community are burnt and destroyed, members of the minority community, besides being intimidated, are not being allowed to reopen their shops. One cannot rule out the possibility of such incidents being driven by interested persons to misappropriate the properties involved, with the help of VHP and Bajrang Dal.

Without a word of explanation for why he had himself done nothing about those covert crimes taking place on his watch, Pande concluded his letter saying that there was 'an urgent need on the part of the state government' to clamp down on the VHP and the Bajrang Dal for 'widening the chasm between the two communities' and to avert the danger of alienated Muslim youths 'taking to violence'. Despite the buck-passing by Pande, no government with any pretence of being an upholder of law could have disregarded the urgency of the matter concerned. Yet, there was no follow-up whatsoever on Pande's letter. Not surprising, given that it was part of a string of documents showing the Modi regime's collusion with the VHP, beginning with the letter given to its leader Jaideep Patel on 27 February authorizing him to take dead bodies from Godhra.

Pande's letter came into the public domain seven years later, thanks to his whistleblowing colleague Sreekumar. As copies of the letter had been marked to him and Chakravarthi, Sreekumar produced it before the SIT in July 2009 during the recording of his testimony. This was followed in December 2009 by the testimonies of Narayan and Chakravarthi, both of whom confirmed receiving Pande's letter. Chakravarthi said that he had advised Pande on the phone to take action if there was any specific complaint against the VHP or Bajrang Dal members. Pande, however, told him, according to Chakravarthi's testimony, that 'the affected parties were not willing to come forward with a written complaint and as such the matter needs to be brought to the notice of the government to control such nefarious activities'. Chakravarthi testified that he had then called up Narayan to 'apprise' him of Pande's views. Narayan, on his part, testified that he had spoken about Pande's letter with not just Chakravarthi but also Modi. The conversation he claimed to have had with Modi, in fact, puts a question mark over the chief minister's motives. For when Narayan urged him to 'use his good offices' with Sangh Parivar activists to 'restrain' them, Modi was apparently reluctant to intervene. Narayan said that 'the CM was noncommittal' even as he held forth 'in a general manner that the state government was committed to the safety and security of all the citizens living in Gujarat'.

So did Modi himself admit that he was 'noncommittal' about Pande's allegations against his saffron supporters? After being shown Pande's letter, Modi was asked during his testimony in March 2010 as to what action he had taken on it. Modi ducked the SIT's question saying: 'In this connection, it is stated that I do not remember now, whether this issue was brought to my notice or not.' Given the immense importance of the issues raised by Pande and Narayan, this was not exactly the kind of reply that would have been expected from an administrator known by then to talk tirelessly about his governance record. Modi made no pretence of being bothered about the Ahmedabad police chief's warning in 2002 that Muslims were being ostracized by his supporters, even after the violence had apparently subsided. The amnesia pleaded by Modi meant that the SIT was left with only one option, lest this issue came in the way of its blanket exoneration of him. The option was silence. The SIT completely covered up Pande's letter. Its report made no reference to the letter, let alone the disparity in the testimonies of Narayan and Modi. For there was no way the SIT could have touched upon the police commissioner's missive without running the risk of admitting Modi's negligence, if not collusion.

All this fiction, which masqueraded as fact-finding on hate-speech allegations against Modi, reveals a grim reality about the status of minorities in India. Especially since Rajiv Gandhi, from the other side of the political divide, had set no better example in 1984. Schooled as he was in Hindutva, Modi could hardly see the folly of hate speech targeting minorities. Take his response to Rashmee Roshan Lall in *The Times of India* during a visit to London in August 2003. Asked if his overseas Gujarat hard-sell conflicted with international criticism of his carnage-related record, Modi defiantly said: 'Yet, no one has asked this question to the USA after 9/11. Delhi is developing fast—no one has asked this question to Delhi after 1984. If it does not matter to Delhi and USA, why should it matter to Gujarat?' This seems to have been the inarticulate premise of the fact-finding that followed years later.

Epilogue

Notoriously intractable, communal violence calls for accountability on two levels. The first, in common with any offence, pertains to the accountability of the conspirators and executors directly involved in the mass crime. The other level of accountability, which is even more challenging, pertains to administrative complicity, whether of ministers, bureaucrats or police officers. The Supreme Court's intervention in the Gujarat carnage has broken new ground on the first level, while drawing a blank on the second. In the violence which claimed over 1,000 lives, mostly Muslim, nobody who was part of the state machinery in Gujarat in 2002 has been found to be criminally liable for any errors of omission or commission.

The fact-finding on administrative complicity, conducted by the SIT set up by the Supreme Court, has ended up eroding the institution of the Supreme Court. Consider the manner in which the main accused in the complaint, Narendra Modi, has exploited the credibility of the apex court to sanctify his exoneration. Asked if he regretted what had happened in 2002, Modi told Reuters in 2013: 'India's Supreme Court is considered a good court today in the world. The Supreme Court created a special investigative team and top-most, very bright officers who oversee the SIT. That report came. In that report, I was given a thoroughly clean chit, a thoroughly clean chit.'

The 'fiction' peddled as SIT findings have not only shielded

Modi but also served to prop up his image as a decisive and impartial administrator. The anomalies of the SIT's closure report filed in 2012 point to far more than the relativism of the truth. They mock India's commitment to its national motto: Satyameva Jayate. The meaning of this line from an ancient scripture is: the truth alone shall prevail. Given the failure of the Supreme Court's initiative to break the impunity enjoyed by high-level state actors in Gujarat, the truth can hardly be claimed to have prevailed. If anything, the voluminous material generated because of the Supreme Court's monitoring of fact-finding has brought out the gap between the findings that have been handed out and the truth suggested by the evidence. It's small consolation that though the scale of the violence against Sikhs in 1984 was greater, a lot more details about the violence in 2002 have come to be recorded.

When it came to the high and mighty, the system betrayed a deep-seated inhibition to take the evidence to its logical conclusion. This is a commentary on how little the Indian legal culture has evolved where it really matters. The cover-up points to the need for a systemic reform which is being promoted by the UN across the world: the enactment of 'the right to the truth concerning gross human rights violations and for the dignity of victims'. The statutory recognition of such a right would be in tune with a fundamental duty enjoined by the Constitution of India on every citizen: 'to develop the scientific temper, humanism and the spirit of inquiry and reform'.

Indeed, one of the great challenges before Indian democracy is to evolve processes that address concerns about institutional bias and impunity and narrow the gap between truth and justice. So long as India does not wake up to its fiction of fact-finding, its citizens are condemned to suffer all kinds of human rights violations, with little redress.

Further Reading

Supreme Court of India

1. National Human Rights Commission v State of Gujarat, Writ Petition (Crl.) No.109 of 2003, Date: 19-09-2003. (*The interrogation of the chief secretary and DGP of Gujarat on the state's failure to seek a retrial in the Best Bakery case.*)

2. National Human Rights Commission v State of Gujarat, Writ Petition (Crl.) No.109 of 2003, Date: 21-11-2003.(*The order staying the trial in nine major cases of the 2002 carnage.*)

3. Zahira Habibulla H. Sheikh and Another v State of Gujarat and Ors, Criminal Appeal 450-452/2004 (arising out of SLP (Crl.) Nos. 1039 – 1041/2004), Date: 12-04-2004. (*The judgment ordering a retrial of the Best Bakery case in Maharashtra.*)

4. National Human Rights Commission v State of Gujarat, Writ Petition (Crl.) No.109 of 2003, Date: 26-03-2008. (*The order appointing the special investigation team under R.K. Raghavan to take over the probe of the nine stayed cases.*)

5. Jakia Nasim Ahesan v State of Gujarat, S.L.P. (Crl.) No. 1088 of 2008, Date: 27-04-2009. (*The order referring Zakia Jafri's complaint against Narendra Modi and others to the SIT.*)

6. National Human Rights Commission v State of Gujarat, Writ Petition (Crl.) No. 109 of 2003, Date: 1-05-2009. (*The order vacating the stay on the trial of the nine select cases and entrusting the security of witnesses to a Central police force.*)

7. National Human Rights Commission v State of Gujarat, Writ Petition (Crl.) No.109 of 2003, Date: 19-08-2010. (*The order in*

which the Supreme Court forbade the SIT to share Modi's testimony with the Justice Nanavati Commission.)

8. Jakia Nasim Ahesan v State of Gujarat, Criminal Appeal No. 1765 of 2011 (arising out of S.L.P. (Crl.) No. 1088 of 2008), Date: 12-09-2011. (*The judgment through which the Supreme Court ceased to monitor the probe of Jafri's complaint and directed the SIT to file its final report before an Ahmedabad magistrate.*)

Gujarat High Court

1. Sardarji Madanji Vaghela vs Union of India & Others, SCRA No. 504/2008, Date: 12-02-2009. (*The judgment upholding the POTA Review Committee's recommendation to withdraw all terror charges from the Godhra case.*)

Trial Courts

1. State of Gujarat v Mohammad Ansar Kutbuddin Ansari & Others, Sessions Case No. 69/2009 & Others, Court of the Sessions Judge, District Panchmahals at Godhra, Date: 1-03-2011. (*The judgment in the Godhra case.*)
2. State of Gujarat v Naresh Agarsinh Chhara, Sessions Case No. 235 & Others of 2009, Designated Judge for Conducting Speedy Trial of Riot Cases in Navrangpura, Ahmedabad, Date: 29-08-2012. (*The judgment in the Naroda Patiya case.*)

Special Investigation Team in relation to Zakia Jafri's complaint against Narendra Modi and others

1. Signed testimony of Narendra Modi, recorded during the preliminary enquiry, Date 27/28-3-2010.
2. Testimony of R.B. Sreekumar (who was in charge of the State Reserve Police before being appointed as chief of the State Intelligence Bureau on 9 April 2002), recorded under Section 161 CrPC, Date: 11-07-2009, 13-07-2009, 15-07-2009, 16 & 19-07-2009, 02 & 04-08-2009.

3. Testimony of K. Chakravarthi (who was DGP Gujarat in 2002), recorded under Section 161 CrPC, Date: 16 & 17-12-2009, 24-03-2011, 30-03-2012.

4. Testimony of Ashok Narayan (who was Gujarat's Additional Chief Secretary, Home, in 2002), recorded under Section 161 CrPC, Date: 12-12-2009, 13-12-2009, 06-04-2011, 17-01-2012.

5. Comments of the Chairman SIT, Gujarat to the Supreme Court on the Enquiry Report in SLP (Crl.) 1088/2088, Date: 14-05-2010.

6. Enquiry Report by the SIT to the Supreme Court in the matter relating to SLP (Crl.) No. 1088/2008 of Jakia Nasim Ahesan & Another v State of Gujarat & Others with Annexures (100 testimonies) , Date: 12-05-2010.

7. Note by the Amicus Curiae, Raju Ramachandran, in Jakia Nasim Ahesan v State of Gujarat SLP (Crl) No. 1088 of 2008 Date: 20-01-2011.

8. Report by the Amicus Curiae, Raju Ramachandran, submitted pursuant to order of the Supreme Court dated 05-05-2011 in Jakia Nasim Ahesan v State of Gujarat SLP (Crl) No. 1088 of 2008 Date: 25-07-2011.

9. SIT Report in compliance with the Supreme Court Order dated 12-09-2011 in the complaint dated 08-06-2006 of Jakia Jafri, Date: 08-02-2012.

Justice G.T. Nanavati Commission of Inquiry on the 2002 Gujarat carnage

1. Testimony of police officer Rahul Sharma, Date: 30-10-2004, 08-06-2006.

2. Report on the Godhra incident, Date: 18-09-2008.

3. Order (Exn. No. 6014) rejecting application of Jan Sangharsh Manch to issue summons to Narendra Modi, Gordhan Zadafia and police officer R.J. Savani, Date: 18-09-2009.

Other official documents related to the 2002 Gujarat carnage

1. Letter from P.C. Pande, Ahmedabad Police Commissioner, to K. Chakravarthi reporting instances of rioting on 15-04-2002 and requesting action against Minister Bharatbhai Barot who is identified as involved, Date: 19-04-2002.

2. Letter from R.B. Sreekumar to K. Chakravathi asking for legal action to be taken against persons engaging in distribution of anti-Muslim pamphlets, Date: 16-04-2002.

3. Letter from P.C. Pande to Ashok Narayan complaining against activities of Bajrang Dal and VHP activists, Date: 22-04-2002.

4. Report from R.B. Sreekumar to Ashok Narayan on the breakdown of the criminal justice system titled 'Current communal situation in Ahmedabad City,' Date 24-04-2002.

5. Election Commission of India Order (No. 464/GJ-LA/2002), Date: 16-08-2002. (*The decision rejecting the Gujarat government's proposal of an early election.*)

6. Fax message (F.No. 012/33/21/02-NCM) to Chief Secretary, Government of Gujarat, from Garbachan Singh, on behalf of National Commission for Minorities, requesting for a copy of the inflammatory speech made by Narendra Modi during Gaurav Yatra, Date: 10-09-2002.

7. Order of the Central Review Committee on POTA (2) in State v Mohd. Ansari Kutbuddin Ansari & Others, Date: 16-05-2005. (*The recommendation to withdraw all terror charges from the Godhra case.*)

8. Interim Report of the Justice U.C. Banerjee Committee in 2005 on the fire in the Sabarmati Express at Godhra (*The findings rejected the conspiracy theory although the final report was stayed by the Gujarat high court.*)

9. Note by the Amicus Curiae, Harish Salve, in National Human Rights Commission v State of Gujarat, Writ Petition (Crl.) No.109 of 2003, Supreme Court, Date: 20-03-2006.

Material on R.K. Raghavan's security lapses in Rajiv Gandhi's assassination

1. Volume I of the report of the Justice J.S. Verma Commission containing its findings, Date 12-6-1992. (*This indicted R.K. Raghavan, who was in charge of security at the Sriperumbudur meeting.*)

2. Volume II-B of the report of the Justice J.S. Verma Commission containing copies of affidavits/statements of officials of the Tamil Nadu government, Date 12-6-1992. (*This includes R.K. Raghavan's affidavit in which he claimed that Rajiv Gandhi had beckoned assassin Dhanu when she had been standing outside the sterile zone.*)

3. State of Tamil Nadu v Nalini and Others, Calendar Case No. 3/92 (Crime No. RC 9/S/91 SCB/CBI/SPE/Madras), Date 28-01-1998. (*The trial court judgment upholding the evidence that Dhanu, strapped with a bomb, had been waiting in the sterile zone before Rajiv Gandhi's arrival.*)

4. State of Tamil Nadu v Nalini and Others, Death Reference No. 1 of 1998, Supreme Court, Date: 11-05-1999. (*The apex court confirmed the findings of the trial court.*)

5. Book by D.R. Kaarthikeyan & Radhavinod Raju, *The Rajiv Gandhi Assassination: The Investigation* (2004). (*Authors supervised the CBI investigation.*)

6. Book by P.Chandra Sekharan, *The First Human Bomb: The Untold Story of the Rajiv Gandhi Assassination* (2008). (*Author conducted the forensic probe.*)

7. Book by K. Ragothaman, *Conspiracy to Kill Rajiv Gandhi: From CBI Files* (2013). (*Author was the CBI's chief investigating officer.*)

Index

About the Author

Manoj Mitta is a senior editor with *The Times of India*, writing on legal, human rights and public policy issues. In 2007, he coauthored *When A Tree Shook Delhi*, a critically acclaimed book on fact-finding done by official agencies in the wake of the 1984 anti-Sikh carnage. A law graduate from Hyderabad, Mitta worked earlier with *The Indian Express* and *India Today*. He is a patron of 'Campaign for Judicial Accountability and Judicial Reforms', a civil society watchdog, and is on the advisory board of Amnesty International India and governing body of Foundation for Media Professionals. Married with two children, he lives in Noida.